This book is for review.

Shubhi Publications
Stall No 42 E 943
Hall 6.0.

Cultural History of
Western Himalayas

Cultural History of Western Himalayas

Dr. B.L. Kapoor

Shubhi Publications
Gurgaon - India

Published by
SHUBHI PUBLICATIONS
LGF-5, Grand Mall, M.G. Road,
Gurgaon (Haryana) - India Ph.: 95-124-5081199 / 5088499

ISBN : 81-8290-061-1
First Edition - 2006

Copyright © 2005 B.L. Kapoor

All Rights Reserved

Neither this book nor any part may be reproduced or transmitted in any form or by any means, electronic or mechanical, including photocopying, microfilming and recording or by any information storage and retrieval system, without permission in writing from the publisher & author.

Printed & Bounded in India at
EFFICIENT OFFSET PRINTERS
215, Shahzadabagh Indl. Complex,
Phase-II, Delhi-110 035.

DEDICATION

*This book is dedicated
to my Late Mother and Father
Althrough in the journey of life
whose love and affection have been pillars of light
and source of strength for me.*

***

Acknowledgement

Grateful acknowledgement is due to

- Dr. K. Mankodi of Bombay
- Dr. O.C. Handa of Shimla
- Mr. Kamal Prashad Sharma of Chamba
- Dr. O.C. Ohri, Ex-Curator of Himachal State Museum
- Mr. Suneel Sethi, Ex-Curator of Himachal State Museum
- Mr. Nandesh Kumar, Curator Bhuri Singh Museum, Chamba
- Mr. Bal Krishan Prashar, Journalist, Chamba
- Mr. Joshi of I.P.S. who was S.P. at Kalpa of Kinnaur in 1975
- Er. K.L. Handa, Retd. Engineer in Chief (H.P.) Mandi
- Dr. L.D. Vaidya, Surgeon, Mandi
- Mr. Birbal Sharma and his staff at Birbal Photo Studio, Mandi
- Dr. B.C. Khanna, Dharamsala
- All of them have kindly arranged photoplates for this book at various points of time.

PREFACE

Of late many a book on various facets of the Western Himalayas which encompasses a large number of erstwhile native states has been written. An extensive territorial area extending from Kishtwar in Jammu and Kashmir, covering Chamba, Kangra, Mandi, Kullu, Bilaspur down to Shimla and beyond including Garhwal and Kumaon in present Uttaranchal and touching the frontier of Kingdom of Nepal were grouped as composite Western Himalayas possessing several common social, cultural and historical linkages. Out of this vast tract of land our study is confined to a present state of India known as Himachal Pradesh. Two strategies are apparent which previously authors had adopted to high light the cultural canvas of their treatises and dissertations. The first group draws their contents from the published materials available in archives, documentation centres; and libraries prepared and composed by various writers, from time to time. It speaks high of reading habits of the scholars which is fast declining but their efforts and attempts hint heavily pertaining to their armchair-attitude. The second group derives requisite strength from the field studies, touring up and down in the dales and hills in the length and breadth of the area. Such narrations and descriptions are of superior nature, more informative and educative. While undertaking the preparation of this work, my endeavor was to make use of both parameters and dimensions. Reading has been my pleasure since childhood and while dabbling in writing the touring took the contours of past time like activity. My visits to various places of prominence while performing the public duties as a government employee stood in good stead and facilitated to quench my thirst to "study on the spot mission". The description of previous authors, scholars and travellers which had fascinated me could only be confirmed and supplemented while combining my enterprise along with government sponsored duties and tours. The extent of assistance provided by such sojourns can only by adjudged by the readers and peers in the field. Some offbeat trips also yielded rich dividends of knowledge and on this score, visit to Hat is an exclusive example. I had no intuition that classical icons of glorious antiquity will be confronted at that place which is so close to my home-town. Similarly my one useful voyage was to village Mangarh in deep interior of District Sirmour of Himachal Pradesh in mid-nineties which unexpectedly opened a new vista of information regarding the antiquities, archaeology and history of this region. At Mangarh, the broken stone icons, the flat roofed temple, the carvings and scrollings on the doorjambs of the shrine, suddenly led me to feel an abundant similarity which I had witnessed at wooden temples of Laxana Devi at Bharmour and Shakti Devi at Chhataari in distant district Chamba. I had to attempt hard to prepare a write up on this place which honestly, I have discrived, as I feel sincerely, "A Sudden Surprise". Later I was given to understand that some scholar had already worked meticulously on the temple and its antiquated treasures.

The caption selected for this book has far and wide reaching implications. It is not a book of history but has been written in the backdrop of twists and turns of history which is primarily local and regional. The regional, local and folk factors contribute significantly to understand the down to earth ethos and issues dominating the psyche of the local populace which as I perceive is the fundamental indicator to unfold exactness and the richness of the past. Similarly, the tradition generated thoughts can not be delinked from the history and historiography which by and large may be highly biased prejudiced, subjective and to some extents directed by the author's own perception. Similarly it is not a treatise of Archaeology which as such is a science learnt by excavations and has been sparingly practiced in this part of the country. Some modest attempts at village Chetaru in district Kangra are in the offing. Again herein also tradition has been the pillar of strength to the scholars. The excavated sites relate to Bhim-Tila and Draupati-ka-bag which give rise to the plea that traditional holds of our epic heros and heroins have a say in a big way while practicing the science of archaeology as well. As a matter of fact, archaeology is a study dating back to customs etc of ancient civilized people and ancient relics, prehistorical remains and antiquities. Our geographical terrain is a rich soil of antiquated wealth in the forms and formation of statues, icons, idols and carvings made up of metal, stone and wood. Primarily they are based on legends of Pauranic lores with essential admixture of folk ethos and issues coming down from hoary past to the present era. The Puranic narrations are suggestive that religion has remained a constant and consistent factor and features of the Antiquarian art and science. Religion do possess exclusive significance and importance in the study of antiquities at local, regional, national and international levels both for elites and the masses. Therefore it is in the fitness of the things to identify and discuss the religious adages and axioms to reach at a conclusion as there is no other way or vehicle available for this most enterprising endeavor. As a matter of fact, religion has been essentially a great protector of Art and in this book the art objects are the main thrust of study.

Scattered all over the Western Himalayas, the Navagrahas, the legend of Samudramanthan, the Vamana avtar and images from the epical texts like Ramayana and Mahabharata can be traced even in the most difficult hinter lands of the Himalayas. The majestic metal icon of Bharmour in district Chamba is the oldest surviving metal statue of lord Ganapati in India. The Vishnu Vaikunthmurti as Hari-rai in metal and Laxmi Narayan in marble at Chamba town have no parallel so far. The Shakti devi of Chhitarari, the laxana Devi and Nar Singh of Bharour in metal are a class in themselves both in religious and artistic parlance. Shiv-Shulpani-a life size metal image in the Laxmi Narain temple complex is one of the excellent masterpieces of Pratihara School of art. Shakti as Mahisasurmardini at Hatkoti in district Shimla is a matchless creation at par with the sculptures of Bharmour. A similar presentation of Durga in the Palal School of Art in slim and sleak contours has been chiseled in the niche temple of Bajaura in District Kulu. Surya: the fifth highest god of Puranic lore has been carved and preserved all over the state and a full chapter has been devoted to Surya iconography. As to how they found places in various manifestations! The answer is simple because they got thoroughly indented in psyche of Himalayan people and were protected due to the associated religious sanctity.

Temple architecture is another aspects which echo the present and past ethos undertaken in this book. Exclusively house like-dwellings which represent shrines is the original form later taking the shape of pagoda style temples made up of local materials i.e. wood and stone superimposed with slate roofs in several tires are representative temples. Hidimba temple of Dhungari, the Tripurasundary temple of Nagar, the Magaru Mahadev temple of Chhatari and the Parashar Dev temple are a few surviving classical examples of this style and shape. It appears the construction activities for temple were on similar pattern elsewhere in the main land of India and its neighbouring countries. A glance of temples of Trichur in Kerala, the Pashupatinath temple of Nepal and Potala palace complex of Lhasa in Tibet stand testimony to our projections. There is an abundant similarity between these shrines and the old wooden temples of Himachal Pradesh. In Kerala, the practice was to provide the kharpal i.e. coconut leaves roofing's to the religious buildings as against slate studded roofs which were in vogue in this part of our country. Though modest, the wooden temples of this area are the finest example of the temple architecture. The shikhara style of temple construction was also not unknown even in the olden days although these stone monuments were later additions to the pre-existing wooden structures. The oldest surviving temple is the Mani-Mahesh shrine at Bharmour. Perched on a huge stone pedestal, a massive shivalinga is housed in garbhagriha without a provision for a sabha mandap. This temple dates back to the era of Meru-varman who ruled over the Brahampura kingdom i.e. Bharmaour in the seventh century A.D. On similar pattern the Nar Singh temple has not been provided with sabha mandap. Although the later shrine is not contemporary of Manimahesh temple, but a practice of simple and pure garbhagriha as worshipping place has had a long sway. Like wise the miniature shrine of Gagat-Sukh, Shiva temple of Nagar and classical Vishveshwar Mahadev temple of Bjaura in district Kullu are also without the additional facility of sabha-mandap. The Laxmi Narain temple-complex dates back to tenth century A.D. after Christ. But for the main temple dedicated to Lord Vishnu, other has only sanctum sanctorum or garbhagriha. The sabha mandap added to the main shrine is the creation of later date. The sabhamandap became an integral part of main temples after the erection of Baijnath shrine dedicated to Lord Shiva somewhere in the 12th century A.D. This wonderful monument gives way to a new elaborate style of temple constructions and can be considered as a prototype for later shrine building activity. A casual study of temple of Mandi Town suggests that their style and shape is entirely on the pattern followed in the construction of Baijnath sanctuary of Shiva.

While discussing the ancient relics, a pertinent query must always be raised? Who conceived, who commissioned and who executed these construction activities? For this we have to go back to the past history of the place. History is pure and simple narration and can not be created or concealed. Although inferences drawn do need scrutiny and correction but the main players can not be ignored. Our approach, while discussing this aspect of ethos, is not an intellectual or an emotional or a devotional exercise. Simply the foot prints on the sand of time have been followed. In this connection, the long list of the names of rulers and the ruled which has come down through authentic sources can not be ruled out. While projecting their name and contributions is not a retro grade or non progressive attempt as off and on some thinkers postulate. It goes to the credit of these creators who not only erected these monuments, commissioned the statues and later on preserved them. Therefore these objects of antiquity and archaeology have survived and survived right to our times. The contribution of local and regional rulers may be a raja, a rana or a thakur is not less significant than the ruling chiefs of the mainland areas. They promoted, protected and assimilated the cults of gods and god lings and acknowledged them as their presiding deities for the family, clan and their subjects. In time almost all of them have been incorporated in the list of Puranic characters

Preface

thereby in people's ethos; they were raised to higher pedestal whereas originally they were down to earth friends, philosophers and guides of the local people. I have devoted a full chapter on the temple and statue of Parashar a most venerable god of the area situated north of the Beas in the erstwhile Mandi State. I think it simply stands for a Sar at a distance i.e. away from the main area of Sanor and Badar which were the earliest part of the ruling chief of Shiva-Badar. Geographically it stands for a lake i.e. Sar at Par i.e. away or the other side of the hill. The ideal location of lake made it a sacred place to the ancestors of the local chief of the place whose progeny later on took over the region of emerging Mandi State. The presiding spirit of this "Para-sar" later got transformed into Rishi Parashar the father of the author of Mahabharata i.e. Ved Vyas. In this way the local spirit was projected as a great Rishi of pauranic lores. This fact can be verified after a analytic study of the icon being worshipped in the nearby temple of the lake which is a human figure with a canopy of nine headed snake. The actual narration associated with this deo does not convey what we know about Rishi Parashar. In fact the antiquity and archaeology go a long way to strengthen the historical ethos. The idols, the forts, the temples, the palaces, the painting, the textiles, the jewelleries, the scripts all edict the local ethos and issues so dearly preserved which is a fertile field to further strengthen the foundation of national history.

The lofty concept and objective of compling to compile this work of mine is to collect and assemble the scattered and fragments of Himalayan antiquity and present them to the scholars and readers in a humble way for scrutiny and analysis. All the chapters convey specific segment of time honoured and time tested thought flows which had appealed to the heads and hearts of the dwellers of this land. This objective has been achieved partly by independent travelling, partly by consolidating the historical datas of the places and party by curating the traditional memoirs percolating from the wisdom of generations to generations which find resonance in this book. It is my pleasure to disclose that most of my write-ups in this book have been published by national papers and periodicals of prominence. With all deficiency in my knowledge, I have with pure and sincere efforts tried to portray what I have read, seen and personally verified. Hopefully, it will be an added source of pleasure and profit to me if my efforts are appreciated by both the peers and casual readers. My readers and friends have a big grouse with my work regarding the language. Their opinion is that I write in a very simple language and it should be made crispy, lively and alluring with the usages of idioms, metaphors and high sounding bombastic words. I appreciate their opinions and advices but submit humbly that there is no harm to utilize simple and generally comprehensible words? Gifted authors like R.K. Narayan, Ruskin Bond and Naipaul are my role models. While going through their fiction and non fiction works, I have never had to resort to the use of dictionaries. My contention is that by making use of simple language and simple style the high-brow and so called boring subjects of history and archaeology can get popular with the lay readers and stimulate them to undertake further studies to quench their thirst for knowledge.

There is also a complaint from my readership that I maintain an element of brevity in my endeavor of writing and fail to elaborate the matter. Yes, I admit. But I feel and do feel strongly that the compositions in short and summary form attract the fascination of a wide range of readers. Short articles are read more often than not and un-necessary stretching of the reading material does not keep up the tempo of the readers. They feel lost in the extensive jugglery of words.

Lastly, I shall appeal to my readers to bear with me the recurring repetition of the events and objects under study and discussion. The reason is being very simple and pure. These compositions were scrawled as independent articles without a distant notion of their being compiled in book form. Lately when the book was under the operative preparation, the process of pruning appeared futile as such unhealthy attempt was erasing the spirit of the contents and the inferences arrived thereafter were getting broadly distorted. Therefore my associates at manuscript level, advised me not to disturb the original form of the essays. It is really a pleasant duty to acknowledge obligation to them. Similarly those who helped by way of counseling', criticism and direction also deserve my thanks and I have great pleasure to express my sincere sentiments of gratitude to all of them, While concluding I wish to place on records my gratitude for the ample and sincere cooperation of my wife Mrs. Narmada Kapoor who seldom grudged my engrossment with the unending process of my studies. I am really grateful to her. Similarly my daughters Pratibha and Pratima do keep constant vigil on my creative activities of penmanship which bestow encouragement and strength to my endeavours. Really I am thankful to them for this silent support which reinforce my tempo in this direction.

Last but not the least, I wish to thank my publisher especially Mr.Sanjay Arya of Shubhi Publications for appreciating my work and to accept it for publication and that is how this pictorial journey of a wonderful saga of Himalayan History, Antiquity and Archaeology could be synopsized in such a handsome format.

— Dr. B.L. Kapoor

CONTENTS

Chapter		Page No.
	Preface	xi
1	SUBJECT MATTER : An Overview	1
2	SUN-SCULPTURES IN HIMACHAL : A Study	15
3	WOOEN TEMPLE OF PARASHAR : A Majestic Sanctuary of Art	21
4	PASSAGE TO MANALI : A Treasure of Curiosity	25
5	VAIDHYANATH : The Supremo of Doctors	31
6	TRIPLE TROPHIES IN A SINGLE SOJOURN : Occasional Episode	37
7	MANGARH : A Sudden Surprise	45
8	KANGRA : An Old Belt of Civilization	51
9	HERE A RANI WAS ENTOMBED ALIVE : A Riddle of the History	61
10	MAHADEVA TEMPLE OF BAJAURA : A Majestic Monolith	65
11	THE SCULPTURE OF THE SHAKTI OF CHHITRARI : A Subtle Statue	69
12	HAT : A Lasting Imprint	75
13	ARKI : A Small Town of Glory	79
14	OLD BILASPUR : The Town That went under The River	85
15	HARI RAI : A Unique Sculpture	89
16	KARSOG VALLEY : A Wonderland	95
17	THE MISSING BOULDER OF BRAHAMINI DEVI NALA : A Rendezvous	101
18	SUJANPUR TIHRA : The Closing Chapter of Katoch Kingdom	105
19	KINNAUR : The Land of Kinnars	109
20	BHIMA KALI : The Ruling Deity of Sarahan	115

CONTENTS - Contd...

Chapter		Page No.
21	AT THE SUMMIT OF SAR-KI-DHAR : A Vast Panorama	119
22	IN SEARCH OF AN INSCRIPTION : No Loss No Gain	123
23	THUS SPEAKS KOLASARA BOULDER : History and Legends	127
24	BRAHMOUR : The Ancient Brahmpura	131
25	THE STUFF OF LEGENDS : Indelible Impressions	135
26	A POETRY CARVED ON STONE SLAB : A Joy Forever	139
27	A PRINCESS OR GODDESS : An Enigma	143
28	A TEMPLE OF PANCH DEV : An Exalted Encounter	147
29	GAURI SHANKARA ICON OF CHAMBA : Unrivaled and Peerless	151
30	A UNIQUE SCULPTURE : Solitary and Single	155
31	SIDH SHAMBU : An Untold Story	157
32	A 'SHIVA' OR 'SIDHA' : A Peep into the Past	161
33	THREE BRASS ICONS : Flight of Imagination	163
34	SMALL BUT GREAT : A Shrouded Fact	165
35	POETIC ICONS : Two Visions	167
36	NAHAN : Grateful to the Royal Ladies	171
37	SAMADHI OF A SAINT : Losing Sheen	175
38	GHATS AMONG THE HILLS : Age Old Tradition	177
39	TEMPLE ARCHITECTURE : A Magnificient Legacy	179
40	SNOWCLAD MOUNTAIN TOPS : Threesome Kailash	183
41	A SAD MEMORABILIA : Rumination	189
	BIBLIOGRAPHY	193

***

Glimpses of Western Himalayas in Pictures

1. The Temple of Kangra in its Present form Dedicated to Brajeshavari

2. The Graveyard of Suhi Rani. It is more than Thousand Recorded Years of this Episode

3. Flat Roofed Narvase Shvar Shrine at Sujanpur

Glimpses of Western Himalayas in Pictures

4. Vishnu and Laxami on Garuda at Neri Temple. The image is not very old

5. Temples of old Bilaspur when the Lake is Dry

6. The Temple of Kangra in its Present form Dedicated to Brajeshavari

7. Shiva as Gauri Shankar of 11th Century made in the Reign of Yogakar Varman

8. A Vishnu Icon in stone in Mamel Temple

Glimpses of Western Himalayas in Pictures

9. Bhairon Shrine at Kothi

10. Temple in Local Style at Kao

11. Kalisthan after Reconstuction in Ninties

12. The Crumbling Fort of Sansar Chand at Sujanpur

13. A Typical Hill Village with Wooden House and Terraced Fields

Glimpses of Western Himalayas in Pictures

14. Main Mahesh Kailash in Chamba at the Height of 18564 F from sea level

15. Churdhar an other Kailash at the Altitude of 2683 m

Glimpses of Western Himalayas in Pictures

16. Bronge Icon Shiv and Parvati of Pratihara Style at Mamel

17. Complete view of Temple

18. Wooden Temple of Tri Pur Sundari at Nagar near Manali

19. Surya Icon of Gum 5th Century A.D.

Glimpses of Western Himalayas in Pictures

20. Kothi Devi Temple of Kalpa

21. Chhatari at Nahan

22. The Kolsara Bouldar

Glimpses of Western Himalayas in Pictures

23. A Replica of Sidh Shambhu at the Ghats of Mandi Town

24. A Three Century old House of Chura where once Raja has his Camp

25. Hari Rai being Displayed at Chamba Chaugan after Recovery from Theft

26. Two Views of Angient Temple of Shiva near Balichowki

27. Old Bilaspuur now Under Lake

28. The Rock cut Temple of Masrur of early 8th Century

Glimpses of Western Himalayas in Pictures

29. Bhima Kali Temple at Sarahan

30. Wooden Temple of Sandhya Devi at Jagat Sukh

31. A Slate Roofed Temple of a Devi in Deep Interior of Karsog

32. An Icon in the Niche Temple of Mandi Town

34. Shiva as Gauri Shankar of 11th Century, Made in the Reign of Yogakar Varman

33. An other Shrine has come to Existence

Glimpses of Western Himalayas in Pictures

35. A Part of Nagar Castel, The old Palace of Kullu Royalty

36. Pandav Shila on way to Janjahali

37. Enterance of 11th Century Temple in Trilok Nath Complex at Mandi

38. The Shiva Temple of Bajaura, Kullu Dating Back to 9th or 10th Century

39. The General view of the Surviving Temple of Mangarh

Glimpses of Western Himalayas in Pictures

40. Chakdini Boulser at Mansi Town at the Confluence of the Beas and Suketi

41. Shiva or Sidha

42. The Kolsara Bouldar

43. Being Further Damaged by the Wild Growth

Glimpses of Western Himalayas in Pictures

44. Sidh Shambhu at the Bank of the River Beas

45. Ghats of the Hills

46. Shiva Temple of Nagar, A post Gupta Relic of Kullu Valley

47. The Temple is Contemporary of Baij Nath Temple
The Masks of Darang, Made up of Bronze,
About four hundreds years back according to the Tradition

48. A Miniture Pahari Temple

Glimpses of Western Himalayas in Pictures

49. Kartikeya on Peacock in Folk Art

50. A Bal-Shiva in the newly found Temple of Harabag

51. Bhadra Mukha at Hara Bag Temple Lying in the Courtyard

52. 14th Century old Temple of Baij Nath, in Kangra, of 1204 AD. Constructed by two merchants

53. An Attempt to Portray Samudra - Manthan in Folk art Placed easily in 16th Century

54. Laxami Narayan Temple Complex of Chamba The Main Shrine Dates back to 10th Century A.D.

Glimpses of Western Himalayas in Pictures

55. Parashar Temple and Lake

56. Lion Icon at House Temple

57. Stading size stone Images of Shiva and Parvati, Damaged in 1905 due to Earth Quake

58. Shiva and Parvati Mounting the Divine Vehicle Nandi Bull in Folk art about four Hundreds years old

59. A Garu Da in Bronze

Glimpses of Western Himalayas in Pictures

60. An Image of Danging Ganesha at Baij Nath Temple of 14th century

61. Shakti Devi Bronge at Chhitrari Dating to 7th century. The Inscription on the Pedestal Records the name of Varman Kings of Bharmour

62. Parashar Sanctum door

Glimpses of Western Himalayas in Pictures

63. A Contemporary Figurine at Chhitrari Temple

64. The Icon of Princess being Projected as Mahisasurmardini

65. A stone image of Surya Partly damaged by Weather and Neglect

66. Durga Temple (on top floor) Prenoualy - Rata's Fort at Pangana (Karsog)

67. In Search of Brahamani Nala Site

Glimpses of Western Himalayas in Pictures

68. Ganesha Icon at Bharmour Bearing an Inscription of 7th Century A.D

69. Narsingha Bronge of 7th Century without clear Inscription

70. Carved Stones of Champavati Shrine

71. Magaru Mahadev Temple at Chhatari

72. Surya from Bajaura in Kullu in Kushana Style, early 8th century now in State Museum, Simla

73. Hari Rai being Displayed at Chamba Chaugan after Recovery from Theft

74. Mahisasur Mardini of Bharmour in bronze in post Gupta style of 7th century. It carries an inscription

CHAPTER - 1

SUBJECT MATTER : An Overview

In common parlance and limited understanding, Archaeology stands for an act of digging; but that is one dimension of this science to procure the materials which after further processing reveals what the past was. Therefore, it is also termed as a study of past i.e. its history, culture, civilization, Anthropology and Geology. Therefore, Archaeology in itself involves all the branches which establish the love of the olden days simultaneously providing it evidence. In its most simplistic definition, Archaeology is a science based on materials, its exhibits and their interpretations. It is of utmost importance not only to scholars but even for lay readers. Surprisingly, the British shied away from retracing the history of India beyond the period of Buddha. Once the inputs of Indus civilization came to light, perhaps they were forced to stretch back our historical existence beyond their stipulated time frame. A new mindset stirred up and now the vestiges of this civilization is found spreading upto Haryana and Gujrat and Rajasthan. The Saraswati river valley is an added dimension in the ancient conceptualization of History in long measurers. Such is the vast contribution of Archaeology to support and strengthen the history. So much that history disassociated from Archaeology is nothing but legend. Even traditions coming down from generations to generation also stand on firm footing once the archaeological remains substantiate them. In the following pages we shall go through the various contours of the history of Himachal Pradesh as a prologue to the sites and places which still have idols, temples, forts and inscriptions spread far and wide in this tract of the Western Himalayas which support and strengthen us to unfold the historical events associated with them. Besides the inscriptions having undisputed value, the style, fashion, design and outlines of the building, forts, temples and icons also take us back to an era when they were actually commissioned, erected, created and established. The religious sanctity associated with them have further made their survival safe; especially that of idols which have been the object of worship whereas the infrastructure and superstructure of the building have undergone tremendous changes with the march of time.

HISTORICAL PERSPECTIVE

Himachal Pradesh as a class 'C' state came into existence only in year 1948 AD. Earlier it was a part of the territory known as Western Himalayan state, which included in it the territory of all the Punjab hill and Shimla hill states. The former encompassed in the native states of Chamba, Mandi and Suket out of which Chamba state formed the district of same name while Mandi and Suket were amalgamated to the District Mandi. The former Shimla hill state of Shimla region were given a composite form known as District Mahasu. In 1984 prior to the present formation of the Himachal Pradesh, it was confined in these four districts only. In the year 1954, the present district of Bilaspur was merged into the Himachal territory which had remained a separate territory as class C state. Earlier Bilaspur was also a native state under a ruler of Chandel dynasty. The march of time for Himachal was still going on; and in this journey, it was at many points to lose its existence. Even the state reorganization commition had recommended for its amalgamation in a neighbouring state. Pannikar and Kungru had proposed to integrate the Himachal to be a part of East Punjab but for the reason that it was overruled by the committee's Chairperson. Ironically he had not visited the place and his two-some colleagues i.e. Panikar and Kungru had made their existence felt in Himachal territory. Thanks to the foresight of Chairman that Himachal survived the holocaust, otherwise it could have lost its identity.

On its inception Himachal was placed under a Chief Commissioner who had an advisory committee comprising of some public figures alongwith other erstwhile enlightened rulers, in year 1952, it got its first elected Legislative Assembly with a cabinet having three ministers. The Chief Commissioner was replaced by a Governor. This arrangement was abrogated soon and in a couple of years the assembly was replaced by a Territorial Council which was primarily a advisory committee with limited powers in the spheres of social services like Health, Education and Building activities. Again in the year 1963, a new legislative assembly came into being including the elected representative of Bilaspur.

A salient landmark was added in 1966 when the state of Punjab was trifurcated on the language theory thereby the Hindi speaking hill tarrains of Punjab were included in Himachal and the present state of Himachal as an enlarged territory came into being. The entire Kangra district including Kullu and Lahaul-Spiti became part of Himachal. Similarly a part of Una tehsil of Hoshiarpur and hilly tracts surrounding the capital city of Shimla, Chail, Kandaghat, Sairi, Kasaul, Sapatoo, Kotkhai and Kotgarh were clubbed with Himachal. Capital of state functioned at Shimla although it was in erstwhile

SUBJECT MATTER: AN OVERVIEW

Punjab. Herewith Himachal got doubled in terms of territory and population. It was in 1971, that Himachal became a full fledged state bigger in area than the states of Punjab, Haryana and Kerala.

In Himachal the pattern of life has remained consistent for centuries. In real sense the modernisation set its pace only after Independence of India but certain mile stones of development were laid down in the times of native rajas as far as health, education and inlaying of roads in concerned. Strictly a new era made its presence felt when a progressive measure of land reform reform was carried out by the Himachal Assembly somewhere in 1954-55. That led to the end of land holdings on which the total economy was based on the grain production and transaction only. So far barter system was the order of the day. As the so called jamindars were devoid of their possessions importance of grains was transferred to currency which resulted into a new concept of economy. Till the merger of the states the medi-eval system of rulers' grandeour and supremacy of the aristocracy remained potential source of power which met a crash when land-holding was transfered to the tillers of the soil.

A sketch of the lifestyle of the then Himachal way of life can be outlined if we try to understand the essence of the followship lines.

A small village, more a hamlet than a village in strict sense, consisting of four or five houses of different or same family, surrounded by some terraced fields, small but well maintained. The principal yield from the land remained coarse grains i.e. Barley, Sarara, Buthu and Kawani that was hardly sufficient to provide two meals a day after year long toil and labour. Nearby there used to be source of water may be a river, rivulet, a babali or Chhuharu meant both for human needs as well as that of domestic animals like cows, bulls, sheep and goats. A place of worship is a must, attach with a village or a group of villages. It ranges from a well carved many storeyed wooden temple or a typical house like building or a place known as 'thaan' (sthan) made up of coarse unchiseled stones in a squarish fashion varying in dimensions supposed to be a resting place of the rulling spirit of the area that may be a god, deo, devote, devi, nag or demigod or demon who terrorises more than pacify the mind-set of the populace associated with the temple. In its annual festival all the members of the area join for a day and night long merry— making, feasting and dancing. The godling being appeased for whatever is needed in an agrarian society i.e. rain, sun, protection from diseases, bumper crops and escape from the ill will of the enemies. The villages were almost independent in themselves in all spheres banking out side only for the salt, crude, muddy-noncrystal both for them and their animals and all else where the produces of the particular localities i.e. the clothes from their own wool of sheep and goats, grains from their fields, milk and ghee from cows, timber and stone for houses from the local areas, oil from the seeds locally available and the fire-wood from the own woods and jungles. They were self dependent and hardly looking beyond their territory. The justice in minor squabble was imparted by the local Panchayat of elders or by the oracles of the territorial godlings. This state of affairs was steady, consistent, unabruptive and long lasting for centuries together.

Actually it is not clear who were the originators to initiate this way of life! The koli-hali-kanet-khash groups are said to be the proginator of this life pattern who were self ruling groups, tribes and sub-tribes. Later on their supremacy was replaced by the Thakur-rana-raja type of polity. Various opinions, conjectures and derivatives have been expressed regarding the information about Koli etc. Who were they and how much is their associations with the Kolarian of Vedic lore and the present segment of present Koli people. Were they only confined to the frontiers of present Himachal or were spread all over the confines of the Himalayas and beyond. Similarly the Kanets are associated with the older Kalinda. Are they separate from Khasha or independent entity? There are confusing and complicated versions to conclude about their ethnic group which are supposed to be earlier inhabitants of Himachal and were practicing almost independent village "Kingdom". This presumed village Kingdom went through multifarious twists and turns till some paramountsy got witnessed in Himachal Polity. References have already been forwarded how in year 1948 Himachal came into existence by amalgamating a few native states of some modern administrative structure under rajas and others were under local ranas and thakurs. The perusal of the age old polity reveals that Thakurs were the first to emerge as the center of power who were confined in their limited territory having sway over two or three neably villages. The supremacy of Thakurs was eroded by the emergence of Ranas who started adding the various thakurains or the territories of Thakurs into their band wagon. Actually some Ranas became overlord by dint of their muscle and military powers whom the Thakurs could not resist and established their dynastic rana-hood and others were confirred such powers by the overlord of the state i.e. Rajas. Eventually Rajas engulfed the Ranas' territories in complete and reduced them to an agriculturist class with some large land holdings. The period attributed to Thakurs and Ranas remains a big force in the Himachal for a pretty long period and important rulers as Rajas came into being mostly in the Post-Harsha-Period. Ranas as political entity were prosperous and powerful and some of them were socially at par with rajas. The inscription of Baijnath temple of district Kangra bears a testimony to this statement wherein it has been confirmed that the Rana of Kiragram i.e. Baijnath was a close relative of the Raja of Trigarta i.e. Kangra. The historian of Chamba state has mentioned several raja-nakas which means just like Raja. The tussel to bring down Ranas under the Raja were long drawn and went up to 15th century onwards. Several battles between Ranas and Rajas are well recorded in the annals of the histories of Chamba, Mandi, Suket, Bilaspur, Rampur and Sirmour. Even in the first half of 16th century, Raja Ajber Sen of Mandi had a tough time in curbing the powers of Ranas. All the high hillocks surrounding the present town of Mandi had several Ranas ruling in their respective territories. The Gandharva hillock had a Rana and similarly there were more near to Sidhani, Kanhawal and Marathu. In alliance they had confronted Raja Ajber Sen in the plain of Bahl where Raja defeated them all and brought them under his supremacy. There was one who was ruling in the capacity of Rana on the present area where the Mandi town stands on the left bank of the Beas and his name in the history has been recorded as Gokal. Due to the limited resources they had to surrender their command to the emerging powers of Raja and thereby the kingship was established in the area of Himachal which later on merged en-mass to form Himachal Pradesh. The states of Chamba, Mandi, Sirmour, Bilaspur and Rampur were having sufficient resources when they agreed to lay down their powers and privileges on being devoid of their rulership. In the present context, the thakurs and ranas as well as rajas have accepted the changed ethos and no longer boast about their "blue blood". Some vestiges of rajahood are still palpable, as they have carved out some political bases by dint of their richness or reputation over their old subjects. Apparently with such background Himachal is still a store-house of inputs about these political upheavals and associated preservation of arts, architectures, sculptures, temples and paintings which narrate the cultural streams of the bygone eras.

Presently Himachal Pradesh is situated in the north west corner of India right in the lap of Himalayan ranges. It is surrounded by Jammu and Kashmir in the north, Uttar Pradesh and Uttaranchal in the south-East, Haryana in the South and Punjab in the west. In the east, it forms India's boundary with China (Tibet). The state is almost entirely mountainous with altitudes ranging from 460 to 6400 mtrs, above the sea level. It has deeply dissected topography, a complex geological structure and a rich temperate flora in the sub-tropical latitudes.

Physiographically the state can be divided into two regions-Southern and south-west part of the state is almost as hot as the plains. While the other region has a temperate summer and a winter with extreme cold and heavy snowfall. Each village in this state has its own deity. This deity is worshipped and is propitiated through its priests. Temples in astounding hill architecture are constructed to house these deities and still the people of the area invoke these deities in order to solve the problems and troubles facing them. There is still on abundant faith in the local devatas. On occasions being celebrated as festivals these godlings are invited on their raths to join the festivities. Still the world famous Dussehra festival of Kullu where although the Raghunath of Kullu proper is the supreme deity, the others residing in their hinterlands are brought to the Kullu town to pay their respect and homage to the central god. In the same way at Mandi on Shivratri they make their presence to the Madho Rai the local overloard of the deities. However the gods of Hindu pantheon has also remarkable places studded all over where they are worshipped according to the age-old-Hindu way of worship. Shiva cult is most popular in these hills. Gauri Shanker temple of Jagatsukh (Kullu), Shiva temple of Nagar and Visheveshar temple of Bajaura are of historical and cultural importance. Similar is the Triloknath in the Lahul-Spiti district and Vidyanath at Baijnath in Kangra district. Balog in Shimal and Sahu and Bharmour in Chamba are known for their Shiva temples. The Gauri Shanker temple with Pratiharas' bronzes of Shiva and Parvati at Chamba town are of much more significant than others due to their cultural and asthetic values. Mandi is proud of its temple of Bhutnath, Triloknath, Panchvaktra and Ardthnarishwar in Shikhara style made up of stone. A peculiar feature is to believe all the high peaks to be the dwellings of Lord Shiva. The Kinnaur Kailash in Kinnaur, the Manimahesh in Bharmour, Chamba and Churdhar in Sirmour-Chopal areas attract huge gatherings of workshippers. With equal favour is worshipped the divine consort of Shiva and Shakti (or Mahisasurmardini) with classical sculptures in bronze at Chhatrari Shakti Devi, at Bharmour as Lakshana Devi and at Hatkoti as Mahisasurmardini are positive indicators of the metal art at its best and finest. Vishnu cult had limited influence and confined in some pockets but could not reach the height of Shiva-Shakti influence. But two grand festivals of Dushehra of Kullu and Shivratri of Mandi have Rama and Krishna the epic incarnation of Vishnu as the Chief-Lord under whose patronages, these festivals are arranged. Nag cult has its own sphere of influence and reverance. Mathod in Chamba, Tandi in Kullu in Sutluj vally, Mahu in Mandi and Nona in Sirmour are some of the temple being worshipped as the Nag Devtas. Gugga worship is another form of Nag cult. The deity is considered effective particularly in cases of snakebites. Jogis and Naths of Himachal hold Gugga as their renovated god. 'Gugga Gatha' are long ballads sung mostly in Punjab, Rajasthan and Himachal Pradesh

Subject Matter: An Overview

in which Gugga is depicted as a valiant fighter who rides a horse. Such images of Gugga on horse in wood and stones are not rare in Himachal. These deities and idols are housed in various types of temples and therefore temple architecture needs a little introduction.

The miniature stone shrine of Gauri Shanker at Jagatsukh in Kullu is supposed to be the earliest surviving stone temple in the State. It has been dated on stylistic ground to the early eighth century. Similarly the most famous and superb in style is the Vishveshwar temple dedicated to Shiva at Bajaura. Here three-some niche temples house magnificent images in Pala arts of Vishnu, Mahisasurvardini and Ganesha. Both of them have only garbhagriha i.e. sanctum sanctorum but the Vaidyanath temple is a classical monument which is in Shikhara style with added sabhamandap. Shikhara style stone temple is not many but those which have survived with the ravages of times are still great cultural possessions of state. Temples of Manimahesh and Narsingh at Bharmour, Laxmi Narayan temple complex at Chamba and various Shiva and Shakti temple of Mandi town are in Shikhara style. A reference of rock cut temple at Masrur (Kangra) made up in post Gupta style of 8th century is a solitary instance of rock cut architecture in Himachal Pradesh. It bears the testimony of influence on temple style in tradition with the peninsular India. Pent roofed structures as temples are situated at Bijli Mahadev in Kullu, Hotkoti in Shimla, Lakshana, Shakti and Chamunda in Chamba. It is the most popular form of hill temples architecture. Several temples with pyramidal tiered roofs which take the form of pagoda are widely distributed in the hills of Himachal Pradesh. This is a unique style of hill temple in which dimmishing roofs rise one above the other and the top are unlike the squarish is round like the shape of funnel which is some-time surmounted with a metal canopy or chhatar. Hidimba, Tripur Sundari, Adi Brahma in Kullu, Parasher and Magru Mahadev in Mandi and several in Satluj Valley like Kao and Mamel are most significant. Domed or deformed shikar temples like Jawalamukhi and Chntapurani are the product of 18th & 19th century and the Jalpa, Tarna, Ganesh and Kameshwar Mahadev temples of Mandi town also falls in this category. These are admixtures of Hindu, Sikh and Muslim architectures. The styles of flat roofed temples are a few but remarkable. Narvadeshwar at Sujanpur Tihra, Ramgopal at Damtal, Mangarh at Sirmour and Budhist Monasteries of Lahul and Spiti are in this category.

A distinguished style of pent and Pagoda temple in common has also developed especially in the Satluj Valley of the state. The Bhimakali temple of Sarahan is a fine example of this style which is one of the finest specimens of hill architecture. The roofs are slanting and slightly concave resembling Chinese pagodas.

History records the existence of a developed culture in the pre-Christian era in Himachal Pradesh. The cultural activity of Himachal is distinct and unique in the sense that it is a continuous historical cob-web woven by various cultural groups of south and north. Herein is found the greatest example of religious tolerance and co-existence. This state in question was settled by series of migration and immigration that continued for centuries. The settlers came from all the surrounding areas, but principally from the plains of India. Four major cultural legacies, each distinguished by its characteristic socioeconomic and ethnic facets can be identified. Firstly the people of prehistoric Indian culture flowed into Himachal areas from the south settling in southern and central parts. The distinctive features of this culture were the Kolarian language an indigenous religious system, and an economy based on live-stock raising and shifting agriculture. The second strain was that of people of Aryan origin; the Khashas was perpetrated from the North-west and settled in the mid-mountainous belt of Himalayas from Kashmir to Nepal and beyond. The principal features of their culture were their language that has close association with Sanskrit now known as Pahari and settled agricultural endeavor. Today they form a large majority of population. The Indo-Mongeliods known as Kiratas in Sanskrit literature came from North-east. The people of this stock settled in the northern most fringes and as time rolled into centuries they got mixed with the locals. This group is characterized by their Indo-Tibetan language, Lamaistic Budhism mixed economic structure of raising live stock and shifting agriculture and trade. The real Indo-Aryan culture penetrated from the south. The people of this group hail from greater Indian plain for variety of reasons. The most important of this reasons include the location of holy places in and around Himachal Pradesh. The intensive thinking on the development of history of Himachal and its people offer these ideas firmly but true authenticity of these beliefs is yet to be explored extensively. Ideas appear to be logical but are largely conjectural and confusing. The fusion of the beliefs, the languages and religious practice give rise to a new picture as a result of amalgamations of concepts and ideals of old indigenous religious systems of Budhism and Hinduism. The old settlers were thus successful in retaining their own culture while imbibing the new. Thus there remained an ideal peaceful co-existence of all the settlers. No confrontation, no apathy but co-operations and empathy with all the ideas of old and new. With this cultural background, Himachal marched on the path of prosperity and many a landmarks were created by the rulers and ruled alike. Vastly they have survived the rigours of time and space to the fact that they were places of workship. Therefore they remained undisturbed. The supra and infrastructure of such places might have got changed with the march of time but the sanctum and idols preserved their original forms and they formed the basis of antiquity and archaeology of this Pradesh. Himachal being a mountainous region, the journey of this area being very unpleasant and time consuming and that is why primarily it remained free from the devastators and iconoclasts. This is the reason as to why the old bronzes, the old temples and the old ruling houses or forts remained preserved till this date. It is a great romance to visit and study these artifices of our old historical records. Many of my sojourns were with this motive to have on the spot study of the glorious objects which are so dear to all the students of History and Archaeology. History, Archaeology and antiquity although provide firm footing to our subject but the fact of the matter is, there is wide speculation about the ancient events which by and far are vague.

Historical linkages are being traced to the vedic and prevedic eras. A large number of establishments are associated with the vedic sages and epic heros. The Aryan's victory on Kolarians is said to be won in the lower hills of Himalayas i.e. in the lap of Shivaliks. Vishwamitra, Lomas, Parshuram, Vyas, Prasher, Shuk and Mandava are all said to have their hermitages in the particularly present Himachal Pradesh and in general all over the Himalayas. Hardly exists any hillock, temple, lake or cave which is not stretched back to be the creation of Pandawas. All these fables, stories and legends have firm bearings on the mindset of the natives of the land. Now some of the writers have become enthusiastic to correlate this history with all the leading kingdom of the greater Indian plains. Chandragupta Maurya is associated with Sirmour as the word 'mour', 'mor' and moriya have some sort of resemblance. Similarly the Gupta empire is said to have been extended upto this region. The iron pillar of Gupta period now in Mehrauli area of Delhi was brought to the capital city from the Shivaliks. In all the important epics, jataks as well as in the Panini's Ashtadhyayi there are vivid narration of small tribal principalities called janapadas which were named after the groups of the peoples or territorial units retaining their own cultural integrity in matter of customs, beliefs and dialects. These were territorial and ethnic Republic units and some were monarchial. The majority however was republican in character and these were called sangha or Janapadas or Ayudhajivi Sanghas who worked under elected or hereditary chiefs and have their own assemblies. Such Janpadas are precisely observed as the Audumbaras, the Trigartas, the Kalutas, the Kulandas and Yaudheyas. One such surviving unity can be ascertained at Malana in Kullu district, which is more a village kingdom reminiscent of olden days polity in village, city and janapadas i.e. the territorial ethnic unit. Malana is a hinter-land of District Kullu in the Parvati Valley situated at height of about ten thousand feet above sea level. The people are still poor, simple and illiterate thriving exclusively on agriculture and animal breedings. So far no person from outside was permitted by the councils of people to enter the territory of the village. Although the population just touches one thousand and more souls but their age old polity in still intact and is the prototype of administration in the prehistoric ages. The administration is run by a parliament type of body which have two houses known as Kanishtag (lower or junior) and Jayshtang (Upper or Senior). The members are partly elected and partly hereditary. The overlord is a village god popularly called Jamaloo but is said to be the Rishi of Vedic era i.e. Jamadagani who was father of well known Parshurama of epic era. Jamalu has his own image and is taken out in procession. He communicates with its people through the oracles or gurs and no one dare to challenge the verdict or judgement of Jamalu. The goat sacrifice is a gala big ceremony. He can pronounce Desh Nikala i.e. extermination and can pronounce death sentence on the culprit. There is total freedom for the fair sex to marry, divorce and remarry all within the frame work of their own native laws. A special dilect with vast sprinklings of Sanskrit words is the language of the people. This village reminds us in actually what were the principles and practices of the law and administration in the olden times; which is not century's old but are prehistoric flashbacks.

In other tribals republic perhaps the pictures was on the similar pattern which might have been the order of the day. Some much celebrated janapadas are discussed to highlight the historical backgrounds of the areas.

Audumbara finds a detailed reference in the Mahabharata. The coins belonging to them are the earliest one found in the various parts of Himachal Pradesh and adjoining territory of Pathankot in the Punjab state. The Audumbara republic flourished in and around Kangra. Their coins mention rulers like Mahadera, Dharaghosha and Rudravarman. Their economic prosperity and building skills can be testified by the study of their coins. One of their rulers Dharmaghesha had checked the advance of Indo-Greek King Demetrious towards the upper Bari-Doab. The growth of this republic their regional powers and material prosperity is evident from the large number of silver and copper coins which date back to the first century B.C. Their power was as far as Mathura and finally they fell before the emerging power of the Kushana Empire which extended its sway over the area earlier held by the

Audumbara. Kuninda was an other tribe of repute.

One of their many their rulers was Amoghabhuti Kunida who existed in first century B.C. as according to the Kuninda coins. There is no mention of Kuninda in the Allahabad pillar inscription of Samudra Gupta leading to explain that by that time their kingdom had withered. Therefore, it may be safely assumed that the Kuninda state did not survive for a longer period and was probably overpowered by the Yaudhayas, which had established their republic on the ruinage of Kushana Empire. They are also known by their copper coins. Contrary to Kunindas they have found mention in Samundragupta's Allahabad pillar inscription in which it is mentioned that they were defeated and subjugated by great gupta dynasty. After Gupta's dis-integration, the plain of Panjab and adjoining hills had years of political stability under Harshawardhan. In post Harsha period the Gurjara-Pratiharas emerged as one of the leading powers in the northern Indian plain. Their influence in Himachal can be deciphered by several bronze and stone sculptures depicting the influence of Pratihara art style and after the collapse of Pratihara the scenes of Rana and Thakurs appears in Himachal Pradesh as local sovereigns which had their sway for a considerable period of time which got replaced by the emergence of Rajas.

Besides Vanshavalies of the rulers the history of Himachal Pradesh during the ancient period has been largely based on inscriptions, epigraphs and numismatic sources. A good stuff is preserved in the traveller's narrations. The earliest rock inscription in the Tons Valley (Sirmour), Pathiyaer and Kanhiyara (Kangra) and Salanu (Mandi) are inscriptions from sixth century onwards. Nirmand in Kullu has an important copper plate issued by Maharaja Samudra Sen.

The most of the early monuments in the Himalayas were made of wood and other perishable materials, and have eventually disappeared leaving us no examples of art belonging to early centuries after Christ. There is evidence to show that Gupta art gained strong foot hold in the hills for the first time in the 6th - 8th centuries especially in the Brahmour region of Chamba from where the Surya image from Gum little known place in the Ravi Valley half way between Chamba and Bharmour is a classical example in stone sculpture. Such images later show the influence of Kushana art as well. Later in the reign of Meruvarman whose time has been dated by paleographical evidence only and scholars differ on the subject. While some experts have placed him in the middle of 7th centuries AD; others prefer the end of the century. There are still those who consider him to be roughly a contemporary with the Kashmiri monarch Lalitaditya

Muktapida (725-5 AD) and in some kind of subordinate alliance with him. On stylistic grounds alone the latter view appears to be more plausible. In this period, Kashmir and the Shivalik parts of Himachal were in close cultural contact as is shown by the architectural designs of temples of such as the Manimahesh, Laxana Devi, Narshimha and Ganesh temples of at Brahmour and by some of the most exquisite of the well known bronzes such as the icons of Laxana Devi at Brahmour and Shakti Devi at Chatrari which all are attributed to Meruvarman the founder of Brahmour. The tradition also has it that it was the last work of Gugga, the master artisan of Meruvarman however the Brahmpura Kingdom formed an important link between Gupta art forms and the expansion of Hindu civilization. The Gupta civilization was later wounded by outer attacks but has left behind its marks in the Himalayan hinterland. This classical art of later Gupta refined and polished in the sophisticated courts of Lalitaditya of Kashmir and Meruvarman of Brahmour clashed with the rustic forthright and down to earth art of Kanauj. The Gupta canon here is still more or less intact but obviously due to early Pratihara influences the sculptures has required a pompous vitality verging on hardness and exaggerated mannerism. This finds its classical example in the Yogakar Varmans idols of Gauri Shanker in one of the temple of Laxmi Narain temple complex in Chamba town. Not only that even other art models also made in way into the Himalayas like that of Pala icons even greater numbers and finally succeeded in occupying a position no less important than that earlier held by examples of Kashmir art. Examples of stone sculptures perhaps executed during the period are the idols of Vishnu, Ganesha and Mahishasura-mardini in the nich temples of Bajaura temple in Kullu. The slender but powerful bodies, the longish faces as well as the over elongated limbs of the pala art of this period are all to be observed in Mahishasur mardini. The sculptures seems to have been carved by artisans from eastern India, as is shown by the marvelous sense of composition and volume to be seen in the arrangement of arms and legs of the goddess and of the demon king, whom she has just overpowered. This is indicative of renewed vitality and vigour of these refugee craftsmen in their new environment. The qualities of their work are also in keeping with the canons of ideal beauty of Meruvarman's brass figures like Meruvarman's images the excessively slim yet elegant body of Mahisasurmardin is dressed in stylized costumes and can even make out the master touch of Gugga's modeling. Besides these classical styles in later Gupta and Pala styles a charming sculptures on an eternal theme by its bold departure from accepted formulate ushered in an era of Pahari style in sculpture mainly based on indigenous resources. A sculpture of Kali Devi is a piece in which the solid objects and rough shape more in harmony with the block or slab of stone art of which the figures are chiseled and in a style which is less inclined merely to respect the cliched set by the accepted schools of medieval India. The emphasis in this style was on the natural shape of the stone a tradition which emerged from the local practice of stone worship prevalent among most Himalayan communities. Even today there are temples in this area where the main deity in some shrines is no more than a piece of stone. A beautiful image of Bhadanti Mahadev, extra ordinary sculpture of five faced Panchanan Shiv as Panchvaktra and that of marvelous piece of icon of Trilokinath Mahadev in Mandi town are the result of this art-activity. Another most interesting sculpture done in the pahari style is Shiva in the form of Ardhanari, half female. Shiva Ardhanari is the logical development of the trend which considered the male to be the personification of the passive aspect, the female the activating energy fused in one. All these art activities right from post Gupta travelling through Kanauj and Pala influences to the folk images are all equally at par so far as the historical background of these activities are concerned. No eye brows are to be raised on the emergence of Folk style as it represents the real creativity and understanding of the man about the great Indian influences on the arts. Actually here is an attempt to portray divine form based on intense insight and spiritual scrutiny of the sculpture that was obviously haunted by the impossibilities of imparting the attributes of an ever sharper symbolic meaning to this idol. With the passage of time the practice became a custom so that even when the temples were more prosperous and their treasury more rich, the images were made of stones the native and down to earth material to transform into divinity. This religio-art tradition in one form of or another was kept alive in the western Himalayas preserved in its indigenous style and ageless symbols.

CHAPTER - 2

SUN-SCULPTURES IN HIMACHAL: A Study

The earliest object which enchanted the human mind was the Sun rising in the morning from the east and setting in the west and was watched with wonder and awe by the earliest survivors of human race. The warmth, the light and the life which it gave to biological beings attracted their fancy. Hardly is there any ancient civilization aboriginel or developed one today which has not taken cognizance of the importance of Sun worship. Sun as Chakra with rays all around, the Swastika and even only a circle constitute the symbolic representation of Sun. These can be deciphered in the old cave markings, coins and un-deciphered scripts. Later the rayed disc was taken as an indicator of Surya which ultimately got an important place in Vaishnava worship as Chakra. On the top of Vishnu temple, the multirayed discs are displayed as emblem or attribute of Vishnu shrines.

In history and legends, the Surya temple at Mulsthan i.e. the present day Multan in Pakistan is said to be the earliest temple dedicated to Surya by the son of Krishna whose name was Shamba. Tradition relates that the Magh Brahamins who were recognized as the main 'pujaris' of the temples were summoned from Shakwdeep which was perhaps present day Iran. Magga or Bhojaki are spread all over the north India and are distinct class of Brahmins. Magi is still a word used in the West for the learned people.

The Sun temple at Konarka is a splendid paradigm of the architectural skills of the 13th century artisans. The history of this magnificent monument dedicated to Surya is also correlated with Shamba the son of Krishna. It is said that centuries after, when Shamba had rebirth as Lingraja Narsingh Dev, he commissioned this shrine of splendeour. It is interesting to note that Konark derived its name from being a predominantly triangular shaped temple when seen from any angle.

The temple in Kashmir near Srinagar situated on a hill even in ruins stands as a testimony of great Kashmiran art and architecture. It is still known as Martanda temple, Martanda being another name for Surya beside Mihir, Prabhakar, Dinesh, Dinkar and Aaditya.

In Himachal my first encounter with an image of Surya was in the temple of Sahibini Sahiba now known as Ekadash Rudra Mandir. The statue is made of marble where the Surya is sitting on the rath driven by seven horses. About one hundred and twenty five years back the mother of Raja Vijay Sen (1851-AD-1902 AD) of Mandi had erected the main Shiva temple with four smaller temples in four corners of the main shrine dedicated to Vishnu, Ganesh, Shiva and Surya. It was in my childhood that I understood that the Sun in the sky is a devta which is worshipped in a temple. I had visited the Baijnath temple in Kangra district while studying for medicine as bus used to be changed at this spot. Here in the niche temple of the shrine; I had seen Surya in sand stone idol shown squatted on a chariot drawn by seven horses. He is decorated with hara, kundala, and kiritamukta holding blossomed lotuses in his both hands. The figure is squarish, rough but bold and is slowly getting erroded by the climatic condition. It was in year 1975, I became familiar with another temple dedicated to Surya in Himachal and it was on my way from Shimla to Kalpa in connection with a mass multipurpose medical camp. To the surprise of my fellow-workers, I got the bus stopped at Nirath a village half way between Shimla and Rampur and visited the Shrine. The temple is in shikhara style with Amalka and Kalash and is dated to the thirteen century A.D. The garbha-griha has a standing idol of Surya. Similarly placed at the entrance is a Sun image of 10th and 11th century. An other full fledged temple dedicated to Sun-god is in the outskirt of Sunder Nagar a sub-division town of Mandi district which is again a sand stone temple in Shikhara style. Constructed much later, it can not date back to more than 300 years. The object of worship is again Surya seated on chariot driven by seven horses. The sculpture is made of bronze and is a product of decadent art more folkish than a refined art object. The third temple which could have existed and primarily dedicated to Sun-god can be conjectured at Bajaura a small township on the border of Kullu and Mandi District. It is thought that the full life size sculpture of Surya in sand stone was worshipped in an independent temple may be nearby the present surviving temple of Shiva known for its high standard of artistic profile. This image of Surya is now in the careful custody of Himachal state Museum at Shimla. It was supposed to be a 8th century creation made up of grey stone but now the scholars are dating it back to 3rd or 5th century. The sculpture was discovered at Bajaura and visualising its shape and size it is deciphered that it had its temple at that side. It is not under Pala influence of art which is observed in other idols of Durga Mahishasur Mardini. Vishnu and Ganesha of Visheshwar Mahadev temple of Bajaura. The idol under description is a magnificent life size image of Surya with sublime face, round contours and very simple treatment without any hint of decoration. The head dress of the figure is similar to the type seen in Gupta style. The gown is going deep down the knee as in Kushana sculpture. The idol possesses a yantra-casket suspended from the waist belt. A long straight sword with sheath is also carved at his left. The two hands hold the non-blossomed lotus flower the main attribute of sun sculpture. The hands have been raised to the level of shoulder giving a royal and majestic posture to the image.

It was almost a surprise for me to locate an image of Surya in the inner temple of Kao in Karsog valley of Mandi district. The main shrine is dedicated to Durga Mahisasur-mardini which has a 8th century's bronze image as the main object of worship. But the most mysterious is said to be a temple of Parashuram in the middle of this temple which is not open to all. I had the privilege to visit it after undressing myself and getting enveloped in a borrowed dhoti when the priest took me to a cave like structure to show the idol of Parshuram. But there was none of Parshuram and I discovered three standing images, two of the height of 3feets each and one Chaturbhuj Vishnu with one face with the usual attributes of gada, shankh, charka and padma and other of Surya holding two blossomed lotuses in its both hands. The third is a small statue of Vaikuntmurti Vishnu with frontal human face with a side faces of bear and lion and the rear one of Kaplika was not shown. When I told the priest that none of them is the idol of Parsuram but only Vishnu, his simple reply was that at Kao, Parshuram is worshiped as four armed Vishnu. It is not clearly understood as to how the image of Surya is the secret possession of this forbidden and secret room temple inside the main building?

Surya in one of the niches of the Shiva temple of Jagat-sukh the oldest capital of Kulu is noteworthy. This piece of art belonging to the 8th century is similar in iconographic conception as that of Nagar again in district Kullu. It is four armed Surya image with long boots and two blossomed lotuses in both upper hands. Surya at Nagar is also in a niche temple of Gauri-Shankar temple. Another broken idol of Surya is preserved in the Roerich Art Gallery of Nagar which is a fine piece of art with serene and sober face. Even in broken state it is capable of lending divine touch to the figure. All these idols have been chiseled under Kushana influence as depicted by their featural configuration. All these sculptures are small objects as compared to the tallest amongst the Surya sculptures in Himachal Pradesh and that is in sand stone preserved in the Himachal State Museum at Shimla. With a height of 30.5 cm another icon is believed to be an 8th century creation and belongs to Masrur in Kangra. The idol is in squatting posture and it possesses great serenity, grace and plasticity.

This idol also depicts, the hands with lotus. Although of 8th century, it possesses the aura and trends of classical period. In the same museum another standing figure of Surya in sand-stone dates back to 9th or 10th century and belong to Sirmour district. Its tight dress and long boots testify it to be carved under Kushana art. It is as usual holding in his both hand, rising to the height of his shoulders the typical lotus flowers in full blossom. Two attendants appear on each side, Dandi and Pingla which can be easily deciphered. At the top corners are Vidyadhars.

The oldest of Surya icon is that of Gum of Chamba district now in possession of Indian Museum, Calcutta. Iconographically similar, there is another stone image at village Gum which is still an object of worship. Bhuri Singh Mueum at Chamba has a privilege to possess one of similar iconography. All the three images seemingly the oldest from the Himachal Pradesh are works of 6th century AD. It is presumed that they are the product of a single artist's imagination and craftsmanship. These Surya images are in squatting posture and in accordance with Kushana trends are having Sassaniam dress and hair style, but otherwise of pure Gupta idiom. The image in the Bhuri Singh Museum Chamba measures 63X51 cms and is shown in squatting pose on a chariot of seven horses driven by Aruna the divine charioteer holding the reigns. Icon is having Kundalas, and holding lotuses in both the hand. Its hair fall down on shoulders in compact position a characteristic of later Gupta period. The arrow shooting goddesses Usha and Pratusa are on either side. On the extreme left corner appears small figure with folded hands possibly Vidyadhara. The girdle is tied over the waist while yantra casket being suspended down. One similar sculpture is said to be at Devi-Ki-kothi in Chamba. These idols indicate the era of their carving when Indo-Iranian influence was decaying and local type of sun idols were being sculptured.

Minor sun images are among the Nav-grahas and can be easily identified on the door lintels of many temples. The examples being the stone temple of Mangarh in Sirmour, the Shakti Devi temple of Chhitrari the Lakhana Devi temple of Bharmour, the temple Dhungari of Manali and Magru Mahadev temple of Mandi. The wooden panels of the Parashar Dev temple have two images of Surya in folkish style. A major wooden panel showing Surya on the façade of Markula Devi temple at Udaipur is of great antiquity in the erst while Chmba state and now in the district Lahul-Spiti. All these images establish the hold of sun cult prevalent in the Himachal Pradesh from very early period to a few centuries back when not only the sculptures were being cast and chiseled but even exclusive sun temples were constructed for this God of life and light.

Bhavishya Purana refers Mega Brahamines as priest of Surya temples. This establishes the identity of Surya with Mirth of Iranian Maga. The scholars hold the view that after the Rigvedic Mitra lost importance, Surya was absorbed into another Braha-manical sun-god i.e. Vishnu. The same Purana ascribes the acceptance of Surya-Mitra to Samba, the son of Krishna, the incarnation of Vishnu in the epic times of Mahabharta.

The earliest Surya icon of Gum in the upper Ravi valley is the oldest of its kind from Himachal now preserved in the National Museum, Calcutta.

CHAPTER - 3

WOODEN TEMPLE OF PARASHAR : A Majestic Sanctuary of Art

A recent visit to Parashar Deo temple opened new vistas and perspectives. Wooden temples and their carvings in ancient times were great preserver of Hindu psyche. Luckily they have come down to our times. How many such excellent harbingers of this art and craft have been lost is beyond imagination! Wood being a perishable material is bound to get damaged after a spell of time. Moreover if these works of art are in exposed condition, the vagaries of weather are also their enemy and sooner or later, they are decayed and get destroyed. Himachal still has to its credit many a shrines in fair condition of preservation. Such temple include the Shakti Devi Temple of Chhatarari, Laxana Devi Temple of Bharmour and Mrikula Devi Temple of Udaipur all belonging to the ancient kingdom of Chamba. Basically these temples undisputedly belong to 7th century although the superstructure might have changed hands several times. The temple of Hidimba of Dhungari in Kullu, Chhatri temple of Magru Mahadev in Mandi and of course Parashar Deo temple of Mandi also possesses the heritage of wood carvings endevours. The master craftsmanship may have disappeared in these later shrines but the process of art creativity in this field had not vanished. May be in a period of decay but still, they reflect the strong impact which the mastercraft-men of earlier period had taken to commanding great heights of glory.

Parashar Dev temple is of early 14th century. Ban Sen was the king of Mandi, when this shrine was commissioned. Situated on the bank of a lake of the same name, the temple is supposed to be dedicated to Parashar Rishi who was father of Ved Vyas. The temple is in pagoda style in three tiers entirely made up of wood and local stone. The roof has been provided of local stone slates to the first and second floor while the third is conical in shape exclusively prepared of wooden planks. The provisions of vertical wooden pieces of one and half foot in length are conspicuous in all the floor roofs. They were designed primarily for decoration but when the wind is blowing they strike with each other giving rise to a melodious note in symphony so charming and soothing which can better be felt only rather imagined. The object of worship is a human figure made up of stone with hooded snake's canopy over it. It is not facing the main door and can only be examined once you are inside the sanctum. A new marble icon of a rishi is a new addition inside this small space.

The most conspicuous feature is the remarkable carvings of the temple. Predominantly it is in scrolls and flora which can not be ignored. The carvings of the scrolls are reminiscent of high degree of such works on the doors of earlier temples as well. The human figures holding garlands, same that of adorers and Kirtimukha resembles early such attempts at Ajanta. Also the prominent inter-twined serpents are a Pratihara motif of Post-Gupta period better known as Gujjar-Pratihara style. Symmetrically carved on both sides the main door is a prominent mask emanating of divinity. Sublime and serene dispositions of there two masks emanating divinity. Sublime and serene disposition of these two masks can be observed on the principal metal masks of the innumerable dancing godlings spread widely all over and every hamlet in the Western Himalayas. An icon of Brahma can be identified in the carving carrying a book in one of its hand. Similarly Shiva reclining on the bull has also escaped the wrath of natural decaying process. A two armed Vishnu carrying gadda and padma on its divine vehicle garuda is still in a good shape and is easily deciphered. Durga-mahisasur-mardini is also carved clumsily. Its stark frontal view exhibits a poor composition holding the tail of the buffalo with one hand and piercing its head with an attribute which looks like a lancer with triangular sharp tip. It appears as if the devi has put its one foot on the neck of the buffalo. Although such representations of the Durga are not rare but this decadent piece of art is not contemporary of the creation of temple and is obviously is a later addition. The scene of Samudramanthan i.e. the tale of churning of ocean is a prominent theme of carving but in Parashar carving, it has been summarised wisely and clearly on a small canvass. A central churning rod is fastened with snake which has been held by two personnels on each side. The churning rod has been put in a vessel rather than in the sea perhaps only to depict the well known legend in symbolic form. Three more deities are shown on a row over the lower two, one among them on the right corner with a prominent mace in one hand may be Lord Vishnu, between Vishnu and the other icon of Ganesha and placed over Ganesha is a Shiva in lingam form being worshipped by row of three human figures the two of them are posed in such a way as if they are more akin to monkeys than human beings. On the left side of the circumambulation on the window frame has a Ganesha icon marvelously carved on the wooden planks which emits all merits of a classical Ganesha image in an excellent state of preservation. While the rest are decaying but this one is as fresh and fine as if carved only recently.

On the whole, the location of temple and lake lends an handsome panorama to this meadow land at alpine height of roughly 9000 feat from sea level. The whole vast tract is grassy with extensive growth of wild flowers of various hues and colours emitting an aroma encompassing entire ecology of the land which is vigourating, profoundly perfuming, cooling and somewhat appetizing also. The wind is almost in blast during the mid-day-time as usual with high land places. The Parashar pasture land on the whole is not an even piece. It is marked by various elevations and depressions and deepest part of the depressed land is the location of the lake which is considered sacred. The temple is on its bank and when the lake is full of water especially in rainy season the reflection of the temple can be observed in the clean watering surface of the lake. A moving island was the pride of this place but due to some geophysical reasons it has got stuck to a side. The trend of rearing fish in this lake; a recent phenomenon has resulted in erosion of the banks of the lake, which is not a positive enterprise. An age old sarai was there which has been improved and provisions of raised platform have been introduced. These platforms are made use of during the fairs when a good number of village deities partake and these serve the purpose of keeping their 'raths' for exhibition to the devotees who propitiate them with deep reverence. This year in March 04, a rath of an old deo of high echelon of Mandi Raj was brought here to expedite the onset of rains. The season was almost dry for months together and the said deo through its oracle had directed the people to take the rath to Parashar to help hem out of lurch and grant the much needed rains for the drying fields. It was deo Chandohi placed very high in the hierarchy in the council of ministers of Deo Prashar considered to be the highest deity of this entire land, comprising Sanor, Badar and Uttarsal. A goat had been scarified in honour of this deo and fresh bloodlines were visible in the temple compound near the place where the rath of Deo had taken position, when we entered the temple. About ten years back a moderate wooden rest house was erected near a hilly elevation but it caught fire and was destroyed. Now a new one had come up just on the entrance of this uneven ground. Nearby the gateway of the meadow land a construction activity for a major building of brick is also coming up, may be a hostel for nomads.

This land is inhabited by nomadic, sturdy and handsome tribe of Gujjars. During our present sojourns all their houselets know as Daware were vacant. All were at stand still. Comes the time, when they return both with family and animals, this place bustles with their presence. The gujjars over here are looking after buffaloes, for seasons after seasons, come and go in search for fodder of their animal wealth. Once they return these sons of nature mingle with the heavenly site of Parashar pasture land and become a part of this small universe of vast un even ground, the lake and the temple.

This time an almost new experience was in store for me, when the entry into the sanctum was disallowed. On previous occassions no such practice was in vogue. The stone image of worship was out of glimpse, for us. It is a storehouse of extremely useful information. The details of the statue could only be elucidated after having a perusal of a photograph of the icon sent to me by a learned friend from Shimla. It is a black stone image? Black stone is rare in this locality. May be a sand stone structure acquiring a deep blackish hue after having repetitions and multiple applications of mustard oil for centuries. History attributes the erection of temple to the period of Raja Ban Sen (Mid 14th Century) but decidedly on iconographic basis the stone image dates anterior to the years of his time. It is a standing image, stout in configuration with round, full and finely chiseled face. Both the legs are muscular and without draperies. The left hand is holding a vase and right seems to be in Abhayamudra. The most conspicuous characteristic of the statue is a canopy of a huge nine hooded cobra which over-shadows the icon. Surrounding from all sides is a number of snake heads more predominantly on the right half of the image. A snake like structure or may be a 'pattaka' which tapers like a head of a big snake is stretching from left shoulder down to the right thigh. It is an admitted fact that details in depth can only be furnished on subjective examination of the object rather than the study of a photograph. No stretch of imagination can classify this icon as that of Rishi Parashar who to an average Indian psyche will match with the recently installed marble statue of a figure sitting in padmasana with long flowing white beard and jattahair falling on his shoulder and beyond. So what message does the stone figure convey? Is it related to a primarily down to earth Naga Cult arising out of snake worship or it is an image of Budhist saint and philosopher Naga-Arajun to whom some of the Budhist scholars claim that it fits in his iconographic pattern. Our inference will remain in the realm of myth till a widely accepted explanation is offered by the authentic sources. So far this single fact will remain crystalised that this image has nothing to do with the Pauranic Parashar who is projected as the father of Ved Vyas the originator and author of the verses of Mahabharta's early version known as Jaya.

CHAPTER - 4

PASSAGE TO MANALI: A Treasure of Curiosity

With Jammu and Kashmir out of easy reach for the tourists Himachal Pradesh emerged as the natural choice for those seeking the cool climes. Manali is easily the most popular tourist resort in the state, visited by tourists both from India and abroad. For those from the plains, the journey itself is a memorable experience. While travelling from Delhi, the hill journey begins after Kiratpur situated in the Shivalik foothills, from where one can get a panoramic view of the Naina Devi Shrine situated on a mountain peak. However, it is only on reaching Swarghat that one really feels the change. The mountain air definitely carries a chill. At Swarghat one can visit a typical hill fort which was built by the erstwhile rulers of Nalagarh although in a state of neglect, the fort calls to mind the glorious history and military traditions of the old hill states to capture a fort in those days meant to capture the land and power associated with it. Most of the forts in Himachal were demolished by the British.

Sawarghat falls in Bilaspur District and the route to Bilaspur involves a steady descent. Bilaspur is a small, modern town situated on the banks of Govind Sagar, an artificial lake created by the Bhakra Dam built on the Satluj river further down-stream. Bilaspur is one of the hottest places in Himachal Pradesh, although not as hot as the plains. During summers, when the water in the lake dries up and the lake bed is visible one can see old historic temples surrounded by huge mounds of silt. They were submerged in water when Bhakra Dam was built. In winters when the lake is filled to capacity, the sight of intense blue water stretching for miles all around is an enchanting sight.

While on the way to Bilaspur from Swarghat, one cannot miss the ruins of the Malaun fort set atop a distant hill. The fort had witnessed several historical battles and survived through several rulers-

the British, the Gorkhas of Nepal, the Sikh rulers of Lahore and finally the hill princes.

The journey from Bilaspur to Slapper is along a level stretch. There is an important hydel project at Slapper. The waters of the Beas and Satluj rivers meet here. The Satluj Beas link established through long tunnels dug through the mountains is certainly a modern engineering marvel. At Slapper we enter Mandi district which came into existence when two hill states of Mandi and Suket were amalgamated after the formation of Himachal Pradesh. Ahead lies a journey as enjoyable as the one to Swarghat. One has entered an area of lovely valleys, bubbling brooks, picturesque waterfalls and towering mountains, a scenery which does not change until Manali.

Between Slapper and Mandi lies the beautiful town of Sunder Nagar which was the seat of power of Suket state for more than 500 years. The snow clad Dhauladhar range is clearly visible from here. Between Sunder Nagar and Mandi lies the fertile land of Balh, a unique flat land well irrigated by the tributaries of the Beas.

Mandi is a historic town of temples, situated at the confluence of the Beas and the Suketi rivulet. It was in 1527 A.D. that the town was chosen as the capital by the then ruling Sen dynasty. At a distance of 20 kms. from Mandi is a place known as Pandoh, from where the Beas has been diverted through tunnels inside the mountains to join the Sutlej at Slapper.

Ahead of Pandoh lies the village of Aut where one enters the fabled valley of the Gods Kullu the sentinel point of which is Bajaura known for the Vishweshar temple and apple orchards. From Kullu, Manali is another two-and-a-half hour's drive away. As you approach Manali, the thick forests of deodar trees welcome you and the soothing sound of the Beas flowing alongside create a beautiful symphony.

Manali offers all comforts to the visitor. There are plenty of hotels and huts which provide all modern amenities. A trek to the Hidimba temple is a wonderful experience. Set amidst towering deodar trees, the temple is shaped like a pagoda, an architectural master-piece of its kind. Nearby is the famous hot springs extremely popular with tourists. A visit to the temple of Manu is a must. It is the only shrine in the country dedicated to Manu Rishi. Manali derived its name from Manavalaya i.e. the abode of Manu. The words "Manav" and "Manushya" are derived from the root word Manu. Manu was the only survivor of the Maha Pralay the great flood and is said to have fathered the human race.

Manali has a lot to offer if one has the time to think and enjoy simultaneously.

MANALI: Once you reach Manali, you are in the land of gods and goddesses, of temples of rare style and also surrounded by the legends and myths of thousands of years standing. Most conspicuous is the Hidimba Temple of Manali situated in a dense wood of deodar trees. It is in pagoda style, about a quarter mile from Manali, connected with jeepable road and is actually in Dhungari hamlet. In folk lores it is connected with Pandavas encounter with Hidimba which later solemnized into marriage with Bhima. Although hailing from a demon cult, Hidimba is considered a Devi who in fact is presiding deity of the Kullu valley. The Raghunath Ji of Kullu can not declare its Dushehra open till the rath of Hidimba has not reached Kullu town. Such is the reverence at its command. The wooden temple was built by Raja Bahadur Singh of Kullu in 1553. It is a square structure and has rich carvings of a devotee perhaps Bahadur Singh the raja who commissioned the temple and other that of Durga can also be deciphered properly. At the centre of the door lintel, figure of Ganesha is shown. On the beam above the door appear the nine planets, navgrahas and above them are carved gandharvas in dancing postures. The upper most part in decorated with. Buddhist box for idols and dorji (Thunder bolt). Some of the panels depict Krishna also. The devotee already described is at the top of the side frame which appears as the same prince riding a galloping horse and on other corresponding side he is shown as a devotee counting the beads. This temple is enriched with an inscription in Tankari engraved on wood informing its creation by Raja Bahadur Singh. It is said this he might have done it in gratitude for the success he achieved in subduing the local chieftains. On the entrance the temple has been provided with big horns of slain animals either for decorative purpose or to exhibit the demonic character of the Devi as her origin is said to be from the clan of demons. The main sanctum has a big boulder and some minor bronze images. As a matter of fact the boulder is the object of veneration.

JAGATSUKH AND NAGAR: Manali including the majestic temple of Hidimba at Dhungari are on the right hand side of the Beas. Exactly the village known as Manali is different and is about one km. from the growing township. A partly paved village pathway leads us to the place where stands the temple of Manu-the first man on the earth and the progenitor or survivor of the human race. There exists modest village temple in Pahari architecture with various deformed idols in the sanctum the identity of which is difficult to decipher. The village guides are generally innocent and ignorant people and for them all these shrines and temples is the creation of Pandavas. Howsoever a strange and unusual description was associated with a semi classical stone sculpture of Mahishasur-mardini in the rear of the temple which was described by our guide a 'rakshak'. I asked him how you say it to be a rakshask or demon. His reply was simple that, that is how his father had told him. Moreover he showed us some old blood stains. Actually the goats and sheep are sacrificed at this point and not in front of main sanctum. Nothing else was remarkable at the village site. The left bank of the river Beas is equally picturesque and charming. On my first visit to the place we followed this pakka motor route because the locality of Jagatsukh on the side of this road is a historical place being the first capital of the first ruler of Kullu. In the genealogical tree of the royal house of Kullu he is known as Vihangmani Pal. He appeared to be roaming here when people are said to have recognised in him their ruler. He made Jagtsukh as the first capital of Kullu kingdom. Later it was shifted to Nagar and lastly to Sultanpur or Kullu proper again on the right bank of the Beas.

Jagat Sukh is a pretty fine village with a Shiva temple of roughly tenth century. It is modeled as a miniature temple in Shikhara style and is in a good state of preservation. The decorative motif on the exterior walls of the Jagatsukh temple is borrowed from the Chaitya-window which is blended with floral pattern. Other motifs are visibly purana-ghata and lotus in ornamental form. The rathikas of the temple are carved out in relief. In the medallion at the facade the usual type of Bhadramukha with three faces of Shiva is shown. Below this is a figure a unique feature, no where else seen in the temples of Himachal Pradesh. This figure is in padmasna with folded hands as if in prayer. Originally temple consisted only of the sanctum; the two pillars together with a corrugated roof are later additions. The shrine is tiratha on plane having a small niche complete with udgama pediments on three walls which still enshrine Surya, Ganesha and Durga mahishasur mardini. A curvilinear rekhanagara superstructure crowns the sanctum. The shrine is simple but elegant. Village Jagatsukh has also yielded some interesting sculptures of 9th and 10th century and some of them are on display in state museum at Shimla. Nearby the Sandhya Devi temple made of wood and stone is perhaps the singular one dedicated to Sandhya Devi. There are several scattered parts of temple assembled to give some organised look to this temple where perhaps could have been a stone temple of same Devi in Shikhara style because I could see a huge amalka lying near the temple complex. The present stone and timber temple dates to 16th - 17th century. Sandhya Devi was being worshipped by the early Aryans and several hymns to this goddess are proud possession of Vedic richas. No where else I have come across a temple for Sandhya. It appears to be an early Aryan settlement which presently is called Jagatsukh and is a monument of national importance.

Lower down about 10-15 Kms. from Jagatsukh is the place known as Nagar.

In the hills generally Nagar use to be a word used for capital and Nagar was capital of Kullu kingdom after Jagatsukh. Nagar has Shiva temple of old antiquity in Shikhara style and on other wooden temple just like that of Hidimba dedicated to Tripur Sundari or goddess Durga. Nagar castle is also a focal point for so many romantic tales and legends and the flat stone placed near the castle is known as Jagatipith an other important place told and retold in folk lores. An art gallery of Russian Painter Nikolai Roerick is also a place of attraction at Nagar. Beside the paintings of this genius his house has large number of stone sculptures displayed in and around this dwelling of a master mind.

Passage to Manali is romantic and Kullu is known as the valley of temples. The valley as a whole has all the attractions of the gleeful fairs and festivals of dances, a scenic beauty of great grandeur and sublimity, attractive ornamental dresses and jewelleries but above all the remains of the historical temples with their architectural grace, grandeur and antiquity in abundance.

CHAPTER - 5

VAIDHYANATH: The Supremo of Doctors

In mid-fifties of last century, I had crossed through a small town of Kangra valley known as Baijnath. It was my voyage to join as a medical student at Patiala followed by many more both to and fro journeys during vacations. From a distance while sitting in the bus or standing near it, I used to admire a meticulous fine piece of architecture which is the temple of Baijnath. Several times, I wanted to have a glance from nearby or enter the temple but always my attempts failed due to the fear of bus being missed all of a sudden and leaving me behind in the lurch. Those were difficult times as far as transportation is concerned. Only two buses used to ply from Mandi to Pathankot and the rest of journey, I used to complete after boarding a train at Pathankot to visit Patiala. Now hundreds of buses, taxis and personal conveniences are available and time has taken a full turn to discard the authority of old monopoly of transport system of government and their drives.

Yes, fortunately or unfortunately, once the bus had a big break down at Baijnath on my journey from Pathankot to Mandi and driver declared unilateral 'ceasefire' till next morning. After depositing personal effects in a moderate lodging near the bus stand, I and one of my fellow-passenger a Namdhari Sikh of Mandi returned to visit the temple. That time I was not familiar with its history and architectural wealth and my maiden visit was simply that of a religious pilgrimage to a Hindu shrine. Of course a person in the premises of the temple told us the age old fable of Ravana worshiping in this temple and other concoction of such legends. There I learnt that religious predilection of Namdhari sect dose not allow them to take meals outside their own hearth and home. I enjoyed to my fill in a cheep road side eatery while my friend kept him satisfied with a dozen or more bananas. My maiden experience with this shrine was worth-while to get acquaintance with a monumental structure.

Later while at Chamba, when I was posted there in early seventies I got exposure to this one of the greatest gift of heritage to the Himachali people in particular and all the scholars and serious students of art in particualr. As a matter of fact, Baijnath is situated in a very pleasant site. It is perched on a ridge of Dhauladhar near the bank of rivulet known as Binnu, which for the sanskrit scholars is famous with the name of Binuka. Its situation at the foothill and the rivulet lend cool climate to this place around the year. In fact Baijnath is one of the few places noted for its breeze in the whole belt of Kangra. A little above the bank of the Binnu there is a spring said to possess peculiar virtues. It is known as Kathog.

It is said that Raja Sansar Chand used to get his drinking water from the spring even while he was in places far away. Once I had a stay in the rest house of Baijnath a site, below which is the over flowing gurgling and dancing river Binnu. The breeze from high hills mingling with the fresh water vapours from the river, keeps this dwelling cool and pleasant in a remarkable state of environment. I was told that, at his place, where the rest house (better known as dak-bunglow) stands, was the site of the castle of the former Ranas, the feudal ruler of the place who owned allegiance to the King of Trigarta i.e. Kangra. About a century ago the remnants of the walls and tanks could be identified on the spot. Small copper coins have been discovered from time to time at this place which might be part of the treasury of ranas of by-gone days. While discussing the Sun-Idols in Himachal, the veteran scholar Mr. V.C. Ohri had hinted about one such idol at Baijnath. For a long time Mr. Ohri was the curator of celebrated Buri Singh Muscum at Chamba and thereafter at State Museum, Shimla. My first endevour was to locate this icon which is situated on the outer-wall facing the bus-stand of the sanctum enriched with three pillar niches of smaller size. The central niche in this east wall contains an idol of the Sun God, Surya wearing a long jacket and long shoes reminding of Kushana influence on the sculpture. It is placed on a marble pedestal which originally must have belonged to a figure of Mahavira of Jain sect; as is proved from a Nagari inscription dated in the Vikrami year 1296 (1240 AD). Similarly niches-temple is on the right and left of the sanctum containing the idols of Hindu gods whereas the niche preserved for Surya is the posterior on the back of sanctum. Similar arrangement is at miniature Shiva temple at Jagatsukh in Kullu district where Surya is on the back of sanctum and other deities like Ganesh and Vishnu are on the right left.

The Baijnath temple is oriented due west. It consists of a garbhaghih, surmounted by a 'Shikkar' of the usual conical shape and hall or sabhamandap, covered with a low pyramidal roof. The adytum which houses the object of worship in a form of a lingum known as Vaidayanath or the overlord of the physicians is entered through a small anteroom with two pillars. The roof of the mandapa is supported by four massive pillars connected by raised benches

Vaidhyanath: The Supremo of Doctors

which form, as it were, a passage leading up to the entrance of the sanctum. The architraves resting on these pillars divide the space of the ceiling into nine compartments, each of which is closed by means of corbelling slab. In front of the mandapa rises a stately porch resting on four columns. Both the south and north wall of the mandapa are adorned with a graceful balcony window. The four corners are strengthened by means of massive buttress-like-projections in the shape of half engaged miniature Shikhara style temples each containing two niches in which images slabs are placed. Smaller niches in slightly projecting chapels are found between the corner projections and the entrance and balcony windows. The outer walls have already come under discussion while having a tryst with Surya image.

As a matter of fact, it is one of the most remarkable monuments of the Beas Valley at the foot of Dhauladhar. Perhaps it was the trend setter of further artistic activities in the adjoining states of Mandi, Suket and Kullu. It is a prototype for their concept ualisation and execution but none of them could reach the architectural loftiness as great as possessed by the temple of Vaidyanath. It was assumed by Cunningham and Furguson that this temple got through restoration in the reign of famous Raja Sansar Chand. But Aurel Stein, who visited the temple in 1892 A.D. is of the opinion that the building has not undergone any alteration of importance. He emphasised that the doorway of the sanctum having the idols of Ganga and Yamuna are part of original construction alongwith the major structure but for the roof which is modern. It was really a fortunate event for this temple to escape the wrath of ghastly earthquake of 1905, which could not disturb it much whereas the nearby smaller temple of Sidhnath, on the contrary was completely reduced to ground.

The name Baijnath is the word derived from Vaidyanath. The name of the place was known as Kiragrama as given on the Sarda inscriptions fixed on the north and south walls of the sabha mandap, the text of which is highly descriptive of the place the persons and other aspects and cultural facets of this region and site. We shall discuss them as much as possible to highlight their contents. Fortunately the date of two inscriptions is expressed both in the Saptarishi and Sakas eras. The Saka date was first assigned by Cummurigham as 726 corresponding with 804 A.D. Further it was disputed and agreed to be Saka year 1126 corresponding with 1204 A.D. We have already mentioned that according to the Baijnath Prashasty the place was known as Kiragram meaning it to be grama or village of Kiras a race about which we know a little. Dr. Vogel of Germany has made a conjecture that perhaps it was a protected garrison where the invaders of the early kingdom of Bharmour were prisoned. Kiras were the people who according to the Chamba chronicles had invaded and plundered this kingdom in 7-8th century A.D. The place is said to be in Trigarta which was the nomenclature used for Kangra territory and the areas beyond it between the Satluj to the Beas and further to the Ravi River System. It is mentioned that on the bank of river Binduka i.e. the river Binnu and this place was ruled over by Rajanaka Laxmana. Here Rajanaka is the word used for rana who was vassal to central power which during the time of composing of inscription was Trigarta whose contemporary ruler was Jaya Chandra of Trigarta. Rana Laxamana's mother Lakshana was daughter of the house of the Trigarta and the name of her father was Hridayachandra. The derivation of this narration is that during that period feudatory ranas or rajanaka were having matrimonial alliances with the central power and although vessals politically they were socially on the same footing. The names ending with suffix Chandra was the prerogative of kings of Kangra till its decadence. Even now the descendants of this clan put the suffix Chandra with their name.

This temple was not the creation of the royalty but some merchants as according to the inscription money regulation and possession was with the rich merchant's class. He is described as Manyuka son of Siddha. His younger brother devoted to him was Ahuka and his wife was Guhika. His Chief mason was Nayaka son of Asika. The other one was Thoduka son of Sammana. They hail from the town of Susarmanpur i.e. the capital town of Kangra i.e. Nagarkot and also known as Bhimkot. Susarman Chandra is said to be one of the earlier kings in the pedigree of rulers of Kangra who had fought on the side of the Kaurava against the Pandawas. It is further mentioned that the merchants erected the temples of Shiva at the doors of which stand the statues of Ganga and Yamuna and other deities.

The perusal of the inscription reveals that most of the names end with 'Ka'. This was the methodology in Sanskrit grammar to sanskritise the non-sanskrit word like Manya, Thodu, Ahu and Nayu. Further it is also stated that the Shiva lingam was Niralaya i.e. without an abode and thereby these merchants provided a roof to it by commissioning the temple over the Shiva-lingam.

The description in the inscription is lyrical with a unique composition. It reads with superb gusto as follows.

"There is in Trigarta the pleasant village of Kiragrama the home of numerous virtues where the river called Binuka, leaping from the lap of mountain with glittering wide waves resembling playing balls merrily plays like a bright maiden in the first bloom of youth." Such is the composition of the verses, really superb to read, the flashback of which remains perpetual for who so ever falls in love with such endeavor and affairs of archaeology and antiquities.

CHAPTER - 6

TRIPLE TROPHIES IN A SINGLE SOJOURN: An Occasional Episode

It was 20th Feb., 2004. The day was clear with pleasant sunshine and clouds were not overcasting the sky. Constant uncertainty prevailing in the weather conditions, this was a good opportunity to move on for shooting of the art objects and sites with camera. An accomplished scholar in the person of Dr. Mankodi from Bombay was with us and also was elderly Inder Singh of Mandi the later was studied a lot about religion and history by dint of his own enterprise and inclination although not much educated in schoolish style.

We left Mandi at 10 a.m. in a Mohindra jeep for our first hunt at Drang about 18 Km. from the town. Drang mines have been a good source of revenue in older times whosoever laid their hand on this site because of its rock-salt deposits. We are told, it has been Rana's territory before its annexation into Mandi state in mid 16th century by a Raja Ajabar Sen of Mandi. Local names like Jaya Pal and Vijaya Pal during Ajbar Sen's time are a little amazing. Such refined named was a rare phenomenon when even Raja himself was having a name like Ajber Sen meaning to me only folkish nomenclature as compared to refined names like Jayapal and Vijaya Pal who were Brahmins engaged by the ruling Ranas of Drang and were fortunate enough to have high sounding Sanskrit names associated with them.

Information was rolled down to us that some old masks have been preserved at a specific place at Drang and our objective was to examine and if possible to get them photographed. A gentleman led us to a small shrine which was nearby on the right of national highway just near the so called bus stop of Drang. The shrine is a small but pucca cement construction of recent origin, dedicated to a female deity and on the right wall of the interior of shrine there were three masks kept up and fixed in a row resting on the wall. It was not difficult to spot and recognise the fact that they definitely were the original masks of 'Bade Nak Wala Devta' as was the deo Chandwali known in Mandi Town. The shrine was locked and the pujari was absent and we had to abandon our photo shooting enterprise. It was postponed to materialize on our return journey.

Now we were in our vehicle, rushing towards Joginder Nagar on Mandi-Pathankot road to locate a old dilapidated temple which recently got wide publicity. Thanks to the abundant proliferation of Hindi daily newspapers.

We had the information that it was near Harabag a small locality on way to Joginder Nagar. Harabag is an open space with fertile fields on both sides of the road and was owned by a landlord of Mandi distantly known to us. We were told that before we reach the vicinity of the Harabag School a small road leads down to the left hand side of the main highway paving the way to the shrine. We could have lost our way but for the help lent to us by a teacher of the school who accompanied us from Harabag down to the projected site.

It was rough pathway with thick bushes on both sides. Majority of them were wild with some plants of known flowers indicating that it was not an entirely dejected place. Ultimately we reached the site of temple which is almost in ruins. When in its actual shape, it was undoubtedly a small but majestic structure. This belief is supported by the remains of its sabha mandap which was centrally supported by four pillars which are made of stone material and can be seen lying on the floor of sabha mandap. A big size beheaded bull in stone is in the centre of sabha mandap and points to the fact, that is was a shrine dedicated to Lord Shiva. Another small bull icon is also there. Two statues still in good form of preservation are that of Bhariawa and Hanuman the later seems to be of recent origin while the former is the work of earlier time dating back to the construction of temple. A half broken stone structure of a scene of Samudra-manthan can be easily deciphered with a rope of serpent around mountain Mandrachala and devatas on one side and danavas on the other. An icon of Kartikeya with its vehicle peacock can be made out after some difficulty as it is mostly in dilapidated form. Indra on Eravat is another statue found in the sabha mandap. A huge amalaka which is really chiseled in classical style is a thing of beauty even in ruins. As usual the Bhadra-mukha has three faces. In this composition central face is sober. The right sided face has a sublime smile and one on the left depicts a state of agony. All the three have jattamukuts and to cast symmetry the right and left are tilted to central presenting it as a single composite piece of art. Such Bhadramukh can be seen on all over the temples of this part of the country. Some chiseled stone with inscription in Tankari are also found lying scattered which can only be deciphered by persons having the knowledge of the script. As you peep into the sanctum sanctorum, a large icon with broken head is conspicuous. It is almost in life size with four arms but the attributes of the hands can not be easily identified. A female figure with folded hands is also in the main frame but its head is also chopped off. Definitely it is a conjoint statue of Shiva and Shakati as the vehicle in their backdrop is bull to the right side and tiger in the left side, i.e. the side of the female figure. The female is shown as a thin lady half in girth than the main figure of Shiva and is clad in a drapery which is having sari like folds. On the whole, it can be conjectured that in its undamaged shape and size it could have been a fine piece of art. The entrance of the sanctum has not yet crumbled but its carvings are beyond identification, due to its state of neglect. Surprisingly even the remaining entrance path also offers some thing to study. In place of two dwarpalas, it has objects standing on marine animals most probably Kurma and Makara which are associated with river Yamuna and Ganga. A proper perspective of details with authenticity will place this temple to be older than all which Mandi town is famous for. All over the main heart land of India, in ancient temple-structures the motifs of Ganga and Yamuna were in practice and not the dwarpalas as in later holy buildings.

Facing in front of the shrine, slightly at lower level is a 10X10 feet step well i.e. wawali another hall mark generally associated with a religious site. It is also not in good shape of preservation and almost the entire upper surface of water has turned into a green sheet due to the proliferation of algaes.

After having a thoughtful inspection of the site the following conclusions appear plausible to explain some facets associated with this old temple.

i) The temple was a shikara style Nagari temple dedicated to Shiva and his consort.

ii) It is older than the other temples, especially that of Mandi Town which is known for its 15-16th century temples. This fact is based on the evidence or the figures of Ganga and Yamuna on the entrance of the shrine.

iii) Its collapse is attributed to the earth-quake of 1905 A.D. known as the Kangra Earthquake.

iv) If really, the earthquake is the cause for its collapse, then why only the icon are beheaded and rest of the parts are still fairly preserved?

v) It is difficult to assign the period when the temple was constructed. Definitely it is not the crude product of the time of Raja Sidh Sen as is inbuilt in the psyche of some people. Definitely on the basis of iconography, it can be placed earlier to him most probably to the era somewhere in 14th century.

vi) As to how and why it remained neglected, whereas the damages of the 1905's earth quake were reestablished and renovated? As it was near a cremation ground that is why none thought to give it its original shape after the collapse. On the left hand side of the temple, we were shown a small green patch which is still used for cremation purpose. To renovate a crumbled structure near the cremation site could not find favour in the prevailing psyche of people who are generally credulous.

vii) This structure became re-conspicuous only in the summer of 2002. It was all covered with shrubs and debris. The place was almost a neglected lot. While working in the wawali which was still sparingly in use, people came across some chiseled stones which after rains had resurfaced. The locals made efforts, cleared the accumulated debris, cut down the shrubs and the place again became a place of worship and that is how again the temple came into existence. A recent parapet of the fine chiseled stones which were the outcome of the collapse is from the old temple structure and has been made use by the people to construct the boundary of the temple recently.

viii) Harabag is a fertile land and is situated near the rock salt mine of Gumma. This was almost a border land between Bhangal and Mandi states of olden times. Actually the state of Bhangal was to the west side of rivulet Gugali but their intrusions upto this place can not be ruled out. It was Sidh Sen who had annexed a part of Bhangal state to his territory. Now who can be founder of this temple! Either of the rulers of these state; because such structures were created under the patronage of rulers only, the ruled were without such extensive means. But was not Baijnath a creation of a merchant. On the same analogy, can this structure be attributed to some one associated with the team of rock mines excavators. This possibility can not be ruled out? But in absence of any inscriptional evidence, it can be mere conjecture only. The Tankari inscriptional stones can tell partially the story of the past if deciphered by some one.

ix) Possibility of destruction by an iconoclast can be kept in mind, on the first examination of the site. It can not be ruled out on the plea as to why the damaged statues have been beheaded only and rest of the body parts are intact. The main Shiva icon is with chopped head and similarly is that of Parwati. The main icon of bull is also without head.

But from the recorded history, no army of iconoclast like Muslim invasion has been recorded in this part of the country. Therefore it is difficult to explain as to why the head parts become the victims of the earthquake or what had shattered this structure.

From Harbagh, our next destination was to visit a temple at Ner south of Jogindernagar. After several inquires we were ready to proceed without the help of any person from Jogindernagar. I had presumed that out of two or three names which were in my knowledge, someone will lend a helping hand, and this remained a presumption only. Some how its location just near the road was a good consolation. After taking many turns from the main road, we landed at the place. The temple is a magnificent piece in Shikhara style temple architecture. A gorkha care taker was of good help for us. The sabha-mandap is supported by four massive pillars leading to the sanctum sanatorum which has stone carved images of Vishnu and Laxami being supported by a large image of Garuda the divine vehicle. Presently the above mentioned image is the object of worship and it is known as temple of Laxami Narayan. The temple does not have much carvings but the pattern of inlaid stone arrangement of the temple walls are highly impressive building lending the notion of its being an older structure than the images of Laxami Narayan. The Bhadramukh is also prominently placed alongwith a sitting statue of lion between the shaba-mandap and sanctum on the top of the temple. A casual look lends an impression that this temple is a carbon copy on lesser scale of the great temple of Baijnath but for the carvings and associated icons of various deities. An idea flashes as to why a temple has been dedicated to Vishnu in the land of Shiva and Shakti. As a matter of fact, in the valley right upto Mandi and Kullu, the Vashanava cult is a later arrival as a form of worship. Prior to Madho Rai and Raghu Nath temples of Mandi and Kullu, no other main temple is primarily dedicated to the Vishnu Cult. Madho Rai and Raghunath were the product of mid seventeenth century but temple under discussion is of earlier date and definitely two or three centuries prior to them. In front of the temple, before we enter the sabha mandap, on the right side is a raised platform having a good number of stones scattered and being worshipped daily, but one of them is conspicuously prominent and well carved shivalingam. It appears that perhaps it was the main object of worship, rather the stone structure of Laxami Narayan on the central wall of the sanctum. It appears that the lingam which was placed in the centre of this sanctum has been shifted to the outer side of the temple. This site has not been discarded but is still the prominent place of daily worship, rather than the carved stone inside. For want of proper documentation, it is far from authentic to elaborate the dating of this temple but on conjectured ground, it seems to be a product of 11-12th century or 12-13th century. Sometimes back, I had seen the photograph of this temple in some local paper. Being on the spot, my thirst to have the glimpse of this object of antiquity much older than its counter parts in the hill capital town of Mandi and elsewhere was quenched Luckily, it is in good state of preservation.

It was about 4 P.M. We had out tea a road side 'Dhaba'. The place was an isolated one, just on the out skirt of Jogindernagar. We were on our return journey. A couple was looking after the dhaba. Later, we had to stop at Gumma where a person known to Inder Singh was waiting for us with tea and snacks. I did not want to miss a stay at Forest Rest House of Urla which has special fascinations for me. Here Mr. Dutta a young and energetic forest officer entertained us with tea and biscuits. The aroma of pine and the fresh breeze of the rest house refreshed us.

We reached back Drang, the pujari of the Jayapal was available. He was kind enough to lead us to the mini-temple which we had as our first trysting site in the start of journey. Now it was dark and the pujari arranged a torch. His wife and youngest daughter also accompanied us. Dr. Manodi took the snaps of the Moharas. In my memory they were four, all identified with prominent noses, but here we saw six, including two more masks of smaller sizes. All the four masks were being used for a small modest 'Rath' like that of the Chuhaar Valley Pagh style as I classify the principal styles of the raths of Mandi region. The four masks were fitted on the four sides of the rath, the central of the threes in the photograph was the front, main and primary mask. Although basically all are on singular pattern hardly dissimilar with each other but for the Mukut part. The main mask has five projections and the others only three. The central projection of this mask is more decorative and broader than the other. Other details like the forehead, nose, eyes, lips, chin and ears with ear jewellery are similar. The entire treatment is folkish and the broad smile is more like a rustic rather the sober smile of divine masks. All the masks have been provided with gala mala or necklaces and the motifs of snakes are conspicuous adding symmetry to the object and mystery to the people. Although in the records of the Dharmarth Department of the then Mandi state, this deity is recorded as Dev Chandwani but popularly it was addressed as 'Bade Nak Wala Deo' i.e. the devata with prominent noses. For last several decades, the 'rath' of this deity has been discarded off. In state times, the management of Drang salt mine had the responsibility to ensure its transportation to Shivratri Fair. With the formation of Himachal Pradesh, this facility was erased, and that is why the rath was also discarded off for want of devaloos (i.e. the retainers of the deo. Various legends are associated with this deity which has come down through ages. Jaya Pal and Vijai Pal the two brahimins are said to be perpetuated as Deo Chindwadi and Deo Kasla. They were involved in casting black magic on the Raja of Mandi by the then rana of Drang. The instigation of the ranas, got leaked. Fearing harsh punishment from Raja, both of them got themselves immolated (in fire). Thereafter as the story goes, they started haunting the royal households. A pious rani who is still known as Praksh Dei got their spirits subdued by deifying them. Later she ordered for their raths and enlisted them in the important devatas of her territory to visit the exalted event of Shivratri celebrated at her capital town. Till early fifties of last century, this practice continued and later got abandoned. This episode further crystallise the opinion that most of the hill gods are head men or women of their areas in the olden times which got deified on one pretect or the other. Roughly at 8 PM, we reached our destination after bagging three trophies in a single day.

CHAPTER - 7

MANGARH: A Sudden Surprise

It was a usual official visit for me. Never had I imagined coming across a unique architectural art in the shape of a temple and sculptural objects in a district where such archaeological remains are conspicuous by their absence.

Mangarh is a small and obscure place with a population of about six hundred souls. It has a Higher Secondary School and a Civil Dispensary the wings of social services which make the presence of government felt in an unknown and offbeat place. The journey to the place is neither pleasant nor enjoyable. Although linked by a motorable road the condition of which is not laudable at all, being partly metalled and partly kucha. From Nahan, which is the district town of Sirmour District, it can be approached via Sarahan a charming little site on Nahan-Shimla road and which is also a tehsil headquarters. Mangarh is only 18-kms, from Sarahan and 70-Kms, from Nahan. Mangarh is also approachable from Solan by road via Narag after covering about 65-Kms. But by far the easier route is via Sarahan only. Mangarh although situated in a saucer shaped depression which is all around surrounded by hillocks is at 5000 feet high from sea level. In itself its terraced fields and a few houses are enough to attract the attention of the beholders. Now this place might have entered a situation of obscurity but in olden days of state polity of native states it was on the important state highways connecting capital town of Nahan with the Rajgarh territory of the state which was abundantly important for the state for its revenues and menpower. Thus being a traditional and strategic pathway it has witnessed the era of glory in those years of past. Actually the name of the place was Sen and the area in between rivers Giri and Jalal was known as Sendhar. The river Giri being famous for its ice cold water fit for rearing trout fish is about ten kms from this place and it joins Jamuna near Paunta Sahib whereas river Jalal derives its name from the colour of its water which is in reddish hue i.e. Jal (water) is Lal (red). As a matter of fact Jalal drains into the area the soil which is full of red muddy hills and is evident while traversing this terrain. Ultimately, it joins Giri at Dadahu near the famous Renuka Lake. One fort standing in its worst decayed and destructed condition is very near to this village which was constructed by one Man Prakash a raja of Sirmour from whom the name "Sen" was replaced by Mangarh. It is said that this fort had many a deep wells which used to serve as repository of "snow" to be used for the house hold of rulers of Sirmour state during the summer season. Obviously it had to be carried by men on feet when means of communication were still meagre.

From Sarahan to a village Jehar one feels that the journey is through hills. On both sides of the road the tall trees of chil and oak are feast to the mind. Jehar was all the more important for me because I had a health sub-centre to supervise here which was found locked and same was the story on my subsequent visits. Ahead of Jehar to Mangarh the physical features of the territory take an abrupt turn. Now starts hillocks of a very strange variety made of rugged stones with scarce cementing mud connecting them. Invariably very scanty growth of trees was visible but for the preponderance of cacti of different varieties and thorny bushes in plenty. To have a departure from the aroma and fragrance of chil to this almost barren land is bit irritating but one has to compromise with the natures, shades and shadows. On entering the village proper, I went straight to the dispensary. Housed in a cowshed type room it is the property of Panchayat; the office bearers of which were more interested to take it back rather than to improve this structure. Suddenly, a young man came running and introduced himself as the doctor incharge of this health outfit. At that point of time he was solitary enough to run the show and had a lot of grievances about the working conditions and professional practices. Ultimately he took me to his accommodation, a rented room which was serving his study, bed room and kitchen, all in one. The doctor was pleasant to talk, good mannered and hailed from a family near Sapathoo a fine good hill resort of Himachal Pradesh. While sipping a cup of tea brewed by him in his room he pointed to a stone structure across the small rivulet and described it as temple. I could not resist the temptation to have a visit to the site.

The temple is housed on the north corner of the village and its approach is possible after crossing a spring of gurgling and clean water. A fine rectangular and well chiseled pillar certainly belonging to the temple premises was being utilized as a bridge on the water spring connecting the village and temple site. Here some village ladies were washing their clothes and beating them harshly on this fine piece of art. Ultimately we were face to face to the temple, the entrance of which although a unique and imposing structure of architectural merits was almost in crumbling state, the pillars of which were being temporarily supported by the scattered stone pieces. If not taken care in time, it may collapse to rubble in years to come. Prior to entering the temple proper, the fragmented pieces of sculptures of considerable merit reveal the glory of the past which the temple structure have had enjoyed. Heaps of chiseled stones were occupying the area all around the temple. They appear to have been excavated from that very site. It is said that about a hundred years back, this whole temple complex was hidden by shrubs and creepers which were gradually chopped and removed by the inhabitants of the village and thereby this place of worship was restored to the present position. A broken, defaced and weathered stone sculpture of a lion attacking an elephant is a beautiful creation of art. Although both the lion and the elephant are broken badly but can easily be deciphered. The lion is in a posture of attack from behind and is sitting on the head of the elephant, which is in a state of grave mutilation and only head, right eye and right tusk are the remnants left behind. The lion is actually in a ferocious pose, having protruding eyes and open jaws. How it got decayed, the evidence is less than certain. Conjecturally it can be as a result of sliding of the nearby hills which might have destroyed various small and big temples of the main temple complex of surviving Shiva Shrines which further got mutilated by the rigours of the weather. There is least suspicion that these sculptures were the casualty by the hands of iconoclasts of attacking armies. The history is silent over it and there seems no local tradition also to speak about such event. Four amalaks; the topmost parts of usual shikhara style temples are also being preserved indicating the existence of minor temples. A stone pillar having two figures is a beautiful piece of sculpture having a figure of a female although badly damaged is shown kneeling with folded hands and the other being that of Nandi; the divine bull vehicle of Shiva walking to the left. The later being a very bold figure is a visual delight. It can be described as the finest figure of Nandi found anywhere in Himachal and fortunately is in good state of preservation. There exists another figure of Nandi sitting to the right with damaged face, very suggestive of an existence of another Shiva temple. It wears a long belt bedecked with well and circular pendant motifs, and a floral garland in the neck. Although again a victim of weather, it is easily decipherable. The sculptor has treated bull lavishly with ornamentations. Another attractive piece is that of Bhadramukh the three faced Shiva as it is supposed to be by one school of though whereas it is told to be a relief of decoration on the top of the main gate of the temple. The piece in question has a central face which is serene and sober while the one on the right is in angry mood and is that of Aghora and the left one is sharp with feminine features. It was gathered from the local persons that a large number of such icons and images used to be there, which have been smuggled out by several persons on one or the other pretext. The whole stone material utilised to cast and carve these sculptures and the main temple is apparently imported stuff brought from far off places as this variety of stone is non existent and non-traceable in this place or nearby terrain. How this material has been transported to this site in those times when there were no means of heavy transport available and could have been possible only on the back of the people or ponnies to any stretch of imagination.

It is true that the entry to the temple proper is imposing but in utter state of negligence. The main entrance has two pedimented niches flanking the main gate which is four feet in height having square pillars with purnaghata or amitaghata motifs. The gate is so designed that a man in erect posture can not enter it. He had to bend his body in forward and downward direction as if he is bowing down or paying his initial respects to the presiding deity of the temple. This has been customary if not mandatory in all entrances of old shrines. The roof of the entire building comprising of Sabha mandapa and sanctum sanctorum ahead is flat with a slight slant to both sides to make it free easily from downpour of rains. It had safety element for long survival of such building which is so much called for also. The plain roof of the Sabhamandap is on four squared pillars. The architraves placed on it divide it into two rectangles. The latticed windows located on north and south walls are carved in stone. It is difficult to comment as to why the structure of the temple is quite in contrast to the curvilinear shikhara style usually found in other temples. Here shikhara is also flat with a slant. Certainly at least it indicates the antiquity of this shrine when Nagara or Shikhara style was still in developing process in this region. The squarish mandapa leads to the garbhagriha which is a rectangular structure housing the object of worship in the shape of a black stone lingam of more than one foot height. Again it appears to have been brought from outside Himachal. Beside Shivalingam an idol of Ganesha and an icon of Uma Maheshwar are also being kept in the sanctum. The doorway of the sanctum offers most interestingly ornamental structure with high degree stone carvings of foliage. The doorway has three distinct parts to portray the right and left 'sakhas' and the lintel overlying them. The two door joints or 'sakhas' are symmetrical each having figures of the Ganga and Yamuna which can be deciphered by their respective symbols of Makara and Kurma. This is the legacy of Gupta art style wherein these two rivers are identified as goddesses and have invariably found places of importance on the doors of Devalayas i.e.

abodes of the Gods. Above these, the door joint vertically divides into two, the inner one possessing floral diagrams rising from the naval of a human figure and going upto the lintel and adjoining panel depicts lotus flowers with five petals. The central joint shows dwarpals one on each side in the lowermost portion and further above them there are three loving couples in mithuna-mudra. The top portion possesses the figures of apasara or flying females having a mirror in their hands on either side. The outermost sakha of the door has scroll work of flowery rosettes. The lintel connecting with outermost sakha has again scroll work with a human face in the center which depicts the face of glory known as Kirtimukha or Bhadramukha. Immediately below in the horizontal row are Navgrahas showing Sun in the center which is riding on a chariot driven by seven horses. In this panel, there is a departure from standard practice as Rahu and Ketu are shown as one and not two distinct graha and an image of Ganesha has been added in the panel of Navgrahas. Just below this panel is a row of human figures in dancing and singing demenour being the representations of 'Apasaras' and 'Gandharvas' of 'Devyoni' as they are described in the scriptures. Rest of the lintel is further decorated with flowers and petal diagrams. On the whole this entire edifice of the doorway is a masterpiece from the viewpoint of art and architectural ornamentations which, in real sense, is the most important and interesting aspect inside a temple premise.

The temples of this style and type are not uncommon in Himachal Pradesh but in District Sirmour it is a unique heritage of the past having no other parallel in the entire territory. Although such settlements of refined artists and their patrons can be traced in other hinterlands of Himachal Pradesh the most conspicuous of which are at Bharmour and Chhatarari in Chamba, Jagatsukh and Nagar in Kullu, Masrur in Kangra and Hatkoti in Shimla areas. All are well known but Mangarh remained obscure. As all of them belong to Post-Gupta-Art- traditions and have been establishments of the art-tradition of 7 - 8th Century. Therefore this temple seems to be belonging to that timeframe as is apparently palpable from its layout, conception and pattern of various sculptural art motifs and decorative idioms. It may be sheer rough estimation but in absence of any other historical, traditional and inscriptional evidences, the conclusion to subscribe it to the Post-Gupta period on stylistic grounds can go a long way to establish its period of construction. As usual for local inhabitants, it is a handiwork of Pandvas; which is deeply in-ground in their psyche.

This place offers a unique experience for art-historians, archaeologists and scholars alike. But undertaking their sojourns to this treasure of antiquity, they should proceed fully equipped with routine, daily necessary requirements of their respective needs as nothing is available in this remote corner of the Shivalik ranges of Himalayas.

On second visit to Mangarh, I was equipped with camera and photo artists to shoot the valuable art pieces and structures.

CHAPTER - 8

KANGRA: An old Belt of Civilization

My first encounter with Dharamsala, the district town of Kangra district was in year 1972. It was a grand ceremony of inauguration of the new building of District Hospital and the principal dignitary i.e. Shri Uma Shankar Dixit was the then Home Minister or Health Minister of India, a grand old man and a close confident of late Mrs. Indira Gandhi, who was Prime Minister of India during that period. Naturally, once the great lord from Delhi was at Dharamsala, the entire cabinet of Dr. Parmar alongwith a large gathering of officials was bound to be there. The Chief Minister himself was displaying unusual loyalty to the central minister. During that period I happened to be looking after the office of Chief Medical Officer of District Chamba. After receiving the invitation for this ceremony, I could not control the temptation to witness this affair. I attended it. On my return journey to my head quarter, my mind was determined not to miss the sites of inscriptions very near to Dharamsala which claim the antiquity of pre-Christian era. Hence next day I proceeded to Pathiyar which is a reasonably big village situated in a vast and open valley giving an impression as if we are right in the heart of the Gangatic plains. Well, we were told to proceed through the road but none were aware about the boulders of Pathiyar for which we were undertaking this journey. All our references proved futile with all and sundry. We travelled about 3 miles on a unmetalled road and found a few pretty shops whose master later directed us to go amidst the fields to locate the said boulder. We were almost lost in our endevour in fields and houses and none were of any help to pin point the place. Ultimately it was a sheer chance that one youngster could gauze our mission and led us to a place. Here stands a boulder with two inscription cut in both Brahmi and Kharoshti scripts, in letters of remarkably bold size recording the dedication of a garden and tank, existing in 3rd century B.C. The perusal of script reveals that here was a 'Pushkarini' or the tank belonging to Rathi Vakul i.e. Vakulasya Pukrini. Vakul was a vassal of some overlord of Kangra which was known as Trigarta and also Jallandhar in their old times and eras. The word 'Rathi' is very significant because even presently Pathiyar has about one hundred family of Rathi clan. The word seems to be a derivation of Rashtrik or Rastriya which might be some official designation of significance. The inscriptions having two scripts also carry in itself vast information of the trend which was prevalent in that period of the popularity of both 'Brahamini' and 'Kharoshsti' among the locals. Surprisingly the 'Brahami' is the precursor of both 'Sarda' and Devnagari and incidentally the Tankari script which was in vogue in this territory in the recent past even during the period of native Rajas under British rule. Although during our tryst with Pathiyar, the voyage period was engrossed with jumping and thumping in the old jeep at my disposal, but by mind was occupied with another aspect of Dharamsala which relates to a time prior to the period it attracted the British fascination for its cold climate. Fairly well known for its oriental serenity and occidental gaiety, Dharamsala was a hot favourite health resort of the British. As a matter of fact, the credit goes to the Europeans for the prominence which Dharamsala attained because the heat of Kangra town was too intense for them. Old European travellers have extolled its beauty in terms unparallel. Prior to the annexation of Kangra into British India, Dharamsala situated on the sunny spur of Dhauladhar was famous for its woods of Ban (Oak) and Pines. When Katoch rulers ultimately lost to Sikh and later to British, Kangra although remained the seat of power but for Whites the lure of Dharamsala was so demanding that they ultimately shifted the seat of administration to the present Dharamsala and the town began expanding its frontiers. Although the District Administration shifted only in 1855, a military cantonment- the backbone for the preservation of foreign rule already existed here in Dharamsala.

In its misty past, stretching perhaps to the time of Pathiyar inscription, because that has a recorded history, the place was known as Bhagasu and the shoulder of the hill was also known a Bhagasu Dhar. The tradition is still preserved in the folk-lores of Gaddies the nomadic pasture-loving tribes of this area. Bhagasu is a hill and its presiding deity Bhagasu Nag, more often confused with Bhagasu Nath. Hence the cult worshiped is 'Naga' rather than 'Nath'. The later is associated with well organised sect of Gorakh Nath etc. but there are reasons to believe that the Bhagasu Naga cult is the down to earth cult of Naga which is widely spread and practiced along and beyond Dhaula-Dhar, throughout the western Himalayas. The salient features of the same are still palpably visible in our own times as well. It is symbolized by snake worship and the main objects of venerations are still water and trees. Here at Bhagasu, the present Dharamsala, the main source of attraction is a beautiful water source surrounded with several fables and legends which inspire the innermost strings of our heart for the love for basic elements of religion which, undoubtedly, is nature. Standing near this water fall and beholding the vast vista down, one is bound to go deep into the mysteries of existence and raptures of Joy. Primarily for the pilgrims and also the visitors of Bhagasu Nag, one building was constructed near the water source which was for all practical purposes, a Dharamsala i.e. an inn meant for dwelling of these pilgrims and when the actual town came into existence no suitable name was found for it and that is why the town goes by the name of Dharamsala.

This visit to Dharamsala remained incomplete for want of time to have a tryst with Khaniyara another relic of prehistoric period. It was a good luck for us to meet at Dharamsala for the annual session of Himachal Medical Officers Association in April 1980 when my endeavour to visit this site could be successful. The place could be reached on foot only. It was a steep descent which was feasible with my health as the ascent make me out of wind even as I start. It is a bridle path. We health as the ascent made me out of breath even as I started. It is a bridle path. We encountered a village of brave Nepali Gorkhas who have settled over here. There we were told to take a small journey by bus. Later a person could point to a site which was being utilized as a cremation ground and there stand several boulders- and one of them to the natives is known as 'Bhutshila' on which are the valuable scripts akin to Pathiyar both in Brahami and Khroshti. The place is actually known as Dari but being famous by the name of Khaniyara, we were slightly mistaken. The scripts reveal that it is here that one Krishanayash had constructed an Aaraam i.e. a Budhist Monastery. Although presently it is not a densely habitated place not there are any evidence left of the building of monastery but one can conjecture that in its good old days, it was an important centre of Budhist learning. The word Aaraam also connotes a garden. Thereby, confusion remains of its being a beautiful garden or temple of learning. Basically it was an important place and that is why there was an attempt to have an inscription attached to it. No other place in Himachal can boast of such inscriptions of the era dating back to 3rd century or of early Christian calendar.

A legend is in currency in the area about this site. According to that, a 'Brahaman Chela' (mendicant) charmed a baital (demon) and made him plough his land and obey his commands. He used to hold the demon, but one day, when he was away, his woman fed the bhut on festival-food which was poison to him, and so he went and sat on 'Bhutshila' and began devouring every living thing that came in his way. When 'Brahaman' returned, he nailed the 'Bhut' down to the stone and, words engraved on it, are the charms he used in the process. Such is our approach to the objects of antiquity. Similarly another man who came to us had his own version about the script. His opinion was cute enough, to suggest that a way to some treasure of unlimited valuables was engraved on the boulder. Similarly such opinion was forwarded about an inscription in Tankari near a 'Pipal' tree in one of the sectors of Chamba town on the way leading to the confluence of the river Ravi with its tributary stream known as Shal just on the outskirts of the town.

As a matter of fact, the period, stretching from 3rd to 6th centuries B.C., the present district of Kangra was a cradle of Buddhist lore the vestiges of the same can be traced down in scripts of these two prehistoric inscriptions which actually extol the presence of Buddhist monasteries over there. Even up to the times of Harshavardhan of Thaneshwar, when the Chinese traveller Hieun Tsang came over to Kulutta (Kullu) he journeyed through one Tamsavan which was perhaps same place near Kangra which the Chinese Scholar has described as Jallandhar, the old name of Kangra. According to him there were roughly fifty Buddha's places of learning and worshipping and about 2500 Buddhist monks were on attendance rolls in them. There is a place known as Chetru near Kangra which had a huge complex of such Vihar. According to one manuscript in the Bhuri Singh Museum at Chamba known as Jallandhar Pith Dipika, this entire land between Ravi and Satluj is known as Jallandhar Khand.

Chetru: The remnants of Budhist civilization are not only confined in the reputed inscriptions of Pathiyar and Kaniara, but in the sphere of influence, Chetru is also a well known place, situated at 60 Km from Bhagasu and 8 Km from Nagarkot i.e. the Kangra proper. Chetru is supposed to be a degenerated from of the word known as Chetya i.e. the place of worship and learning of Budhist school of Philosophy. Stupa is another synonym for Chetya. The remains of Chetru is a vast hillock or mound called Bhim tila which is about 830 feet in circumference, situated at the confluence of two streams Manji and Gurulu. During British times a Budha icon and a detached Budha head were discovered at this site. They were actually sent to Lahore Museum now in Pakistan for preservation. Now this site is in active process of excavation as prescribed by the eminent archaeologists. Bhim Tila as well as Draupati Garden are two sites which appears to be originally one only separated later on by a man-made canal system, otherwise both these sites are of contemporary importance. Various objects i.e. gray wares have been traced from this sites which resembles those which are obtained by excavations from Kurukshetra and Hastinapur- the sites related to the period of great epic of Mahabharata. This lends evidence of Chetru's association with that period. At Draupati-Bag there is a statue under worship and according to the locals it is an icon of Drupati but on iconographic collaboration, it is not a female icon but that of Budha. The bricks measuring 36X23X7 cms discovered at Chetru belong to Kushana period which was again a glorious page so far the rise of Budhist cult is concerned. All this reveals that about 2000 years back Chetru had a great tradition of Budhist culture which has remained in one form or the other till this date, along with a place known as Chari which is 12Km from Kangra. Another object of excellence of workmanship is the Budhist statue measuring 30 cms in height and wrought in brass and inlaid with silver eyes was obtained from an inn at Fatehpur in Nurpur tehsil. It is preserved again in Lahore Museum. The elaborate pedestal bears a dedicatory inscription; from the character of which it may be concluded that the image belongs to the 6th century A.D. But in case of a portable object like the present it is not possible to tell whether it originally belonged and was cast at Nagarkot. At this place were found the foundation of a temple built of large size stones which were fastened together with iron clamps. An inscribed pedestal which once must have supported the image of the boarheaded goddess Marichi or Vajravarahi proves that the temple was a Budhist shrine. Although the inscription had no date but on the character of letters, it was attributed to the 5th or 6th century AD. All these Budhist remains collaborate with the references of Hiuen Tsang- the celebrated Chinese scholar and traveller of 7th century during the region of the district in which it was discovered. Otherwise also the Nurpur area appears to be the main fort of Budhism. Its old name is Dharmethi which seemingly have been derived from the word Dharāmgiri, very close to other names prevalent in Budhist literature.

According to Hiuen Tsang, in the kingdom of Jalandhar, there were no less than 50 convents or viharas harbouring about 2000 monks who were students of both Mahayana and Hinayana of Budhism. Here again you will find it difficult even to know the road leading to the sites of Chetru and Chari, as I had during my sojourn to these places. The local population is so much unconcerned about these places, that once you ask them, the reply is never forthwith. A lot of churning about the one or other aspect of these sites ultimately arouses them from the deep slumber of sleep about the historical, religious and archaeological importance of these valuable places which are in their vicinity.

Masrur: By far, the mot remarkable place in the Kangra valley is Masrur which can be described as the Ellora of Himachal. Here, one comes across a group of rock-cut temples, unique in designs and architectural excellence. Standing on the summit of a sand-stone range of hills which are 2500 feet in elevation form sea level; Masrur is not very far from the ancient capital town of Haripur, which was a state in itself. From Haripur it is about 12 Kms and 20 Kms from Nagarkot. From these places it was connected by only rough inter-hamlet tracks when this unique structure came into prominence. Even now you ask any person at Nagarkot and Haripur, they are totally lost about the existence of a place known as Masrur. Such is our concern to our heritage!

Its inaccessibility explains why it escaped notice until the year 1913 when it was first noticed by one Mr. H.L. Shutle of I.C.S. and subsequently surveyed by Mr. H.L. Hargreaves of Archeological survey. The temples of Masrur are a unique class in themselves being rock-cut shrines, so common in western and southern India, but are wholly unknown in the western Himalayas. Here this structure consists of fifteen shrines of Shikara style of Indo-Aryan architecture profusely decorated with sculptural ornaments. The main shrine is known as Thakurdwara the name for Vaishnava temple and contains three stone images of Rama, Sita and Laxman, but these are recently introduced. The presence of figure of Shiva, in the centre of the lintel of the main shrine, affords a strong presumption that the temple was originally dedicated to Mahadeva. There is no inscription to fix the date of construction of the Masrur temples, but on the evidence of style Mr. Hargreaves concludes that the monument can hardly be assigned to an earlier date than the 8th century of Christian era and may possibly be somewhat later. Even among the scholars, the rock-cut-temples are not well known as these are situated at an out of the way place. The reports about these temples were first published in Archeological survey of India, Annual reports for 1912-12 and 1915-16. Thereafter some scholars made brief references about the art of the temples and sculptures of Masrur. It is hardly possible to do justice to these magnificent and unique temples in Northern India in a brief note. These monolithic temples are chiseled out of a rock at this ridge and present a fascinating view. Whenever the rock was not hard and suitable enough to be carved out, loose sculptures were inset to fill the gaps. The sculptures are characterized by poise, grace and smooth plasticity. There are several carved penal on the temples with figural and decorative work.

These temples could not have been commissioned by a local Chieftain. It can not be said with certainty that who had got the work done. Possible the rulers of the Jallandhar Kingdom had made the place, Masrur, their capital when they withdrew from plains and settled here. A splendid temple complex was conceived, but carving on certain temples were never completed which suggest that the place was probably later abandoned and the famous Kangra fort was occupied because of its strategic location. It first came to notice in the early eleventh century when attacked by Mehmud of Ghajani. Relics on Kangra fort area of period contemporary with Masrur have perhaps not come to light. Although stylistically of early 8th century, the modeling and other details, the sculptures of Masrur possess the characteristic of the classical period. The Surya, Varuna, Shiva, Kuber and a head of a Deity all belong to this category and is now prize possession of State Museum at Shimla hailing from Masrur.

Kangra: The town of Kangra is famous for two monuments which are of great antiquarian interests. Firstly it claims to possess one of the oldest Shakti Shrine of Northern India and secondly for its fort which had the reputation of being an impregnable fort. The town carries a long variety of name i.e. Nagarkot, Bhimkot, Sushumanpur and Kot Kangra although the last one is its latest transformation of big row of nomenclatures. When I first passed through Kangra, tempatation to visit both the palces was really beyond words. It appears that in its olden imperial times, the place was stretching right from the fort to the town proper which presently is a modest place known for its renovated Shrine or Devi Kangravali or Devi of Bhawan. Although there is nothing of antiquarian importance now left with this temple but relics of old shrine i.e. one amalak lying in the circumambulation of the temple which was reduced to ruins in the devastating earthquake of 1905 AD. In the temple proper the object of worship is not any idol but a piece of stone given facial decorations like eyes and nose. Similar is the fate of the massive fort of Kangra which was really an imposing structure but could not escape the wrath of the earthquake. The old photograph taken prior to those tragic days extols the grandeur and strength of this structure. The fort in its ruin age is surrounded on three sides by inaccessible cliffs, appears on imposing structure of stone and in its highest part were the dwellings and the temples of the Katoch Kings of Kangra, but after the earthquake the whole structure is nothing but the surrounding wall which is left. So ghastly was the earthquake of 1905, that all its buildings and ramparts, which took the enemies many months to scale were crumbed down in a few seconds by the mighty hand of nature. The description of the fort in the Kangra District Gazetter is relevant presently as was in 1928 when the book was published from Lahore. The fort is entered through a small courtyard enclosed between two gates which are known as Phataks and are only of Sikh period, as appears from an inscription over the entrance. The gates have no archaeological pretensions. From here a long and narrow passage leads up to the top of the fort through the Ahani and Amiri Darwaja, both attributed to Nawab Ajij Khan, the first governor of Kangra under the Mughul. Some 500 feet from the other gate the passage turns around at a very sharp angle and passes through the Jahangiri Darwaja. This is said to have been the outer gate of the fort in Hindu kingdom and that its original name remains unknown. The Jahangiri Darwaja, however, has entirely the appearance of a Muslim building and judging from its name would seem to have been raised by Jahangir after his conquests of the fort in 1620 AD. There are some reasons to assume that a white marble slab bearing a Persian inscription of which the fragments were recovered in 1905, originally occupied a sunken panel over the gate. It in all probability was a record of Jahangiri Conquest of the fort, an exploit on which he prides so like an original conqueror. Both Amiri and Jahangiri Darwajas received serious injury in the earthquake, but could be repaired. Not so the next two gates called the Andheri and Darshani gates which were totally damaged. The Darshani Darwaja, when extant was flanked by defaced statues of Ganga and Yamuna, and must date back to the period when it was not yet plundered by the Muslims. It gave access to a courtyard, along the south side of which stood the shrine of Laxmi Narayan, Shitala and Ambika Devi. Between the last two building a staircase led up to the palace, a part of no architectural significance. To the south of the Ambika temple there are two Jain shrines, facing west. One of them contains merely a pedestal which must have belonged to a Tirthankar image. In the other is placed a sitting statue of Adinath with a partly obliterated inscription dated, according to Cummnigham, in 'Samwat' 1523 (Ad- 1466) in the reign of Sansar Chand-I.

Although in history and legend this fort is described as most protected structure but several references are available when it was looted and plundered. Mehmud of Ghazani was the first who was described by his chronocoliers as the first to usurp the fast possession of this fort. The amount was such that the backs of camel could not carry it. Such vast accumulation of wealth was stored within the walls of the fort. It was contained in several hundreds vessels as writers had recorded it, and is beyond the imagination of an arithmetician to conceive it. Farishta states the amount as 7,00,000 golden dinars, 700 mans of gold and silver plates, 200 mans of gold, 200 mans of silver bullians and twenty mans of various jewels, including pearls, corals, diamonds and rubies and other valuable properties. All of it was taken to Ghazani and displayed on a carpet spread in the courtyard of the palace. The idol in the temple of Bhawan made up of precious metal was also removed but the temple does not seem to have been demolished. Such a vast treasure being built up and protected by the Katoch Chiefs for centuries was made good within months by a foreign invader. Really a big tragedy of its time!.

CHAPTER - 9

HERE A RANI WAS ENTOMBED ALIVE: A Riddle of the History

It is more than a thousand years, when a strange and terrifying event occurred in the annals of the History of Chamba State now a district of same name in Himachal Pradesh. It was the ruling era of Sahil Dev Varman of Chamba when his beloved daughter took fancy to this place now known as Chamba town and wanted her father to rule from this place. Accordingly Raja established his capital over there which was predominantly a land of Champa trees, a picturesque site surrounded on two sides by high hills, remaining two sides by the swiftly flowing the Ravi and its tributary the Shal, forming a natural capital fortress of the kingdom. A wide open green land added beauty to site and the snowy peak of the Chowari pass was visible from their new home reminding them of the peaks of Mani Mahesh in the backdrop of their original capital i.e. Bharmour. After establishing over here the biggest misfortune was the paucity of drinking water. Therefore to meet this exigency a canal was dug up from the nearby rivulet and surprisingly the water did not enter this newly created water duct. In reality this mysterious phenomenon was not only unfortunate but unexplainable as well. But more mysterious was the dream which the King witnessed which was less of a dream but more of a nightmare. The spirit in the dream advised him to sacrifice a member of the royal household who is dearer to him and thereafter the water will enter the new duct prepared for the purpose of water supply to the town.

This made the king sad and sullen. No one could know the cause of his agony till he disclosed the content of his dream, to no other than his spouse. The much loved and admired rani offered herself to be sacrificed to fulfill the demand of the water supply of the town. In spite of all persuations as told and retold in the ballads still in currency, she did not budge an inch and was firm in her contention for self sacrifice. Ultimately her journey started from the place to Sarotha Nala about three kilometers from the town followed by her people. I was told that even after the passage of full one thousand years, the pathway on which the rani travelled can still be traced.

In year 1970, with the help of Mr. Kamal Prasad Sharma, I also trekked on the beaten track of the rani. Although professionally Kamal is qualified and competent surgical theatre assistant but his flair and inclination of mind for and about the history and art of Chamba is a by-product of deep love for these subjects and in my opinion he is a living repository about the cultural and historical wealth of Chamba.

It was Sunday a holiday for both of us. Luckily the sun was not warm. He accompanied me upto Sarotha Nala-the place of sacrifice. We started from the place now known as Panihara or the water-point and climbed the steps made of stone. Originally this track might be a goat route but later stone ladder steps were added upto the place where there stands a wooden structure known as Suhi-mata-ki-Mahari. It is said while on her journey, she took rest over here. Now a metal mask has been embedded on a cement platform, the mask representing the rani Suhi. This concrete platform had added further charm to the place. The pathway running from this resting place to the Sarotha nala is almost horizontally running with the town lower down on the shoulder of the hill. Presently the entire route is in good shape of preservation although is still a kacha road. Eventually it leads to the site on the bank of the rivulet where the rani is said to have been entombed alive. It is recorded in the pages of history that already a deep pit was got prepared, the rani voluntarily sat in that and was covered with stones and debris. It is embedded firmly in the psyche of her people that as soon the cruel act of entombment was complete, the water from nala suddenly started flowing in the duct leading upto the nauna-panihara of the town proper from where both of us had started our trekking to this place. This event of history or that of legend is still remembered as a week long celebration at the place of her resting i.e. Suhi-Ki-Marhi with all gaity and enthusiasm. Interestingly this gathering is entirely the privilege of ladies; the gents are seldom allowed to participate. Especially the ladies drawn from Bharmour dance and sing in their best attires. Although the rani has been deified as goddess but the occasion is not marked with enchanting of bhajans and singing of religious songs as is done in religious congregations. Not surprisingly, the conspicuous feature is the singing of Ghurians or love-songs in the melodious voices of gaddi ladies. While dancing, their wide 'ghagharas' or 'lehangas' flow circularly as an open umbrella, down their waist and it looks like a butterfly of very huge size. Free feasting is a hall mark to honour these ladies. During state times, the raja used to stand the expenditure and presently it is done by government and philanthropists. The most important song of the occasion is Sukhrat praising the rani for her act of sacrifice. "How shall we utilize this cold water without you, we wish to live while beholding you, oh rani."

Actually the place of sacrifice has no remnants of antiquity available. Some boulders are present where the event is said to have occured. Even Kamal was not able to pin point the place. Whatsoever may be the merit of this episode, it is true that human sacrifice was in vogue in this hinterland of the Himalayas. Such human sacrifices had been witnessed and narrated by European travellers at Nirmand in Kullu known as Bhunda. Later, even at Nirmand such human sacrifice was abandoned and replaced by a goat during Bhunda.

Sahil Dev was the first Varman King who ruled from Chamba. He has been described as a great warrior. His chroniclers and successors have mentioned about his virtues in high sounding phraseology. Also he was a remarkable builder of idols and temples. The marble statue of Vekunth-murti-Vishnu in Chamba dates to his rulership which is a skillful piece of art and architecture. Being a Vaishnavait himself, it is not understood as to how he yielded to sacrifice his wife which is not prescribed in Bhagwat or Panchratra cults worship. May be the Kanphatta Yogi Charpatnath be the visionary for this act but that also sounds unconvincing. The meeting of raja with the yogi is the event in the later phase of his life when he was old enough but the demand of water supply to the town is the requirement at the establishment of the capital at Chamba which definably seem to have occurred in the prime of his life. Many a time without proper documentation, it is difficult to assign yearwise events. When history and legends mingle and blend with each other; in the span spreading one thousand and some more years, the conclusions are bound to be arbitrary based on traditional parables passed on from generations to generations.

CHAPTER - 10

MAHADEVA TEMPLE OF BAJAURA: A Majestic Monolith

Bajaura is an open fertile flatland on the right bank of the Beas in Kullu district of Himachal Pradesh almost half way between Mandi and Manali. Situated on the border between two principaliaties of olden times, this fertile valley has always been a temptation to rival kings. Today it blooms with modern buildings and moneyspinning orchards, but it also remains an attraction to art historians and scholars because of its famous temple of Vishveshwar Mahadev. The approach to the temple is easy as it is only 100 yards from the main road.

Built in 'Shikhara' style, the temple has a huge 'amalka' at the top. Every stone used in the temple is well carved with pot and foliage patterns as decorative designs. Some figures of snakes and maithunmudras are also seen.

The main object of worship in the sanctum is a huge 'Shivalingam' in stone, locally known as Mahadev of Hat. It is not without significance that the territory surrounding the temple is known as Hat. In the hills the name of a town ending with Hat indicated that at some time it was a capital town. So it can be safely presumed that 'Bajaura or Hat' had the distinction of once being the capital town of a ruler who was either a sovereign or a vassal of the states of Mandi or Kullu. Moreover, the place was on the old trade route to Lahual and Spiti and further to Ladakh and Tibet. Before the construction of the present road the track touched the main door of the temple. It is said that the Beas once flowed close to the temple which had a stone "ghat" built up to the river. Later the Beas changed its course and drifted away from the shrine. Stone images have been found scattered in the area around the river. One such image of Vishnu belonging to the eighth century is still lying in a box in the compound of the temple. No one in the village is able to say who packed the image in the box and for what purpose. But it is presumed that local sentiments must have prevented the Vishnu from being tansported elsewhere. Another eighth century masterpiece is a broken but majestic idol of Surya, now kept in the Himachal Pradesh state Museum at Shimla. This sculpture, althogh discovered at Bajaura, is different in style and decoration from other idols in this temple. It appears that different styles of idol making have been in vogue at Bajaura. The Surya idol suggests that it was the main idol in an independent temple. This leads one to the conclusion that the Vishveshwar Mahadev Temple is a survivor of a large number of temples, which were once in existence there.

The msot conspicuous and elegantly featured are two almost symmetrical female figures, which are carved on the two sides of the entrace of the porch. They are shown standing on lotus pedestals. On casual examination these statues look like "Dwarpala" but a careful examination reveals almost unrecognizable head-parts of "Makara" or crocodile on the right side and "Kurma" or tortoise on the left. Considering that these symbols represent the sacred rivers of India, these female features are those of Ganga and Yamuna. The figures have their attendants as small figurines as well as the holder of a canopy over the heads of the goddesses. The backdrop of abundant flowers and foliages has been carved with meticulous care. Although damaged over the centuris, they still remain specimens of the art of sculpture that must have flourished in this area.

Bajaura has three life size images of Vishnu, Shakti and Ganesh in its west, north and south niche temples. The west niche has a statue of Vishnu in standing position with two miniature attendant figures, holding 'chamars' in their hands. The statue has all the four attributes of Vishnu-shankha, chakara, gadda and padma. From the upper end of the slab, appear two figures fo gandharvas with garlands in their hands as if worshipping the lord. The sacred thread and the long garland, vaijayantimala, of Vishnu are well preserved but the face of the image has been damaged. A halo encircles the head.

In the niche temple on the north is a big slab of eight armed-Mahishasurmardani. She is shown in the act of plunging the trishulla in the body of the demon whose hair she holds in her other hand. In her other hand she holds a vajra, an arrow, a sword, a bell, a cup of skull and a bow. Two demon figures are also in the same statue perhaps those of Shumbh and Nishumbh. It also shows the buffalo demon with the buffalo head severed and a demon in human form emerging from the trunk with a mace in his right hand. The sculptor has beautifully condensed the whole epic of the goddess in this single slab sculpture.

The south niche temple has an image of Ganesha seated on a throne of lotus supported by two lions on both sides. As usual Ganesha has four arms, a huge trunk which is touching a hand holding a vessel of ladoo. Ganesha wears a huge garland and the sacred thread of snake.

Both the idols of Shakti and Ganesha have conceptful resemblance with the metal icons of Menuvarman of the seventh century at Brahmour in Chamba although they have iconographic differences showing the different period of their constructions. The Vishnu differs from Chamba's Hari Rai and Laxmi Narayan as these are four faced Vaikunthamurti Vishnu whereas the Bajaura Vishnu is Ikamukhi. Brahmour and Chamba idols are constructed under the influence of Kashmir art where the figures are bold and the faces are bloated and round a characteristic of the post-Gupta period. The proportions of the figures, the anatomical treatment, the hair style, the costumes and ornaments all belong to the post-Gupta period. In Bajaura the idols have slender but powerful bodies, the longish faces as well as over elongated limbs of Pala art. Most conspicuous is the statue of Mahishasurmardini- the slayer of the buffalo demon.

Bajaura being easily approachable has been attracting a large number of scholars and art historians but so far its antiquity has remained a mystery. There is a difference of opinion about the period when this masterpiece was built. Perhpas William Moorcroft and G. Trebech were the first Europeans to mention it in their "Travels in the Himalayan Provinces of Hindustan and the Punjab" published in 1841. They passed through Bajaura in August, 1820. A detailed description, but not so scholarly and analytical, is available in the HFB Harcourt's "Himalayan districts of Kooloo, Lahoul and Spiti" published in 1871. Dr Vogel has written an authentic and intellectually sound article on this temple in the Archaeological survey report of 1905-06 but has not committed to any period of the construction of this monument and its sculptures. According to him "the exact time of the execution is not so easy to establish but the excellent workmanship of the large base-reliefs and in fact all the sculptural decorations on the Bajaura temple points to an early period". J.N. Bannerjee thinks that the temple belongs to the seventh or eighth century and Dr. Herman Goetz suggests that it was built in the middle of the eighth century during the period of Yashovarman of Kanauj.

All these opinions are based on the style and decorative details of the temple's architecture and the idols' configuration. There is no documentary or inscriptional evidence. A later inscription done in clumsy Tankari, details the gift of some land to the temple by Shyam Sen, a raja of Mandi in the 17th Century. But it does not lead to any evidence about the founding of the temple except that once the temple was in the territory of the erstwhile Mandi State.

CHAPTER - 11

THE SCULPTURE OF THE SHAKTI OF CHHITRARI :
A Subtle Statue

I was on a return journey from Bharmour the ancient capital city of Bhrahmpura kingdom. The day had moderate temperature and month of year was October 1970. The experience of Bharmour was still exciting and the impressions gathered there were of profound dimentions. A kingdom about 14 hundred years back had such sophisticated heads and hands who could cast marvelous metal sculptures of human heights were beyond my imagination. What I read about them, I confirmed and discovered them of more significance than what I had found on first introduction. How prosperous was the ruling era of Meruvarman! What were the resources of his mountainous kingdom! How he chose such a strenuous place to rule over! Who was this Guga- the master craftsman, who knew in detail the iconographic knowledge about the Hindu gods and goddess as laid down in the scriptures of architecture of old Indian texts. All such notions were clouding my thinking when my companion in journey Kamal Prasad Sharma came out with a new idea. "The best amongst all bronzes in the area is at Chhitarari, he told me, but the impediment was how to ascend to that height! The only course was by foot- march. Chhitarari was not yet connected by the motorable or jeepable road. Now in 1993 I was told that an all weather road connects the shrine of Chhitrari with the outer world. I could not say no and decided to make an ascent. It was told that there are two foot paths, one at Luna-ka-pul which is more steep but short and other at Gehra which was somewhat sloppy, easy but takes longer time. We left the jeep at Luna-ka-pul place and our uphill journey started. The jeep driver drove to Gehra where we planned to meet him after covering the sojourn to Chhitrari.

Shortly after a few feet ascent; I started feeling out of breath. The perspiration was so intense as if I was having a complete bath of sweat from tip to toe. The sun was at its majesty. The pathway was rugged, stony, shade less and vertical at almost ninety angle. I developed intense thirst also. Many a time I thought of telling Kamal to return back to the main road but my false sense of pride did not allow me to disclose the desire lest my companion under estimate my physical strength. Slowly but steadily and breathlessly I was keeping both face and pace. The government agencies had laid down water pipe lines of polythene material. Had there been water in them at least my thirst could have been quenched but it was not in my stars. Here was a clear picture of human vandalism and the non co-operative attitude of the inhabitants of the area that deliberately they had broken the lines of water supply. No other natural source of water was visible, so with great physical and mental agony; we climbed the hill to have the glimpses of the area which is proud to process the best specimen of Guga's craftsmanship.

Once this village was on the main foot path from Chamba to Brahmour which was the traditional route. With the opening of vehicular traffic though it is not on the main road but still is visited by thousands of people every year and Chitrani still possesses its own religious charm on the psyche of people who are 'Gaddies'- the pastural, migratory tribe who still proudly call their heards of sheep and goats as 'Dhan' i.e. wealth. Chhitarari falls for all practical, cultural and ethnic purposes in the Bharmour tehsil but has been made a part of Chamba tehsil of the district of the same name. The village has an era of 530 acres and is inhabited by 500 and has not shown much increase in population even presently.

As we reached the vilalge, which is a fantastic fertile land and of a mountainous track, Kamal had understood my need and led me to a house of a school teacher known to him. The owner of the house was fair in complexion, soft spoken and humble in demeanour. I had four to five tumblers full of cold water which made me at ease. With cool breeze my bush shirts and trousers wetted by my own sweat started drying up. Then there came a plate full of freshly cut pieces of apple. I did full justice to this delicacy. The apple produced at Chhitrari is really of full size rather extra large in gradations, juicy and appetising to look at. If I am not wrong it is not inferior to the apples of Kotgarh which has been made famous as the best apples of Himachal Pradesh.

After resting a while, I hinted to Kamal to hurry up for the visit to the shrine of Shiva Shakti, as the presiding deity is designated. On first encounter, the temple appears a simple structure of wood and stone constructed in age old Pahari style. It can be disputed whether the same dates to the era of its erection by Meruvarman or have undergone repairs, additions and alterations. But one fact remains undisputed that the sanctum sanctorum housing the idol of Shiva Shakti in its interior is same site where it was in the reign of the

Meruvarman in 700 AD. The Sabha mandap is conspicuous by its absence and approach is straight to the garbha-griha with circum- ambulance or parikrama path all around. The roof is pented and overlaid with slates. It is said that before the earthquake of 1905, it had a flat gable roof. The twelve thick deodar pillars exhibit the elegant and rich carvings and similar are the entrance doors of the shrine. The pillars have brackets carved like lions and other animals, flying Gandharvas and scrolls of flowers. The shrine door has richer feast for the eyes of the beholders. Besides many animal headed structures, the Kartikeya with six heads with divine vehicle peacock, Indra and Shiva are conspicous on the left and on the right the four headed Brahma Prajapati with two 'hansas' are still maintaining their minute details in spite of bad rigours of the weather for centuries. The goddess Mahisasurmaridini, the three headed Vishnu with the human face in front and bear and lion on the sides alongwith goddess Yamuna and Ganga are in good state of preservation. The lintel has a row of 13 sitting figures depicting the nine planets i.e. Nav-grahas and dig palas of four sides Uttar, Dakshin, Purva and Paschim are well executed. The post Guptas style of showing stylized scroll work sprouting from long drawn creepers growing out the mouth of two sitting Yakshas are at the bottom in the same manner as can be deciphered in the stone door frame of the Mangarh Shiva temple of Sirmour which I encountered after two decades.

The metal image of the Shakti Devi is the main object of worship, also it is the greatest of the great pieces of surviving art. Its epigraphic richness to understand or rewrite the history and art- history of the region is also of great significance due to the lengthy inscriptions of the Brahampur which as Bharmour was known in the glorious days and the name of the artist which sounds like typical pahari names still prevalent till the last century. Therefore, the idol of the goddess invites some detailed observations. It is about 4'-6' high image standing on a pedestal fashioned as a big lotus with reverted over-ripe petals. The goddess is shown as a very slim figure described as Sumadhama in the text and its elegant body is covered with a transparent skirt falling down to the ankles. The rich belt or Mekhla have strings of pearls. The scarf is hanging over her shoulders and necklace, armlets, bracelets and ear-rings are all of classical designs. A big mala of pearls hangs down from her neck between the heavy bossom to her thigh. A high majestic mukuta decorates the head part. The idol has four hands. In her right upper hand she has a lance and lower one has lotus and correspondingly in the left upper hand a bell and a snake in the lower one. All these attributes have significance both religiously as well as metaphorically. The lance is a symbol of divine power and eternal energy and the idol is known as Shiva Shakti; lotus symbolizes life and urge for living. The bell is a substitute of Nad-Brahm or entire universe whereas the snake is a symbol of time and Goddess's control over the death. Thus a poetry in metal is before the beholders rather simply a sculpture to worship. As in literature poetry is the supreme form of expression heading over dramas, fictions and essays similarly the Shakti statue is supreme over the Lakshana, Ganesh and Narsingha of Bharmour which are again the works of master craftman Gugga. The degree of technique, craftsmanship and the knowledge of ancient texts can be visualized by the following description.

"One leg of Shakti Devi is firmly planted on the ground and maintains the position of 'Vaishavasthana'. The other is extended sideway 'Iryka', the distance between the two unequally divided in relation to vertical median or 'Brahm-Sutra'. The character of the torso of the Devi maintains a 'Nirbhugna' position and is marked by a degree of tight and erectness of the back lending majesty. The long strand of pearls that makes its way coyly between the cup shaped breasts of the Devi acts as pendulum and shows its swings towards the right, the deviation from the 'Brahamsutra' or the plumb line. This gentle stance adopted by Shakti Devi necessitates the rising of her two arms in 'Katashista' posture. There is a slight variation in Hasta mudra as the thumb and forefingers do not meet each other. The other two arms are raised upto the shoulder level and then form two triangles with their apex at the elbows. These geometrical figures in space are the manifestations of Shakti and represent Shaktimay."

To describe the beauty and grandeur of the image, one can not but quote Dr. Philip Rawson. "The face is broad like a full moon, the nose having delicately arched bridge like a parrot's bill typically of Aryan origin, the lips full and curved like petals of sesame flower, brows curved like a bow, eyes long like a fish or a willow leaf. The image of Shakti Devi is one of these rare images which strictly conform to the cannons of ideal beauty as contained in the ancient texts. Not only face but the limbs of rest of her body as well are borrowed from vast animal and vegetable kingdom. This sculpture of Gugga is correct as well as beautiful and is carved according to the well understood law of proportions". However the ancient texts on econography do not provide for such type of images in these terms and perhaps it is for this reason that the image of this type bearing similar iconographical traits and attributes is not found anywhere in India remarks one of the art lovers. In short he means that no 'Dhyan' of this Devi Pratima is described in any of the texts.

Besides this main object of worship, the sanctum houses three more brass images of varying size and shape. There is a male mask figure which is an old brass idol confined into a bust above waist upwards emerging from a copper pedestal. Its two hands bear a rosary and a lotus respectively. A high pileup hair represents jatta mukta with a diadem on the forehead. Ringlets from both ears flow down the shoulder. It is said to be either Surya or Shiva. The lotus in one hand goes in favour of Surya while its resemblance with the image at Hatsar on the foothill of Manimahesh suggests it to be an idol of Shiva as the Hatsar image is worshipped as such till the scholars have these two opinions fixed up in their psyche and none is clear about the exact nature of the deity. Both conjectures have its own pros and cons but it is clear that the mask is cast under Kashmir's school of architecture and is contemporary of the Shakti Devi idol.

Two small figures of females much smaller in size, short and stout also can not escape notice. Scholars used to call them 'Yoginies'. They are not the product of primitive art, but of perfectly of provincial origin, though decadent, but art pieces of highly refined tradition. Recently it has been suggested that there were also miniature attempts before the final image of the Shakti Devi was cast.

In early seventies an image of a royal person with a lamp in hand was discovered at the sanctum which is made of brass; the treatment as a whole is of high degree and face is by far the most chiseled one in the whole list of Brahmour- Chhatrari images. Its hair are matted and it is bearing a Janeyu with a dagger in the fold of its dhoti makes it a royal personnel perhaps the Raja Meruvarman who had commissioned the Shakti temple and icon. There was such a tradition even in the far south when the kings used to cast themselves to perpetuate their existence or memory. Now it has been suggested, that this image is that of Gugga, the master craftsman but this settlement does not appeal as no such tradition had ever existed.

The art activity in the area remained continued even after this post Gupta era of 700 A.D. The nearby temple of Shiva and Parvati has stone images reflecting Pratihara influence. Therefore, the Chhatrari was an unique center of creative art along with Brahmour for such a lengthy span of time.

The epigraph on the pedestal of the Devi has an important message to convey. It is one of the sources of the early history of Chamba dating back to rulers earlier to Meruvarman and the cause for which the shrine of the goddess was commissioned by him. The epigraph extols the notable victory of the raja over his enemies for which he thought that the Shivashakti was the real power behind him. In gratitude for his victories and extensions of the boundaries of his kingdom the temple and idols came into existence. The further proof of the enlargement of his kingdom from Brahmour in the Buddial valley down to the banks of river Ravi nearer to Chamba is substantiated by a stone-inscription of Asadhaya Dev a feudatory to Raja of Brahmour who has claimed in the inscription of Gum that Meruvarman is Maharajadhiraj and he is his vassal king.

How Chhitrari got its name is also mixed in legends and fables which are still preserved in the psyche of the inhabitants. Nearby the main shrine of the village is a 'samadhi' of a 'sidh' who, once in hoary past, was residing there. The village being without water source, his disciple went to fetch water but got killed by wild animals. The sidh was upset and decided to invoke his spiritual powers to provide water at the spot. It is said he made thirty six holes with the tip of his trishul and to the surprise of all water gushed out at 36 places. Presently there are 36 such water springs or Paniharas which are attributed to the power of Sidh and leading thereby to get christened the place as Chhitrari. Also it is said that one ruling chief of Brahmour donated 36 Lahari a local measurement of land to the shrines of Devi and thereby the place acquired the name Chhatis-laharis in due course got recognised as Chhitarari.

Our return journey was not rigorous. We descended via a mild sloppy and wide pathway down to Gehra. I am at ease going down hill rather than going up. Here at Gehra we made use of our vehicle to return to Chamba.

CHAPTER - 12

HAT : A Lasting Imprint

A prompt decision to visit Hat was a wonderful experience when in year 1975, I had joined the services at Civil Hospital, Mandi. That was a fine morning, and in an old second hand jeep, a retired engineer was on the driver seat with a learned teacher of mine on the front seat myself sandwiched between the two. Both of them were comparatively of thinner physique as compared to mine but to travel on a precariously adjusted place was neither comfortable for me nor for the other two.. The journey was short and that is why the discomfort was tolerable.

Hat is now a village of a few houses with sprawling grain fields spread for miles all around it. The entire area is called Bahl which was described as the "Pet of Mandi" as it used to be major source of grain production; meeting the needs of the entire area. Otherwise Bahl means a level, low-lying and fertile track of land situated near and around the perennial source of water which, on being used for irrigation, can give good yields of crops.

The temple at the Hat was a simple one roomed structure with an idol of Kali mode up of black stone, with protruding red tongue heavily covered with various layers of silk draperies. It was enigmatic and it still is so, as to what sort of statue it is various versions are available, but only the pujari knows the actuality; although different mouths give rise to different stories. Nearby was a room, which we enter through narrow doors and therein were various sculptures displayed. The room is on lower level than the main shrine. Why was it conceived to construct it in such a way. No clue was forwarded by the people who had assembled there by noon when were relishing the food the thick stuffed 'paranthas' brought by my teacher, an eminent writer, poet and painter in his own right. We had our meal under the shade of a mighty pipal tree with a circular platform. This cemented platform was our place to take and talk about the meal, the people, and the history with its multiple horizons and dimensions. Surrounding the thick trunk of pipal were numerous sculptures some of them definitely of fair artistic taste and contours; one was a horse headed deity with a musical instrument in his hand. Was it 'Havagrihya'? Or was it a 'Yaksha' or 'Gardharva' carved in stone? We get references in old scriptures of these 'Devyonis' in such forms. On my salesequent visit such sculptures were missing; taken away by art thieves or art lovers! Basically in this context, both belong to one category, which is tribe of thugs indulging in antiques thefts.

The two idols as referred above are really fine pieces of art, which on iconographic and stylistic studies are unique treasure of antiquity dating back to 10th or 11th century. So far nothing as far as art or religious objects corresponding to this era have been acquired from not only this central place but also entire length and breadth of the erstwhile Mandi State. These two stone sculptures are amongst the finest examples of late Pratihara School of art. Naturally, question arises how to highlight their creation? Are these the works of local craftsmen? Chances are rare. Otherwise it is possible that they have been brought from the main land during the post Harsha period when the nation was in turmoil and such objects were being pushed to safe hill zones by the cadets and collaterals of various big and small kingdoms of north India. But there were no tangible replies worth offering.

Out of the two, one is a Vishnu sculpture, three feet in height, although preserved but in a badly damaged state. It still constitutes one of the objects of worship in this tiny room and therefore is not totally neglected. Herein, Vishnu and his consort Luxmi is depicted sitting on a standing stout Garuda: The divine vehicle of Vishnu, with bold and conspicuous wings. With usual attributes, the idol of Vishnu is six armed; two additional with usual Vishnu images. Around the deity there is a large lotus halo shown in prominence. The whole concept is so presented as if it is full temple in itself. Various flying figures and Chamarvahanis can easily be identified. To top most parts of the idol on the far corners are reserved for Shiva and Brahma thereby the three trinity of Hindu pantheon is on a single stone slab. Being less damaged Shiva can be spotted but Brahma can only be deciphered by the flowing beard. The other details are obscure.

Almost on an identical pattern, on a slightly smaller stone slab is mainly an icon ofShiva. Shiva and Parvati are both in standing posture and Nandi- The divine bull shown on their posterior part is reminiscent of Pratihara school. It is as if a representation of Shiva image in metal in Laxminarayan Temple complex of Chamba town dating to 11th century. Shiva with jatamukat with usual attributes in the hands is chiseled by meticulous craftsmanship while the Parvati idol is having a crown. Here again the top right and left corners are reserved for Vishnu and Brahma out of which the later is totally damaged whereas the former can be recognized. One statue each of Narsingha and Ganesh also finds place in this room but obviously they appeared to be late additions and do not belong to early school of antiquity. Totally in folk pattern they are works of local artists. The casual examination of the main idol of Kali or Hateshwari also is moulded on folk art which is also creation of some local artist of by gone time.

In the history of Mandi state, it has been recorded that the present village Hat was the seat of power of the area surrounding which ultimately emerged a native state as an off shoot of Suket. Here Bahu Sen had established his capital after having quarreled with his elder brother Sahu Sen; who was ruling Suket in the 11th century. A relevant conjecture is justified that the present temple complex was part of his palace area. The present temple was the principal shrine of the ruler and he was belonging to the sect of Shakti worshipers. With passage of time the palace crumbled down but the temple survived evolving into many shapes and sizes and finally taking an entirely different architecture as is presently in 2001 A.D. The remnants of previous temples like amalaks and idols which were scattered around during our first visit lend testimony to our version. There was a huge granite amalak partially sub-merged in the soil near the gate of temple complex also known as Pandav Ki Paroli i.e. the gate of Pandavas. This gate is attributed to Mahabharta's heroes as is usual in these hills. Anything magnificent, strange and extra ordinary is said to be the creation of Pandavas. The gate structure is also gradually on the path of further damage and decay due to consistent neglect.

According to the historical data available with us, Bir Sen; the common progenitor of both Mandi and Suket states had is original capital at Pangana in the Karsog valley in the 8th century. He was followed by six rulers and then emerged Sahu Sen. Mandi traditions narrate him to be eccentric and inclined to be misanthrope. His courtiers had plotted to replace him by his brother Bahu Sen. The plot was discovered and Bahu Sen had to pay the price by withdrawing from the original capital palace to his estate at Hat about 20 kms. from present Mandi town. Later he moved to Manglour and made himself its master. It appears, from the narration of the history and substantiated from traditions that Hat had its glorious and palmy days when Bahu Sen had settled there and its sculpture and shrine dates back to the period of Bhau Sen in early 11th century.

Presently in 2004 A.D. an ultra modern temple has been built at the previous site of main temple. 'Hat' - as a proper noun is used in the western Himalayas with a special connotation. Although in general parlance, currently it is a substitute for a market place. But in by gone days 'hat' was the word used for a capital town. Generally the capital had the privilege to have shops and bazaars, and the entire rest of the territory of the Kingdom used to have rural orientation. Therefore, so many places known as hat were at a time of history, the main place from where the rulers used to reign as the chief and the master of the land.

CHAPTER - 13

ARKI : A Small Town of Glory

In early seventies of the last century, I had a long spell of posting at Chamba town, which is rightly described as a treasure-house of antiquities. Bhuri Singh museum set up during 1908 A.D. was a right step to retain and maintain the regional history of the then State known as Chamba. I was introduced to a book under the title "Himalayan Art" authored by J.C. French a civil servant of British colonial rule which contain a touching comment on the kingdom of Bhagal presently in district Solan and its capital town Arki; which enthused me to visit this place. In 1929, J.C. French toured Arki and had published his impressions in 1937. He states that Arki town is like Chamba. It is dominated by a fortress palace and below there is an open space in the center of the town. Its wall defending the palace is in some places carved out of the long rocks and precipices continue them. The vista, up the narrow streets of Arki town to the place is old Italian, and even finer is the view from the west, of the fortress palace and overhanging a mountain torrent in sombre steepness. In the last month of 1986, opportunity was in store for me to visit this place. The location of this township was a labour of wisdom. Almost a small fortress in itself surrounded and protected all around by hills of considerable heights, Arki appears a flat land which is a rare sight in the mountaneous country. It is recorded that prior to shifting the capital to this place, the ruling dynasty had their dwellings at village Dundhan. Somewhere in 1650 A.D., Arki was selected to be the seat of the ruling chief.

The fortress palace although presently not in its due royal grandeur, still commands and demands attention. Its foundation dates back to year 1700 A.D.. Later additions were a matter of rule from year to year and from ruler to ruler. In Chamba, the town spreads all around the palace but here it differs. The whole inhabitation of the area, the bazaar, the streets, the grounds, the state buildings of administration are all patched below the foothill of the palace; as if it is supervising all the activities taking place in the township.

The fortress is unique in a sense, that it is out of a few fortress palaces in

Himachal, other being at Nahan of Sirmour rulers, at Nalagarh of Hindu dynasty and one obscure at Kuthar near Solan on way to Mahalog. Other ruling houses who merged to form HImachal Pradesh did never fancy to give fort like semblance to their palaces. Rana Sabha Chand when transferred the ruling seat from Dundhan, naturally a palace was to be proclaimed as a dwelling site for the chief, and he selected present Arki.

The construction of the present fort palace came into being in 1700 by the descendant of Rana Sabha Chand, Prithavi Singh followed by Rana Bhup Singh who finally completed and shifted to this palace-cum-fort. The initial dwellings of the Rana were near the present Laxami Narain temple. Soil erosion near this site led to its complete abandonment somewhere in 1760 A.D. Further aditions were effected by this ruler in the fort which virtually and eventually became the official court.

As a matter of fact, the ruling dynasty claims their origin from Ujjain. This is how it has been recorded in the history. As to why and how they left Ujjain and settled in this tract is not clear but it is clear they claim to be Panwar Rajputs who added "Singh" as a suffix to their name replacing the original Chand. This trend of changing over the clan name is evident in many a ruling dynasty. The ruler of the house of Chamba to whom French have referred with a remark that Arki resembled Chamba. In matters of changing suffixes in Arki from Chand to Singh and in Chamba from Verman to Singh is a further example of similarity.

Although the fort is in decay and decadence, it is still majestic and magnetize the imagination of the passers by. But still more rewarding is an opportunity to enter the interior of the fort, and to get spell bound by the still surviving effects of its wall paintings, the frescos and miniatures which can easily be deciphered and interpreted. There extensive decoration of the painting process is the Diwankhana where the ruler in his palmy days used to hold his darbar and interact with his audiences and subjects. Mr. M.S. Randhava a great art historian and civil servent had planned visits to this place after hearing the merits of the paintings. His words are really imaginative and worth quoting. According to him this school of painting is an admixture of Rajput and Pahari school encompassing variegted themes at Arki. He notes: "Arki frescos are a visual record of contemporary life in the hills of the Punjab in the middle of the 19th century. Apart from illustrating religious themes, they tell us how the people amused themselves and what were their geographical conceptions. The overall compositional arrangement of the subjects and their designs give the onlooker a sense of mystery and suspense. Monotony is avoided by the thematic contrast of form and colour. However, the overall balance of the colour and design in maintained."

There are discrepancies and difference of opinion about the style of paintings. Realistically they emit the aroma of painting which we presently call Pahari school of painting banking heavily on Kangra and Guler styles but distinctively giving it a local feature known as independent Arki sub school of Pahari Kalam. J.C. French propounded it on these lines and later on was endorsed by M.S. Randhava. The paintings are immaticulate execution of themes borrowed from religion, history and culture beside other thematic concerns for amusements. The Kama's death by Shiva's arrow and Kalia Mardan are prominently displayed. When Himachal came into being, N.C. Mehta was its first chief commissioner in 1948. He was a scholarly person with a mental make-up and desired bent of mind to patronize art and was the rightful authority to get it interpreted. According to him these paintings of the Diwankhana were primarily works of Rajputana school performed by artists of Jaipur.

Broadly the paintings portray the flora and fauna for decorative purpose. The religious thematic narrations of 'Puranas' are conspicuous by their presence and this is an integrated part dominating the Kangra school in general. Raginis can be made out and similarly the war scenes. The most attractive parts are the decorative design having floral and figurine compositions. A female figure with two prominent wings and riding a horse with a small lady figure sitting behind her seems to be purely imaginative. Like wise a royal lady mounting an elephant is again a creation of fantasy. The lady is perched on the back of the massive elephant between two figures which are partly human and partly animal. It is difficult to conclude what massage it has to the on looker. Basically the royal woman depict the fundamental spirit of Pahari (Kangra or Guler painting) but lacks the elegance and beauty of female figure for which Kangra school of painting is so famous. An attractive piece of art is frescos depicting acrobats in action. These nats and natinis were major sources of amusement for the hill folks. Most curious contribution of the painting is the portrayal of foreign places like London, Florence, Portugal, Paris and one of course is that of Goa. It is said they have been copied from picture post cards and are in European style but other imaginative and religious themes are purely influenced by Mughal or Rajasthani or Pahari shool when it was on the decay and decline. Curiously enough a family of King of China are painted with neck of horse and face of cat. In another frescoe a Raja is atop a horse who has tail turned into a female figure and the body and leg of canine family may be cat or tiger.

As a matter of fact the fort is the sole and major attraction of the town and the paintings are its soul but due to neglect in preservation and suitable protection, they are steadily and slowly loosing their shine and beauty. After all, the site belongs to the erstwhile Raja without power, privileges and resources to maintain. It is beyond the means of a single person to manage their upkeep who is no more a ruling chief now. Actually the most of the part of the building i.e. fort is crumbling down to ruins. A part of it is a royal resort and another part is a private residence of the Ex-Raja. When I visited the palace partly it had been rented to some government agencies also. In such state of affairs the proud possession of the by gone days in the nature of paintings and frescos are bound to get neglected. Otherwise the palace fort is situated in such manner that it lends commanding view of snow capped mountains and also gives glimpses of once important hill stations like Shimla, Kasauli and Subathu. Arki fort shared its misfortune during the rise of Gorkha in Himachal hills when Amar Singh Thapa used this fort as garrison for his troops. The Raja was made to stay at Nalagarh and near by Punjab area of Ropar. Later on finally it was the British forces who handed it over to the ruling family of Arki in the middle of 19th century. And the ruler was upgraded from Rana to Rana due to his loyalty to new empire. Raja Ajay Dev had created the new state of Bhaghal in early 13th century and finally Bhaghal was stripped of its autonomy when in 1948, it got merged to form Himachal Pradesh? Why it is called Bhaghal? There is a stong view that this territory had a vast population of Bhaghs i.e. tigers and that is why the name Bhaghal came into being. Again Arki is a uncommon name which was chosen capital town. Lal Chand Prarthi had the opinion that this is a derivative of a vedic name i.e. Aryaki which originated from Arya. Lal Chand Prarthi who had drawn some such conclusion in his book 'Kuluta Desh Ki Kahani.' According to one learned Sanskrit scholor of Batal, a near by colony- village of Brahmins, Arki is an other name of Saturn that is Shani-a Grah known for its bad effects. As Shani has a soft corner for this place and is said to be merciful for this place, the name Arki was bestowed upon this new town. The other story is prevalent that it was called Har ki Nagri. Har is Shiva. From Har-Ki-Nagri, some words were dropped as well as nagri so. Arki evolved from Har-ki-Nagri thereby getting shortened to be more popular in the populace. Such legendry explanation is really an interesting piece of information. It appears that its name as Har Ki Nagri is not beyond doubt due to the existence of cave temple dedicated to Lord Shiva who is also known as Har. One such cave temple is that of Lutru Mahadev situated high up on the hill top. From the town proper it can be easily spotted. While approaching Vatal village midway there exist a temple of Durga and nearby is Gangeshwar Mahadev with a perennial source of water. Wherever there is water, to the Indian psyche, it is Ganga. Besides Lutru Mahadev there is a Mutru Mahadev also in a small cave just across the main market in a cool thickly wooded and serene surrounding. Here the natural phenomena of constantly dripping water is most exciting. The Har-ki-Nagri has temple dedicated to Hari i.e. Vishnu also and this shrine is known as Laxmi Narain Temple. That is how Shiva, Shakti and Vishnu the major deities of Hindu pantheon were worshiped in the old kingdom of Arki.

A casual look at the main bazaar beyond the central age old massive pipal tree is also as enchanting as the excellent wood work of some of the window frames of the old elites of the towns are still surviving which throw flood light on its glorious days. The temples, the fort palace inter- twingle with various convolutions of history and legends along with its paintings and frescos can remain memorable part of our sojourn to this historic town.

CHAPTER - 14

OLD BILASPUR : The Town That went under The River

More than three hundred and fifty years ago the Raja of Kehlur founded a town on the left bank of the Satluj, little knowing that it would eventually be submerged and the river in the part of the region, would come to be known as Gobind Sagar.

The Raja was Deep Chand, who moved his seat of power from Sunhani to this site of his choice. When the town submerged under the water of Govind Sagar, it lost all its historical monuments, mainly temples and valuable pahari paintings which were earlier viewed and reproduced in their works by eminent art historians and European travelers like Fortster, Moorcraft, Trebeck and G.T. Vigne.

The Major extant source of information on Bilaspur today is the work of Huchinson and Vogel, who compiled the history of the town and its people in their celebrated book. "The History of Punjab Hill States". The authors drew heavily from a vernacular history in verse, "Shashivansh Vinod", written in the late 17th century by Ganesh Singh Bedi. The last ruling chief of Bilaspur state, Raja Anand Chand (1927-194), also authored a book on the state under the title, "Bilaspur-Past, Present and Future". Much of his information was also based on the "Shashivansh Vinod".

Although Bilaspur town became the seat of power of the state only in 1654, the ruling dynasty controlled the territory on both sides of the Satluj from a much earlier period. According to Bedi the foundation of the state was laid at Kot-Kehlur, a small town on the foot-hills of Nainadevi Dhar, by Vir Chand in 697 A.D. Huchinson and Vogel however, claim that the state came into existence in or around 900 A.D.

What is certain, however, is that Bilaspur was the seat of the powerful hill state whose paramountsy extended over the ruler of Bagal (the present Arki), Kunihar, Beja, Patta, Dhami, Mangal and Kunthal states of the Shimla region. Till the transfer of power to the British, all these and about 12 hill states were vassals to the ruler of Bilaspur. It was mandatory for them to be present at the festival of Sairi on first Ashwani, with an annual gift of cash and kind.

Bilaspur is spread over moderate hills and vales, and with his control extending over seven hill ranges, the Raja was described as "the lord of seven hills". A folk tale set in the period of Raja Kalyan chand narrates how a tragic quarrel broke between the King and his queen over the issue of seven hills. A ballad was being sung in praise of the lord of the seven hills while the king was playing chess with his queen, who was a daughter of the Raja of Suket. Her plea that one of those hills belonged to her father made the king so angry that in that furious mood he hit the queen on her nose. She went to her father, who engaged his son-in-law in battle at Mahadev (now in Mandi district, then part of Suket) and the Raja of Bilaspur was killed. Consequently, the queen committed Sati.

Before the advent of Gobind Sagar which finally submerged Bilaspur the township went under water in 1761, when heavy landslides turned the Satluj into a lake for 45 days leading to massive loss of life and property. Huchinson and Vogel also had taken note of this event.

When Gobind Sagar was carved out the displaced persons were paid compensation. But when the water recedes in summer, many residents of the old town nostalgically point out to places where once stood their hearths and homes.

Scattered in the vast sandy spread one can make out that large flat of green land known as Sandu-Ka-Har, the remains of old palaces and temple tops.

The palaces, themselves exquisite structures, were noted for their wall paintings, which attracted the attention of that administrator scholar, J.C. French. He also mentions them in his book, "Himalayan Art". According to him, the palace incorporated two styles of architecture-the older part was built in the Rajputana style, and the later addition by Raja Amar Chand (1833-88), was in the hill style.

The frescos in the upper storey had for their theme Radha and Krishna, and floral designs in a rough Kangra style. The walls of the Darbar Hall were painted all over with flowers and birds. At the end of the hall above the windows were the frescos in the late Kangra style.

Also notable were two temples in Shikhara style. According to the German art scholar, Dr. Herman Geetz, the temple of Shan-Mukheshwar, dedicated to Kartikeya, may have been connected with the vassal state of Satadru (on the

Satluj), under the paramountsy of Hanshvardhan of Thaneshwar. The repetitive use of angular and cushion moldings under the plinth of this temple possessed characteristic similarity with the post-Gupta ruins of the 7th Century Sarnath Shrines, but the lintel over the door had been treated with motifs of flying figures in the style of Lakasana Devi temple at Brahmaur in Chamba.

The other temple that of Ranaganatha, dedicated to Shiva, can be estimated on style and structure to be of the 8th century. The architectural elements in the plinth portion of this temple were almost identical to the later Chalukian shrines. Thus, this temple signifies the spread of Chaluklan art in this region when the Gupta tradition declined with the invasion of Kashmir style during the region of Lalitaditya (725-756).

Today the state museum of Himachal Pradesh at Shimla has in its possession two graceful figures of Digpala which were brought from the hindniches of the Ranganatha temple. According to Dr. V.C. Ohri they are a mixture of Chandela art, which was a late manifestation of the virile development inspired by Gupta art with stylized, well developed limbs indicating muscular strength without disrupting the smoothness of the form. There are 16 Digpalas in Hindu mythology. Each responsible for the protection of one direction. Temples were built as a symbol of the universe, and in the earlier Hindu Shrines all Digpalas were given a place, a tradition which is not observed in the later period.

The temple is said to have been commissioned by Aildev, who enshrined his own idol in it as a personification of Lord Shiva the Ranganatha.

This reference indicates that Bilaspur had a well developed cultural activity much before the founding of Kehlur state of Kot-Kehlur. Perhaps history may have been repeating itself and the town may been abandoned and sumerged in the river many times.

When the seat of power was brought to the place, the old temples may have been renovated because on iconographic ground the superstructure of the temples belonged to a style of a much later period, not fitting with the structure up to the plinth level.

That these temples were excellent relics of the past is certain. The Shan Mukeshwar temple, the temple of Karikeya, son of Lord Shiva, was a singular example of a shrine dedicated to him not only in these hills, but all over north India.

Now a new town is emerging on a nearby hillock. The clusters of small houses with a modern touch; a modern market, a busy bus stand was the dream child of a planner setting out to create a small Chandigarh in Himachal Pradesh. The nucleus is there, but how it develops in the years to come remains to be seen.

CHAPTER - 15

HARI RAI : A Unique Sculpture

My stay in early seventies at Chamba town of Himachal Pradesh had opened new vista of knowledge. The existence of a museum having innumerable pieces of antique and good stock of books of lore coupled with temples of unsurmountable beauty and their idols were enough to extoll the peace, prosperity, vast learning and insight of the era when Chamba was at its glory.

The exposure to an idol of Vishnu with four faces had singularly added to my sphere of understanding about the iconography of this great god of Hindu pantheon only at Chamba. When I first visited the temple in August 1970, in the temple complex of Laxmi Narayan is the presiding main idol of Vishnu with four faces out of which rear one is not visible. The idol is more than life size in height, made of marble and tastefully decorated with costumes and costly jewelleries. The main face is that of human while to the right and left are that of lion and boar representing the Narsingha and Varaha incarnations of lord Vishnu. It is true that Vishnu in its various forms and postures are widely spread in the age-old temples but such an idol was my first encounter. Those who were close to my circle could not highlight about this presentation of Vishnu. Ultimately Mr Ohri the learned curator of Bhuri Singh Museum of Chamba came to my help. He lent to me a book on Hindu iconography by Bannerjee by the aid of which I could make out the pros and cons of this school of worship where Vishnu is worshipped as Vishnu Chaturmukhi Vaikuntha Murti.

Till that time i.e. one May night in 1971, no one had the slight idea that one more an idol of Vishnu similar in design and concept in metal co-existed in another shrine of Chamba known as Hari Rai temple.

Cunningham, Vogel, Huchison and later chhabra wrote extensively, about the history and heritage of Chamba but surprisingly they are all silent about the idol of Vishnu in metal which is older and cast even earlier than the metal idols of Bharmour and Chhitrari made during the reign of Raja Meru Varman of Bharmour kingdom. Perhaps, one may only conclude that as the icon of Hari Rai temple does not bear any inscription where as the others do, it escaped the attention of these celebrated historians and art-lovers.

Once the statue of Hari Rai was found missing, the news spread like wild fire all over the country and more so in Chamba where the citizens resorted to agitations, bands and dharnas for many days. I have witnessed those days how the gloom loomed large in the psyche of the residents of Chamba. Later when this idol was recovered from a gang of smugglers at Bombay and restored to its original site. The way all this followed in quick succession was something rare in the history of crime detection. After the recovery, Chamba was festive for many days. Prior to its installation in its original place, the idol of Hari Rai was kept for public darshan in the Chaughan a nearby wide tract of land near its temple.

It goes without saying that a wonderful statue is a beauty to behold. When without its usual attires and fabric coverings the whole treatment of the idol is visible which is nothing less than immortal poetry in metal. It is a massive structure weighing 400 kg and measuring 1.17 mtr. The whole anatomy is not only superbly executed but particularly remarkable for its muscular modellation in a very naturalist way. The four armed Vishnu is shown with four faces, the frontal one is that of human one which is serene and sober with downcast eyes which are inlaid with silver. On the right side is a face of lion representing the Narsingha incarnation and the left one is that of Varaha. Although these animal faces can be easily deciphered but are highly stylized and made more decorative than the real faces of the animals. In the rear is a face, which is horrifying and remains hidden when the figure is studied from the frontal exposure. The human face is called Vaikuntha of the Chaturmukhi Vishnu. According to the scripture these faces represent the relatives of Krishna i.e. Balarama, Pradyumana and Aniruddha. Other elaborate explanations are available in the scriptures for their association with the Vaikuntha Murti Vishnu. However the frontal face is that of Vasudeva which is the main object of worship according to the Bhagwata cult. In this Vaikuntha Chaturmukhi pratima, the god is represented with all its powers of creation, perpetuation and destruction of the universe. The decorative aspect of the image can be summed up in the following description according to which the central figure of the image, with a pronounced well modeled chest and waist, is clad in a dhoti with prominent but delicate folds, arrayed artistically. Fastened to the waist by strings held together by four diamond-shaped floral classic, the dhoti cover the major portion of the left leg of the image and only the upper portion of the thigh above the knee. A folded scarf-encircles the thighs. The figure is elegantly decked in beaded anklets with pendants, brackets, finger rings, armlets, with diamond- shaped central pieces, a beaded 'hara' elaborate with pendants, flower shaped Kundals and a Mukuta with three ornate triangular projection: a full blown lotus crown the mukuta. The hair is arranged in schemetic coiled locks, falling on shoulders and back. Along Vaijayantimala, encircking the body extends almost down to the anklets and a beaded upavita down to the waist. While the neck is marked by auspicious lines, the central part of chest bears a diamond-shaped jewel (Kostubhmani). With eyes inlaid with silver, the central broad and globular face is saumya and sudarshan i.e. placid and highly pleasing to look at. The idol stands with slight flexion, wellbalanced and graceful poise on a moulded spouted pedestal. Emerging from the pedestal, is the upper portion of the Earth goddess between the legs of the god. Her stretched palms are partly placed below the feet of the image. Richly be-jewelled and adequated draped with a sari a scarf and a short blouse, she is looking up towards the lord in respectful wonder. Of the four hands of the main idol two are depicted with a fully blossomed lotus in right upper hand and a sankha in the other. The lower left hand is shown as Chakarpurush while the right lower hand is that of gadadevi which are all beautifully and appropriately cast and the Lord is shown as placing his hands on them.

The whole treatment to this idol is nothing but a poetry in full symphony. It is a poem in metal, the idol is all together, a delight of devotees, iconographics, art-lovers and antique hunters.

"It is fantastic, it is invaluable. It would cost much more than 50 lakhs (in 1971)" exclaimed, Dr. Moti Chandra, Director of Bombay's Prince of Wales Museum, who was called in by the police of Bombay to assess the antiquity of the idol. "In all world" said Moti Chandra "no idol of this kind" is known to exist." He placed the age of the image as 800 AD approximately. The date of the image remained controversial. Following the recovery of the image, it is noticed that various dates, ranging from AD 400 to AD 1200 were suggested for it. Extensive study assigns the idol to the reign of Avanti varman of Kashmir (855 AD-83).

As a matter of fact there is no inscriptional ground to assign the exact date for the idol. All efforts have been concentrated to place it in 9th century on the stylistic basis only. Moreover, even the temple known as Hari Rai temple made of sand-stone where this idol is a object of worship is not attributed to any ruler and this is an exception to the rule in the history of temples of Chamba proper. Almost all the important temples are ascribed to one or the other ruler but the history and legends are silent about this temple. There exists one copper plate deed in the Bhuri Singh Museum which details about a land donation to this temple and it dates back to the period of one King Somavarman (11th century) son of Salavahana (or Salakaravarman) who accordingly to Kalhan, was stated to have been deposed by King Ananta (AD 1028-65) of Kashmir but the charter recording the grant was issued in the first year of reign of Asata, the brother and successor of Somavarman. In spite of all the opinions, the imprints on people psyche is that this temple belongs to the era of Raja Sahil Varman who had founded the capital town of Chamba. But this image of Vaikunth Murti Vishnu belongs to two centuries period earlier than the reign of Sahil Dev Varman. Certain valuable collections of Bhuri Singh Museum of Chamba reveals open the mystery of the antiquity of this magnificent icon which again lend support to the antiquity of this image. Several broad bricks collection in the Bhuri Singh Museum was brought here from the temple complex of Laxmi Narayan. It is said that these bricks were unearthed while doing some development of site. It appeals to the mind, that a temple made of bricks was dedicated to Vaikunth Murti Vishnu, which was the object of worship. Later when present Hari Rai temple came into existence, this idol was placed/installed. In this way this impressive structure of mid-eighth century fired the imagination of Sahil Dev Varman when he selected Chamba to make his permanent capital after abandoning Bharmour. Although the marble icon of Laxmi Narayan does not reveal the round face and trinated mukuta of Kashmir influence but for all practical purposes, it is a replica of the Vaikunth - Murti - Vishnu now worshipped at Hari Rai temple.

History of Chamba is not silent on the founding of capital town of Chamba by Sahil-dev-verman in 10th century where in Sanskrit Shalokhas, it is clearly mentioned that after defeating 'Khashtriyas' in a battle the Varman dynasty chose the present platau of Chamba as its administrative head-quarter. Again there is a mystic interpretation which suggests us to believe that this town of Chamba used to serve as the second capital of Bharmour kingdom. The rigours of Bharmour used to so intense in winter that but for old, infirm and delinquent persons all used to migrate to Chamba till recent past. What about in those days of Varman supremacy? How it was possible to gain and retain territory in these olden time when snow was abundant and forest were dense. Now the rigour is still tolerable, but in the olden times, Chamba was much more comfortable for the kings and his subjects to come down to have a migratory office at Chamba. Perhaps during that span of time the Vaikuntha - Murti - Vishnu was cast at Chamba housed in the brick temple the remains of which are still available at Chamba Museum. Contemporary of this icon and slightly later, the masterpieces of Gugga also were being created at Bharmour and Chhitrari which are in existence on date as Ganesh, Narsingh, Laxana and Shakti Devi metal sculptures.

During my stay at Chamba, I had heard about the legendary knowledge of history and society of Chamba of one Pandit Thakur Dass. It is said that he had unique knowledge about the temple of Chamba. Even Vogel and Huchinson used to consult him to reach their inferences. Thakur Dass had access to the old books and manuscripts housed in Laxmi Narayan temple which unfortunately got destroyed by a sudden fire which broke out later. It was he who had made it known that there was one Vishnu temple as mentioned in the old manuscript, in the eighth century. There exists no doubt about the founding of Laxmi Narayan temple in 10th Century with marble icon. It is beyond doubt that the Vishnu Murti Vaikuntha, was an object of worship in Chamba town prior to the founding of capital by Sahil Dev Varman and the icon was none other than Hari Rai - the poetry in metal, a masterpiece, marvelous and magnificent object of art and indicator of artistic and cultural height of that era in Chamba - Bharmour kingdom.

CHAPTER - 16

KARSOG VALLEY : A Wonderland

I had no good perception of the valley known as Karsog. It was described as a rustic land situated in deep interior of the then Suket State, now a part of District Mandi. All the misinformation and disinformation sublimated into deep esteem and admiration for this tract of land when I first visited the place near the end of year 1975; the occasion was a multiple specialities camp organized by the Goverment Medical College of Shimla. I was to look after the service part for eye and ear, nore and throat patients who fall within my speciality. Karsog valley is a wide and vast fertile land and in that part of year its fields and forest were lush green with nature's bounties and on my first contact I got allured and attracted to its location and its possessions. Nature has placed this valley in such a way that on its northern end, it is wooded with Deodar jungles with intense cold climate suitable for the first grade apple cultivation and on its southern tapering tail it touches the bank of the river Satluj which form an ideal site for rearing mangoes of all varieties. Topographically being so rich, it is a contradicts of area which has a gradual gradient from the high mountain to the foot hills giving rise to varying climates and varieties of crops. I have yet to see the such a dense net work of irrigation channels (although modest but so profuse) in any other place as seen in this part of our hilly country side. On my first visit I was so charmed by the abundance of its greenery and natural scenic panorama that I thanked my stars for having been invited to the Multiple Medical Services Camp, which caused brought about my visit to this countryside of extra ordinary landscape.

In my childhood, while in our country house in an area near Chhatari, I had heard of Kao and Mamel temples. My mother used to talk very high of them. The impressions of early pre-school days suddenly propelled me to visit them when I came to know that these shrines were part of this valley, not very far from Karsog proper. This was a humble place in 1975 and now had suddenly become a full fledged market place of fairly good trade. My colleagues also accompanied me from our Karsog camp to village Mamel now can be described as a suburb of township of Karsog. Mamel was reached after walking down an uneven track, which was although, fit for jeeps, but was not suitable for a stroll. The most conspicuous structure of this hamlet is the old wooden temple of Mamel Mahadev which is in pagoda style with outer sabhamandap leading to sanctum sanctorum. A narrow circumambulation has been provided around the sanctum. The idol at Mamel is now addressed as Mamleshwar which is a inscribed bronze image. It is a rare metal sculpture of marvel of Gauri-Shankara. The idol is on the pattern of Pratihara period and might have been commissioned when this region was under the sway of Gujjar Pratihara kingdom. It appears some representative of the then kingdom might have settled at Mamel and ruled from the site. The idol of Gauri - Shankara has an inscription on it which I was given to understand, has not been deciphered as yet. Another rock inscription existing at Mamel is a fine source to throw a good deal of light on the history and art of Karsog valley. The idol is unique antique and is akin to the Gauri-Shankara of Chamba commissioned by Raja Yogakara Varman in 11th century. Herein Mamel the statue is half the size of Chamba but in iconography and perception both are almost identical in which Shiva and Parvati are standing with the divine bull Nandi behind both of them. The sabhamandap has been provided with a "githa" - a deep pucca pit in which wooden sticks have been burning since the creation of the shrine. The doorjam of the sanctum has decorative motifs of flowers with Navagrahas at the lentel of the framework carved systematically in somewhat folkish style. In the sabhamandap two sculptures of Vishnu and Laxami are in good state of preservation, which again dates back to late Pratihara period. The figures possess fluidity and softness. The faces are full and sensuous. A big drum is a pride possession of the temple which is said to be made up of Bhekhali plant. Similarly a piece of wonder is a big grain of wheat weighing about half a kilogram. Both of them according to local legend and prevalent belief belong to the times of Mahabharata when Pandavas had halted at this place. Although the so called wheat grain exactly look like that but it appears to be cast by making use of mud. This item is properly preserved and occasionally exhibited.

Presently the temple is in typically Pahari wooden style with three tiers taking a shape of pagoda with a chhatar at the top. It is a fine piece of surviving wooden temple with slate roofing, ideally a shrine made up of entirely local materials. Although the present structure is not more than three to four centuries old but some remnants of old stone temples are conspicuous by their presence i.e. amalak and stone sculpture of olden days. Nearby is a bhandar of the temple storing the valuables of the deities. This treasury house locally known as 'Kothi's is also a traditional Pahari building of considerable merit. In the circumambulation of the main sanctum are two wooden 'raths', they belong to the Mamel Mahadev and his subordinate, Kodu; are decorated during special occasion and fairs. This custom is prevalent in a vast area of inner Himalayan range of Dhouladhar stretching from Bara Bhangal to Mandi-Suket and beyond to Shimla hills and Kinnaur. Such customs of assumed godhood are controversial, which have been superimposed? The traditional local cult of dancing Gods with 'Raths' and the Puranic Gods represented by metal idols and kept in the sanctum have intermingled in such a way that it is really an uphill task to separate and split them to project independent and sovereign entities.

During this camp period which lasted for six weeks, we had journeyed to village Kao which is also famous for an ancient shrine dedicated to Kali which is situated on the south of Karsog. We marched through the ripe fields of maize on narrow pathways, and crossed two small wooden bridges on Bimla and Amla: two small rivulets considered to be of religious merit. To reach Kao, it took more than an hour as we trekked roughly five kilometers of footpath. The entire pathway was serpentine and zigzag. Again in 1991 this village of Koa was connected with Mamel by a jeepable narrow road and we made use of this alternate road which again took not less than an hour to reach from Karsog as the road has been built in an entirely different site ignoring our trodden path of 1975. At Kao, a wooden temple for Kali is constructed on a rectangular platform which is about four feet in height. The walls of the temple are built above the platform leaving a passage, two feet wide, for parikrama, the wooden planks of which are slanting outwards. Apertures appear at regular intervals near the base of the slanting planks of ventilation of the circumambulation. The inner walls are made up of wood, rubble and mud. The pradakishna path has separate roofing with wood and slates at a lower level than the main edifice. Out of the roof of the main building rise two pagodas like structure, which make the view attractive. Each pagoda with two roofs is capped by gilded amalaka. The upper roofs are covered with well-chiseled slates. Below, the caves have wooden pendants for ornamentation. This temple has an elegant metal sculpture of Mahisasurmardini a very popular icon in these Himalayan regions. This idol is on the pattern of Gauri Shankar of Mamel and is on the Gujjar Pratihara style. A Parashuram cave is said to exist in this temple proper. I had a desire to examine it myself. A lot of mythical legends are associated as usual with this cave. When I visited the place in 1991, I expressed my old craving to the temple priest and he was gracious enough to agree to my plea reluctantly. As the custom goes, I had to put off my clothes and use a clean dhoti to enter this sacred shrine. A friend from my department made arrangement of dhoti and I was led to the so called Parashuram cave which is a small one room structure having three stone sculptures. One of them is three feet high Vishnu idol with four arms havng usual attributes of shankh, chakra, gadda and padam. The second one of same height is that of Sun God having blossomed lotus flowes in its both hands signifying the cult of Sun worship in this land of Shiva and Shakti. Of course, Vishnu's idols were observed in temples of Kao and Mamel which show the vast canvass of Hindu Pantheon was known in the territory. The third icon which is half the height of the former Vishnu is Vaikunthmurti having three faces. The frontal face is a human and that of right and left of this are that of lion and boar respectively. My eyes were searching for Purashuram's idol but here in this cave none fit the description to pronounce them as Rishi Parshuram. The keeper of the temple pointed to the image of Vishnu to be that of Parashuram. I disagreed with him. His version was they worship Parashuram as Lord Chaturbhuj Vishnu as the former was one of the incarnations of the Lord himself.

Similar to Mamel Mahadev, the Kamakhya Devi of Kao has also a wooden rath. A usual with necessary decoration it is a source of attraction and veneration to the masses. Her assistant is Nag whereas the assistant of Mamel is known as Khodu. Nag of kao has also been provided with a wooden rath. Dushehra is a time of great festivities at Kao where surprisingly buffaloes are sacrificed in the most inhuman way. In entire land of present Himachal Pradesh only, Kao is only practicing this cruel ceremony. This Devi has great influence in the psyche of its people. It has well demarcated area of jurisdiction known as Har and the rath of Devi is never taken beyond that territory but for Mamel. Usually Shakti is supposed to be the consort of Shiva and on this analogy Devi of Kao is better half of Devta of Mamel. I had occasion to enquire from the retainer of the Devi as to who was superior between the two. A simple and unexaggerated reply was both were in their own territory - a very earthy reply but appropriate and to the mark. In our male dominated society, this rustic thinking is in proper perspective, throwing aside the bondage of male preponderance in the maintenance of the affairs of the temple, the statues, the Rath and its jewellaries. He further elaborated his version which was really informative. According to him whenever the Rath of Mamel Mahadev is brought to Kao, the Devi Rath of Kao is taken to receive it at a specific place of the village and its Rath is titled first in salutation to the Mamel Devta. On proceeding to the temple the Rath of Mamel Mahadev is followed by the Rath of Devi. Similar practice is at Mamel; where the Mahadev receives her at a specific point in the hamlet, offer salutation and the Rath of Devi paces ahead of Mamel Deo; thereby proving the law of equality, fair play and justice among the two sexes which are kept at par. Also here in hills the Deo-Parivar retains some bondage with each other but neither they are subordinate nor challenge the superiority of the other. This is an ideal example of code of conduct and practice.

The survey of the antiquities of Karsog will be incomplete if Pangana is ignored. Pangana is hardly twenty kilometer from Karsog proper and is identified as the ancient capital of the proginator of Suket and Mandi states who was known as Vir sen. After settling down at his capital, he and his succesor ruled over the entire hilly region between the Bears and the Satluj. A wood and stone structure attributed to Vir Sen's time, i.e. 8th century A.D. is still in existence. It is a several storeyed building the uppermost of which houses a Devi. The passage to reach this part is cumbersome from the groundfloor upwards with a number of narrow and tortuous staircase. Each story is provided with holes in their walls which were made use to fire at the enemies and thereby protecting the edifies from the external dangers. The fort appeared to have been repaired and renovated according to the needs of the times. This Devi also possesses a Rath as at Memel and Kao. The structure has survived due to the placement of the uppermost storey for religious reasons, otherwise the scant care which can be easily visualized could have led to its collapse much earlier. The religious protection accorded to it is the hallmark for its survival down to our times.

CHAPTER - 17

THE MISSING BOULDER OF BRAHAMINI DEVI NALA : A Rendezvous

Was it my last visit to Bharmour? This is how I thought in 1975 A.D. No; it was destined that I shall serve Chamba again. So, I am not sure when, but suddenly in one of our Eye Service Camps, I decided to climb to Brahamani-Nala to get a glimpse of all the mural drawn on the boulder. Generally first two or three days are very busy in eye camp. Thereafter it is only aftercare of the patients; and there is a lot of free time. Now here was the opportunity to combine business with pleasure. Most of my sojourns to the sites of antiquity, the study of icons and sittings at temples and forts are the outcome of the opportunities offered by work and-pleasure combine, wherein the real assigned task was also never neglected.

Bharmour has an alternate approach also from Kharamukh which is merely a bridle path other than the motor-road. The rustic path is typical and traditional roadway on which falls a village of a comparatively populated nature having good number of houses and is called Khani. All the previous scholars who had the first surprise of the magnificence and remarkable achievements of erstwhile Bharmour kingdom have beaten this track only, because the motorable road is a recent development in this early site of civilization. Between Khani and Bharmour is an all weather rivulet which collect the water from the high mountaineous ranges and is called Brahamani-Nala or small rivulet known as Brahamani. Incidentally this 'Braham' is the precussor of the name of Bharmour which is decadent derivative of a Sanskrit word Brahmpur. It has been recorded by Vogel that Bharamani Nala boulder depicts all the images still under worship at Bharmour's temple complex which is called Chaurasi. Chaurasi means eighty four. According to local tradition, there were eighty four, temples at this site and that is why the place became famous by this name. An other version is that the spiritual guide of Raja Sahil Dev Verman of tenth century was one from Nath sect and he was no other than Charpat Nath and he had a bigger group of naths with him and they were eighty four. As they had camped at Chaurasi, so naturally the place got this name. Brahamani-Nala flows exactly in between Bharmour and Khanni. I in the company of my friends and assistants endevoured to climb from Bharmour to face the traditional route. As we reached the Nala site I was overjoyed to become familiar with the celebrated reliefs on the boulder. We were jumping like hill goats from boulder to boulder to trace this remarkable landmark but it was not possible to spot it. A number of local residents were amaged simply to know our curiosity but none was aware of the particular rock. It was really a uphill task. I simple could not imagine how our European scholars had confirmed these out-reach objects of antiquity. Suddenly a wiseman came to our rescue. With his simplicity and humility he confirmed to have seen the rock. We happily followed him. To our surprise, it was a flat rock with recently written slogan of family planning that 'Dusara bacha abhi nahi, tisara khabhi nahi.' It was a very popular slogan of early seventies preaching two child norm. We were shocked at his stupidity but reconciled to his plea that he had come to my medical camp at Bharmour and thought we were supervising the works of wall slogans. Actually he had no knowledge whatsoever of the stone-reliefs of this place. Steadily we marched up to Khani to trace some person of old generation and to our dismay, he recalled that in one of the recent floods, the boulders having the 'gods' of Bharmour has been washed down. Thereafter no body bothered to locate it. There was no Vogel or Goetz to find to take fancy to trace the clues of our heritage.

As Khani was on the tradititonal old route leading to Bharmour and Bharamani Nala was the landmark to their destination and that is why stone reliefs were carved to expose pilgrims to the gods who were being worshiped as Bharmour's Chaurasi. There reliefs revealed what is in store for the pilgrims as they reach the capital of the Brahmpur Kingdom. The Suryamsa Lingam, Shiva Shilapani, Ganesha and Lakshana Devi are said to be on the stone boulder and they exactly fit in the scheme of temples and icons of the village-capital. Howsoever the prominent Narsingh incarnations of Vishnu is missing from the relief which has a life size bronze image in one of the Shikhara style shrine in Bharmour. The Suryamsa Lingam seems to be identical with big Surajmukh (Rameshwar) linga, still standing at Chaurasi on a big copper yoni once set with silver flower-rossttes. The Shiva statue, once probably eight feet high seems to have been very similar to a statue excavated at Avantipur in Kashmir. It depicts Shiva standing in fronto of a standing bull, a very particular iconography of Shiva under the Kushanas, Sassano-Kushanas and Kidara-

Kushanas. The statues and temples were destroyed during the attack on Bharmour by some barbaric tribes may be Tibetan in origin under Khri-sron-Idebtsan. The present temple of Mani-Mahesh with a massive stone lingam was later on built in the tenth century by Sahila-Dev-Verman. Only an asthadhatu bull survives that era and is presently facing the Mani-Mahesh temple in a small shed in front of the temple. Ganesha relief of the boulder has a grand bronze statue of Ganapati partially destroyed in the invasion but its temple had been completely destroyed at the hands of the invaders. It is a very powerful image sitting on a lion. The temple of Mahisasurmardini as Lakshana devi is intact in its original form. Here the four armed idol of Lakshana Devi has a trident, sword, bell and the demon's tail in her hands on the pattern of Chalukya icons of the Devi. Her slim anatomy, fine jewelry and silver-inlaid eyes are similar to late Gupta art-objects. It is beyond imagination as to why the invaders were choosy in their act of destroying. It can simply be guessed that they were some uncivilized and barbaric lots. They destroyed completely the human like images of Shiva and perhaps Surya (which is now Suryamsa lingam), destroyed partially the animals like icons of the Ganesha and bull in front of Mani-Mahesh temple. The lion-human admixture of Narasingha image (if it pre-existed the date of invasion) escaped completely and the temple of Lakshana and its object of worship survived as such may be because the former was more animal like and the later because the devi's image looked like the icons which the Tibetans venerated themselves as Lha-mo. The boulder images were in themselves a complete miniature guide for Bharmour.

After visiting both sites, I have made certain observations and drawn conclusions. It appears that Bharmour had eighty four images but five great temples were dedicated to Panch-Ishwar. The temple in the centre was the principal one dedicated to the Lord of lands-Shiva and at the four corners were the temples of Ganesha, Shakti as Lakshana Devi and Vishnu as Narsingha and Surya. Surya on the fourth corner, at the head of Mani-Mahesh road was perhaps like the Surya of Gum, an icon of fifth-seventh century. It being altogether a human figure was smashed completely as Shiva-Shulpani but the people have not forgotten its existence. After the withdrawal of the invaders, a Surya lingam was substituted in place of Surya icon and temple as the Brahmpur Kingdom of Bharmour had lost its palmy days of abundance.

We were unlucky to miss the boulder as it woudl have been a useful clue to the age-old shrines and statues of Bharmour. The invader's spared the magnificient statue of Lakshana Devi from destruction. Similar could have been the fate of Shilapani-Shiva and Surya as precious art-objects in metal.

The image of Ganesha in bronze has no parallel in any other North-Indian shrine. All these images are the workmanship of one master-artist known by the name of Gugga. Luckily all the surviving icons have inscriptions on them with the mention of the name of artist. It is not without firm perception if we assign the image of Nar-Singha also to Gugga as in concept and design/style botth he Ganesha and Narshingha are similar. It is not clearly understood as to why the Brahamani-Devi-Nala has Nar Shingha omitted from inclusion on the reliefs over the boulder. May be, some Shivait had knowingly omitted the Vishnu icons thereby highlighting the age-old rivalry between the Shaivaits and Vaishnavas. The inscriptions are of great importance historically as they record the names of king meru-Varman who commissioned their constructions as well as Gugga, his master-artist who gave size and shape to the images. These are the remnants of the last phase of great Gupta art tradition.

I think my visit to Brahamani-Devi-Nala was not futile. It never the less, bestowed on us the insight to visualise the long-lost architectural and religious forms of Bharmour as they stood during the period of king Meru-Varman.

SUJANPUR TIHRA : The Closing Chapter of Katoch Kingdom

The year 1980 was about to end. I had organized a huge eye service camp at Sandhol, a fertile tract of land on the bank of the River Beas where the river forms the boundary between Mandi and Hamirpur districts of Himachal. We had to approach the place via Sarkaghat, by traveling in the stony bed of the Khud Bakkar which was really a unique but bitter experience. Irony was, although the village and 'Ilaka Sandhol are important parts of Mandi District they are not connected with an all weather road. What happens in rainy season is that Bakkar drains all the water from the western part of district Mandi and it becomes a horrible site, when Sandhol turns into an isolated island in itself. Only when the water recedes, it is becomes possible to reach the place through the rivulet's bed and not bank. This is the height of callousness on the part of bureaucrates and politicians who ignore public interest. Even when the weather is dry the passage through the bed of the Khud is never comfortable. The constant tossings and turnings in foreign donated government jeep make you really a condemned creature rather than a citizen of a free country. Therefore, I made it a point to return via Hamirpur, when I had gone for second time for the follow up of the cases. This change in programme of journey made me visit Sujanpur Tira or Tihra Sujanpur.

After traveling through almost plain track of Hamirpur through the pine woods the encounter with Sujanpur Tira was all the more enlightening. The situation is really remarkable where this small town is thriving. A spacious flat land called a 'maidaa' is really a site to admire. Rarely in the towns of Himachal we come across such a vast piece of level ground. The 'maidaa' has in its back drop a hillock of considerable height on which are situated dilapidated pats of the palace of the Katoch Kings the most prominent of which was Raja Sansar Chand-II. Its location on the bank of River Beas adds to the beauty of the scene immensely.

The grandfather of Raja Sansar Chand was Ghamand Chand who ruled over Kangra for twelve years from 1761 to 1973 AD. It was he who laid the foundation of this town, which which was later on improved and enlarged by his grandson who ascended the throne of Kangra in 1779 AD. As Kot Kangra had already been lost, first to the Moghals and later to Ranjeet Singh, the ruler of Kangra preferred this place along with the nearby Alampur for his dwelling. As a matter of fact Sansar Chand gave this town a shape of a fort. On one side was the river Beas and on the three sides of town a strong wall was constructed to make it a walled capital city to disable the on-slaught of the invaders. The wall, partly intact is about three miles in length and encircles the town. The population of the town was allotted residences on the periphery of the ground and the palace was commissioned on the hill top. It was at its glory during the reign of Raja Sansar Chand. Even now the high walls of the central hall with its various gates extoll its architecture of significance. In this hall the raja used to hold his 'darbar' where all the hill chieftains were supposed to be present compulsorily, especially during Holi and Dushera. Each Raja was allotted a specific gate for making his entry. On one end was the mighty gate and on the other end used to be the palace for the King of Kangara. Now almost in ruins, one can imagine how magnificent would this building have been. Presently the only part in good state of preservation is the palace which houses the metal idols of Shiva and Parvati in almost human heights which are a fine specimen of Pahari art. It is said that the Shiv statue was moulded in such a way that the fascial anatomy of the idol resembles that of Raja Sansar Chand. Same is true about the Parvati who is said to possess the facial replica of his gaddian rani whom he loved and admired much more than the other 'ranis' of his household. This Shiva statue is known as Sansareshwar clearly indicating that Sansar Chand had commissioned it and supports the notion prevalent that it is based on the anatomical configuration of the Raja. The local tradition also endorses this viewpoint. But there is a snag and no one has cared to investigate. In all the miniature paintings of Kangra art, Sansar Chand is invariably shown sporting a beard but this bronze icon is without any facial hair. It needs explanation. Perhaps it is to bestow godhood onthe icon as Lord Shiva does not support a beard.

As the Beas forms the natural boundary of the town and the mighty stone wall streching four miles in length encircles the town, the gate of the locality is based at the confluence of Pungh Khud with the river Beas. It is called Bhaletha in the local dialect. Sansar Chand was also a patron of the Kangra school of painting and many paintings were produced in his time. The wall miniatures of the Shiva temple bear testimony to this concept. Although this temple of

Narvadeshwar is a flat roofed structure but its walls still exibibit the master strokes of the Kangra school of paintings. The Shiva here is in Lingam form and on the four corners there are small temples dedicated to Vishnu, Surya, Durga and Ganesh, thereby forming a unique conglomeration of all the principal gods of Hindu Pantheon. This seat of worship is devoted to Panch-Parmeshwar, uniting all the five great schools dedicated to the five great Gods of Puramic Hindu concept. Besides the fort and palace of Sansar Chand this great temple of Narmeshwar is second greatest. Ghamand Chand, the founder of town ruled for twelve years and succeeded by his son, Teg Chand (1773-79) after whom finally Sansar Chand became the King. During the period of Sansar Chand both Sujanpur Tira and Kingdom of Kangra were at its height and he slowly paved the way for tis decadence as well. Sansar Chand was the first son of the hills who dreamt of capturing the throne of Lahore. He not only dreamt but made many attempts but failed and failed miserably. In the court of Sansar Chand at Tira, the salutation to the King in vogue was "Lahore Prapat" i.e. let us win Lahore. When he became vassal to Sikh Kingdom, Ranjeet Singh used to taunt him with the same world. Perhaps even in his bad days, he kept up his composure and wit. His reply used to be "Jo Mila Ohi Prapata" i.e. it is enough ultimately what fate brought to me.

The events in his rise are a steady feats of his valour and ambitions but his over-wrought ambitions are what ruined finally. Moreover, he appeared to be capricious to his other hill chiefs and was rough and tough with them to the extent that he lost their loyalties. Little did he realise that history was being written elsewhere as two great military powers the Sikhs and Gorkhas were preying on him. In those times he might have achieved much greater heights but for the presence of these superior forces in picture at the time.

One singular event extols the remarkable reputation of Sujanpur Tira palace. It was during the annual regular attendance of Raja Sansar Chand that the King of Lahore inquired of him about the glory of his palace at Tira. Sansar Chand could understand the intension of Sikh Ruler that he was planning to acquire it for himself just like Kangra fort. He returned a quick reply for which all praises for his presence of mind and told the overlord of Punjab that in bygone days, these building had been in good royal shape but at that time they were crumbling down. Simultaneously he despatched one of his loyal servants to Tira to partially pull down some part of his palace and there start the story of the damage to the fall of these building. Ranjeet Singh the shrewed king as he was also sent his persons to inspect the site and on their reporting the damage to the palace, gave up his intention of grabing this palace from Sansar

Chand. The local people come forward with another explaination. According to them one of successors after the demise of Sansar Chand was constantly under debt to one tradesman who was a dogra brahmin and was functioning as 'modi to rajas' household i.e. the suppliers of various requirements to the palace especially eatables. Despite several requests, Raja did not make his payments. One day the 'modi became anxious, realising that his daughter was to be married, he went with a sword in hand, determined to commit suicide if he could not retrive his money. Since the Raja could not fulfill his demand he killed himself and threw his blood on all the walls of the building and cursed the Raja that his palace will be uprooted and destroyed. He became a Brahamrakashash and his soul dwelt in the palace and thereafter the Raja was forced to leave this building for good. A very confident person told us that the said Brahamrkshash can still be spotted in the damaged and destroyed building. Such are the lasting impressions of the so called fallacious narrations?

CHAPTER - 19

KINNAUR : The Land of Kinnars

In September 1975, I had just joined District Hospital Mandi, when a telegraphic order along with telephonic directions was conveyed to me to join the Multipurpose Medical field camp of Kalpa in Kinnaur organized by the Medical College, Shimla. I had not yet settled down after getting relieved from Chamba, when this summon for the distant and difficult Kinnaur land was not at all a welcome news. After a little persuasion with the then principal of that college who was reckless and unconcerned to listen as the prevailing internal emergency had made him larger than life size autocrat. Although distantly known to me, he hardly appreciated any thing to discuss. Time and again his version had the ring of name dropping of Health Minister and Chif Minister and so on. I perceived correctly that it is fulite to prolong the matter with this high-headed man and ultimately the fear of emergency made me yield to his dictates. Arrangement for my tramsporation was with district Chief of our Medical Department upto Shimla and thereafter it was the camp bus of Mobile Hospital of Medical College to arrange the onward journey to Kalpa. My apprehensions disappeared as soon as I got introduced to the staff and students. I had preconceived thought that doctors serving in Medical colleges generally denigrate the doctors in the field but to my surprise most of them; I found friendly and accommodating. As I stepped down from the jeep a group of housesurgeons and interns gathered around me inquiring my relationship with their teacher Dr. Mallick. He was professor of Surgery for sometimes at Shimla and later preferred for gulf country after relinquishing his job of Professor. Perhaps I had some physical resemblance to the person so that was the curiosity among these who knew him. I had simple reply that not even once I had occasion to meet their professor. So such was start of our journey and later two months fellowship with them grew with all affections and mature understanding.

Kalpa was a place to see during that season. The apples were ready, so heavy was the crop that the trees had to be supported with huge stakings from many sides. Similarly for first time I saw a foot-ball size carrot, a tomato weighing half a kilo a piece, and fine red juicy and extra large apple of Kinnaur. Not only that the grapes, the almonds and Zeera condiments had their own importance, there was the Chilgoja which in my childhood I used to have pocket full everyday. Kalpa offered the special attraction of the Kinnar Kailash visible from the hospital campus where we were serving and from that place we had glimpses of special optical phenomenon of changing colours of the solid rock worshipped as the Shivalingam mounted on the perpetually snow covered Himalayan peaks high above sea level.

But I was searching for something else. Something which is of archeao logical importance, a thing of past, having antiquiterian value and linking the area with the main land of our vast country. I think I did not fail in my endevour. A small trip to Koti near Kalpa offered much of what I was craving for. Some 4-5 doctors on one Sunday started the foot march on the goat track to reach Koti which is about 5Kms from Kalpa. Our trek was through the thick deodar jungles and then along the fields with a stream of water perhaps a 'Kulh' following the track till we reached the gate of the Koti village. On entering the village the most conspicuous structure was a hill temple dedicated to the Devi of Koti one of the powerful goddesses of the region who is feared most. The rath of the Devi was on its 'annual inspection' tour of its jurisdiction, but the structure and maintenance of her temple made in wood and stone in alternate layers, with pented roofs of wood was really remarkable. By this time the village folk had gathered around us and we were being fed with the stories and legends of this devi of their locality. The legends were not exactly fitting with in the canvass of the fables of Devi as narrated in Puranic literature but still she is worshipped as Chandika of Kothi. As her area is pargana of Shuwa, she is addressed as Shuwang Chandika. Although held in higher esteem and feared universally for her wrath in her area, her legends and stories are a-kin to any other village goddess of Himachal which are scatterd all over and are rather more numerous than the villages and hamlets. Nearby is a pucca pond full of water, common elsewhere but unique for this village and for the entire territory of Kinnaur. It is called 'Kund' and is associated with Pandwas. Whatever may be the truth, it is one of the vestiges of Hindu belief prevailing in this area in good old days. The Kund is several feet deep, and several steps down, the walls are paved with chiseled stone. It is square in shape and tapers towards the bottom. I was very excited with this 'finding' and when I tried to go up to its bank I slipped and was about to fall into it but for the help of my friends. It was a consolation that one in our group was a good swimmer and was able to save a young life at his own life when the Beas in Mandi was in spate due to rains. Somehow the 'Gods' or Kinnaur were kind enough to salvage me from the slip.

At this point, I was further obsessed, when the black stone sculpture though deformed was conspicuous by its unique presence. From a distance, the sculpture appeared to be that of Shiva with four arms although three were missing from the idol. Some human figures near the main idols could not help to establish the identity of the icon but for a bull which lent credence that it is a Shiva idol. The hair style and the cosmic aura behind the head look to be the work of a mature craftsman. The aura was designed in such a way that it looked like the bright petals of the Kamal. The flying Gandharwa couple with chamars in their hands were seemed to be worshiping the lord. Although no historical evidence in the form of inscription or any event of the era is associated with the sculpture but from stylistic and iconographical view the figure may be of Pratihara period and this sculpture can be safely placed in the period of 10th to 11th century. Although Shiva idol has got an easy exposure. Anyone who is nearer the pond will be fascinated by this sculpture as stone images appear scant in the area.

Kothi can also claim several idols of Bhairava housed in a nearby dark room. The idols are in a bad state of preservation. The face part is totally deformed and the vehicle or the constant companion of Bhairava i.e. dog is missing. The idol has ten arms and most of the attributes are beyond indentification. But still after a little effort, it can be deciphered that right hand is in var Mudra i.e. granting all comfort to its worshipers.

Besides the commanding idol of Bhairva there are twenty or more statues but once you enter this dark room without proper light and guide it is difficult to make out their composition. I could find out that one having Veena in the hand may be the goddess of learning i.e. Saraswati and another one that of Shiva with Parvati. But these are hasty and instantaneous conclusion from distant after casual observatios. Proper study of these idols may add new chapter in the hsitory and art- history of Kinnaur. The visit to Kothi was a new experience. In a land-locked country where there is total sway of local gods and goddesses, the presence of the gods of Hindu Pantheon is significant. The village itself is also well environed. The fields and fruit orchards and grapevines in bloom are abundant all around. The perennial small stream with its gurgling water lends a sense of mystery. In the backdrop, the perpetual snow clad Kinnar Kailash adds spiritual aura for any visitor. Kothi is also known as Koshtampi. In an era, told and retold in the folklores, it was the residential place of the local ruler who was known as Thakur. They had their Kothior magnificent dwelling over here and that is why the place got the name Kothi. These Thakurs later on were made vassal by the Chandika of Koshtampi whose temple is also a landmark of hill architecture. In its annual fair hundreds of goats and sheep are scarified to please the goddess and the tradition is very much alive to this day.

While camping at Kalpa, the beauty of Vaspa Valley was extolled in so many ways by one and all. The Vaspa is a tributary of the Satluj river which joins the later at Karcham. The area all around this river is known as Vaspa valley, a valley of thick woods, vast fields, a variety of flowers and fauna of high altitude and along with the snowy cold water of the Vaspa which always comes in torrens, becomes silent only when it meets its principal river. We were determined to visit this place and one day Mr. Joshi the local superientendent of Polic of District Kinnaur came to our help. He gave lift to all of us, five doctors, and himself on the steering wheel of his jeep. We had plenty of food all pre-cooked to be enjoyed at Sangla the important village of the sub-division of the same name. This journey stretched from Kalpa to Karcham and from Karcham to Sangla. It was not only refreshing but almost a discovery of wonderland of Kinnaur. Not only did we find it to be one of the prettiest valley of inner Himalayas but also the vast flat land like this to be conspicuous by their absence elsewhere, in such a geographical situation. We reached the village Sangla which is at an elevation of 2620 Mtr above the sea level and is proud of having a well maintained rest house. All of us had our hearty meal of Puri and Potato-bhaji with extra helping. Perhaps I took large share as during travelling my appetite gets enhanced. This had resulted as I used to take avomine to which later on I said good-bye when intensive touring engaged me almost daily in connection with official duties. Sangla offers natural beauty in abundance and the rest house is so situated that alround view extends for miles together and its panaromic view is gratifying. Far distant to its south we were told is the location of village Kamaru which was visible from the rest house. At Kamaru, placed on the shoulder of hill is a tall building inviting attention almost automatically. It is a fort said to belong to Raja of Rampur-Bushair. The local information says it dates back to Mahabharata period. As usual the spell of Mahabharata is pervading. Being conversant with this phraseology and phenemonon although not satisfied, my mind was excited to see this fort which I learnt was the early palace-fort capital of Bushair from where the Raja of the state used to rule till he shifted to Sarahan another alternate site in Himalayas. The local people prefer to call it Mone rather Kamaru and both names have got mingled up

KINNAUR : THE LAND OF KINNARS

while describing the place. Till 1948, such ws the importance of Mone and its fort that till the raja did not used to get enthroned over here, he was not recognized as the ruler of the erstwhile state of Rampur Bushair. After trekking for roughly 4 kms we reached the fort site which is surrounded by scattered buildings. The fort is constructed on a land, which is 24 "Hath" by 24 "Hath". The basement is solid and rocky and a stair leads to the first floor which has five rooms. Each room has its own function and is used as store, bathroom, water storage, kitchen and kotha. All are small, dark and dingy when housed in a total area of 96 sqr feet. In the second floor there are three rooms and a spare room, which generally remain unused, an other is worship room and third one contains the Rajgaddi and eight idols in bronze known as thanapatis, which literary can be translated as the lords of the place. The third floor again has five rooms each having its own use. One room remains closed, second is the slaughter house for goats and sheep, third is to skin these butchered animals and maintaining their parts, the fourth is reserved to the Bhima Kali which while on tour from Sarahan, is kept in its rath overhere, and fifth contains the luggage of Raja of Bushair like the antiquearian weapons, gunpowders etc. Fourth floor is designed for exclusive use of Raja's household which contains one darbar hall, second reserved for ranies, third bathing room, forth kitchen and fifth is small room which has the dwelling of protector of the fort known as Batkul Devta. The fort on the whole is made up of stone walls with timber arranged in layers by layers. This used to serve as the palace as well as the defence- mansion for the area. The location itself is being on the raised shoulder of the hill used to make it impregnable by the enemies who were attacked from height with arrows and stones. This is another illustration as to how defence was organised in the olden states in the Himalayas. On the same pattern, there is an eighth century palace fort at Pangna in the District of Mandi, which was the capital of the joint states of Suket and Mandi.Here also the fort has five storeys and upper most is reserved for the local goddess. Perhaps the forts and palaces would have crumbled down but for the temple portion of palaces. The Pangna fort is almost like the Kamaru fort. Another conspicuous structure of Kamaru is a temple in Pahari style dedicated to Badri-Nath. Badri-Nath has its own "Rath" and claims to have brotherhood with the famous presiding deity of the Adhi Badri-Nath Shrines of Garwal. Another rath is kept in the same temple made for one Raja Kayan Singh of Kamaru who is also worshipped more as a godling of the place than a departed and dead raja. Hills are full of such myths and legends that need to be analysed and related to each past event or happening.

It is presumed that Kalpa which was previously known as Chini might have possessed such a fort of its own which was destroyed by a devastating fire. The name for Kalpa which is still prevalent in Bhotas is Gayal-S-China meaning thereby the capital town of Chini. It is felt that at one time in history, the place might have been under a ruler who called the place Chini. Later this thakur of Chini was subdued by the princelings of Kamaru and even now in one of the fairs held at Kamaru a person from Kalpa (said to be representing the area) is insulted (only in a symbolic way) to commemorate the victory of Kamaru over Kalpa. It was said that in Kinnaur all Budhist Shrines were store-houses of bronze idols of Lamaism but we had no such opportunity to come across any.

CHAPTER - 20

BHIMA KALI : The Ruling Deity of Sarahan

While returning back from Kinnaur, it was but natural to visit Sarahan which is also shrouded with myths and legends. It is not exactly on the Hindustan-Tibbet road but from a place Jeuri one has to travel uphill on road to reach this picturesque place, situated at the height of 2154 m. above sea level and roughly 230 Kms from Shimla. It was not at all in our scheduled official programme but students were to be prepared mentally to visit this place through repeated persuations. Ultimately they prevailed upon the inept principal to agree and therefore they raised three cheers to him. While reaching Sarahan one Dr. Larjoo who was a house- surgeon that time arranged a sumptuous lunch in the military rest- house near the main Sarahan temple of Bhima Kali. The temple has its importance in so many ways. Bhima Kali as such is described to be the incarnation of the Aadi-shakti in Kaliyug as recorded in Durga-Saptashati. It is not only at Sarahan but shrines are dedicated to Bhimakali at Kalka in Haryana and Mandi in Himachal, but the temple at Sarahan is a wonderful creation in wood having multistoreyed buiding dedicated to the Kali.

Sarahan is said to be the old Shonatpur capital of Banasur, a contemporary of grandson of Lord Krishna, who had his capital at this place. Mythology is full of events as to how Banasur brought the River Sutluj from Manasarowar and further how he controlled its flow up at Shonatpur or Sarahan.

The goddess is not only the spiritual ruler of the place but was the temporal authority of the area. The raja of Rampur was only a Karder who used to rule over his territory, on behalf of Bhima Kali. Therefore during the state period a large amount of revenue was collected for the temple which used to have a grand coterie of officers and workers. Actually it was Sarahan which was selected as the site for captial by the ruler of Kamaru when they shifted to this place prior to establishing Rampur as the captial town of Bushair.

Years back, 'Himalayan Art' was a book written by a European traveller J.C. French who had left no stone unturned while discribing this place. Although he has been an art-critic, his narration of nature is superb in this book. The ditant snowy peaks, the thick deodar jungles and the ever green panorama of meadow had captured my imagination and longed to behold this beautiful place after reading his graceful description that is true even today although the scenario has abruptly changed due to the inroad of modernisation. The main entrance of the temple is approached after climbing the stone steps and the entrance is on a pedestal several feet above the ground. The main attraction on reaching the gate is the silver sheet plated doors depicting flora and fauna along with some depictions of Mahabharata and Ramayan tales. As you enter the door the small rows of dark rooms are shown as the old palaces where the Raja and his family used to stay. The rooms are really small and suffocating. The main attraction was temple but there are two, an olden one which looks like a miniature from of the leaning tower of Pisa and has been abandoned. The objects of worship have been replaced in a modern replica of wooden structure, which is the present abode of Bhimakali. The attendants of the temple were confused about the year of construction of new temple. According to one version it was a product of post-state era while other insisted that the temple came into being during the period of erstwhile rajas of Bushair state. No doubt the olden temple is several centuries old. Previously the entry to "Outsiders" into the temple was prohibited and outsiders were all who were not the inhabitants of Bushair state. Had I come here in my childhood, I could have been considered an outsider, but these days entry is not so strict.

The temple is a multi-storeyed structure. The first storey has five rooms. One is a treasury room or a strong room of treasury, in strict parlance, which contains the account books and cash and other four rooms are used for havan and butchering animals which are continually offered to the goddess. The second storey has four rooms out of which one is reserved for the main idol of worship which is about three feet high bronze statue of standing goddess and other three have sotre-house of utencils, bathroom and storage for shibu or the red wine. Similarly the four rooms on the third floor has the statue of Kumari, the main treasury, water storage room and one vacant room. The fourth floor is having the big kitchen for non-vegetarian meals, a small second kitchen and another vacant room. The fifth is just under the roof and is not used for any purpose.

To upkeep and maintain the records, accounts of income and expenditure, a "Cabinet" of Bhima Kali is always in attendance headed by one "Bist" who is the first and most important out of the rest. He is assisted by two kaiths (clerk), bhandari (store/clerk) shikaru (hunter) who mainains the offering of goats and sheep; two gatekeepers two supervisors of inner complex, two gardeners, one water-fetcher, one cook, one Bhojahi, one prohit, one rasiya etc. Besides these the maintainer of bands are also in attendance and are several in number. A close perusal of this discription reveals that devi was rich according to the local standards who can employ such a large cabinet. Still, on top of them was the Kardar who was no other than the Raja of the state and had authority to appoint Bist.

Most interesting part near the main temple is the well of death which recently has been topped with a stone structure. It was believed to be so deep that its bottom was patal-lok where the demons re-side. Whenever they used to have liking for human blood, there used to be grand noise inside the well. On that occasion some (one may be a person considered prejudicial in the eyes of the ruler and his associates) was dropped in to the well and killed. It was not the noise of demons, but the demonic desires of the courtiers or their ruler to finish someone under the petext of demonical desire. Hopefully in future, none will meet this fate which so many Busharies were subjected to, under the autocratic regime.

This is another story prevalent as to how the Bhimakali cult originated. It is said that two Rakshashas Shiv and Kut were plundering this area. Getting terrorized by them the local Jabli Devta under took penance and Lord Shiva appeared and killed both the Rakshashas and blessed the Jabli Devta with a daughter endowed with all godly powers and privileges. She was to rule after the Devta and eventually called Bhima Kali and became the sole spiritual and temporal head of the area.

From archaeological point of view this is unusual pagoda style of Pahari temple architecture is the sole proud possession of the place. A small museum has been added in the temple complex recently with some articles of interest like the old musical instruments, the pots and vessels for worship rituals, bells, swords, and dhaal which are old time warfare armaments.

CHAPTER - 21

AT THE SUMMIT OF SAR-KI-DHAR : A Vast Panorama

In the pages of history, it has been recorded that a fine temple of stone was erected by Raja Suraj Sen of Mandi (16637 A.D.- 1644 A.D.) as an act of thanks to Naina Devi i.e. The goddess of eyes, as he got cured of an eye ailment. His favourite, Chief Mason had created his wonderful palace, which was considered by the raja to be the only one of its kind. Similar opinion he had about this temple also. And in term of rewards what do you think was in store for the mason? Mercilessly both his hands were chopped off so as to prevent him form repeating his skill of construction elsewhere. To spot the site and the shrine, one fine morning; I, my wife and daughters set out to get visit this place. We were in a Jeepsy being driven by an experienced driver. Our journey started from Rewalsar.

Rewalsar a small town, is only 25 kms from Mandi the district headquarter of Mandi District of Himachal Pradesh and is famous for its lake of floating islands. Set in a natural surrounding, once a circular lake with one mile long circumabulation now stands sacrificed on the pretext of beautification. Situated at the height of 4500 feet above sea level it is sacred for Hindus for their insatiable love for water may be a river, a glacier, a lake, a spring or a fall. Likewise the Budhists of Lama cult claim it to be an abode of 7th century missionary Padamsambhav and the Sikhs have fascinations for the place as the tenth guru is said to have once presided over here over a congregation of hill rajas and chiefs in the early 18th century.

But still if you are in search of nature and want to behold it in its magnificent grandeour away from the filth and squalor, your scenic destination is Sar-Ki-Dhar on the southern side of Rewalsar lake. It is also called Naina-Devi-Ki-Dhar as on its top is a temple dedicated to a devi of same name. The hilltop can be reached through a serpentine motorable road recently constructed or by trekking against gravity up the steep ascent on a traditional path way of 3 kms, whereas the motorable road through its curves stretches the distance to 8kms up to the Naina Devi Temple which is at 350 feet above the Rewaloan lake. Whatsoever may be your route of journey, the entire land as you ascend high offers you vast feast of variety of flora which grow in plenty partly natural and partly by the human endevour of growing more trees. The bumper bloom of wild but beautiful flowers lend majesty to the site. The fast growing and imported cosmos flowers in various hues and colours are a pleasant phenomena to look at. Its seeds disperse fast by swift winds and can germinate without any care. On your way up, there are stone-caves where young and enterprising foreigners from various countries are busy with their mystic prayers and meditations in exclusive solitude.

After a steep ascent you reach a comparative flat land and come across a lake more splendid and larger than Rewalsar on virgin soil, unspoiled by human hands. Its water, although crystal clear, reflects blusish hue and thereby called Nilasar: "sar" means lake and "Nila" is a word for blue in vernacular. It is also called Kuntbhayo-Jhil. Myths and legends associate it with Mahabharat's heroes Pandavas. A belief is widely prevalent in the Himalayan hills to attach claims with Pandavas with all that stand beautiful and awe-inspiring. As the folklore goes; once royal mother Kunti felt thirsty and her duty bound son Arjun shot a swift arrow in the soil nearby and there water gushed up and not only quenched the thirst of Pandava's mother but steadied as a lake for posteriority down to us. Just a walk of a few meters separates Nilasar with Kalasar having water emitting blackish colour. Do not try to approach the water level lest you are lost in the slippery and deep mud surroundings all round these lakes. As you approach higher from a spur of a hillock a third lake namely Sukhasar becomes visible with brickly and turbid water. Ordinarily it remains dry but for during rainy seasons when all the mudy water collects to fill up this natural reservoir. Needless to add the beholder gets wonderstruck to watch three deep and silent lakes presenting three distinct colours blue, black and brick just adjacent to each others existing like three neighbours with their distinct identities but living in tranquility and preaching same to our sectorian society.

Throughout the track, the environment is studded with numerous small water ponds which are primarily the collections of excessive rain water but four of them have very curious down to earth names like Tawa, Kundi (bowl of large size), Kauli (Katori) and Karachi. A village lady was shy but curt enough to enumerate these household names of daily kichenwares. Actually these "Sars" are named accordingly and this so natural and practical nomenclature is worthy of complements for imagination and originality.

Throughout your sojourn in the Sar-Ki-Shar the hillock of lakes, clouds are touching you; touching the earth and in a minute the sky. As the clouds ascend up suddenly everything is visible and in flash of moment you are covered with them and so are the lakes of joyous beauty. It does generate a rupture of emotional and psychological touch of relaxation once you see the Nilasar, Kalasar and Sukhasar together for a while and then all of a sudden the thick curtains of clouds take them in their bondage. A unique game of hide and seek is constantly being played by the nature with you and you have to submit as a silent and meek spectator.

Once on the hilltop, witness a temple made of sandstone which had crumbed down in the earthquake of 1905 A.D. Various temple parts like amalak and carved stones are still scattered in the courtyard of the shrine. The object of worship is a stone idol of mother goddess profusely covered with thick layers of silken draperies. It is not possible to study the details of the icon. A new temple in its place is fastly coming up.

Black but syrupy tea is available in a solitary shop near the temple and for your meals you have to come down to Rewalsar to have the cuisines of your tastes with pre-placed orders. Rewalsar has suddenly become more a market place than a tiny village of a famous lake. Its inborn natural charm is shrinking and a steel and concrete jungle is coming up so fast that only Sar-Ki-Dhar remains a solace for the naturalists.

Such aimless wandering in the natural environment of the hills does not yield any material gains but there is a fairly plentiful source of delicate and soothing touch for the traumatised emotions and hurt feelings in the serene and solemn hill surroundings. Otherwise the man of our times remains a constant victim of tinsel-world with all its modern amenities. Sojourn of this kind is a short escape from the humdrum which is surrounding us from all sides, in our endevour, we had failed as the original shrine erected by Surj Sen as is recorded in history, was a crumbled heap of stones, no more in its original shape as envisaged by sovereign. Our only satisfaction was to witness the miracles of nature at their best. It was rainy season. The prevailing lush green environment were indeed a refreshing treat to the eyes. The ponds and lakes were overfilled with water and there was a boom of natural flowers all around. Predominant were the cosmos, famous for their wide spread. Although cosmos are a highly prized handsome flower, callousness on our part has made them a wild growth all over the hill. The play of hide and seek with clouds again and again remains an unforgettable experience. This journey was first undertaken in year 1991, now after a lapse of twelve years in the winter of 2002 when we drove up to hill top the, picture was entirely changed. The old shrine had been transformed in totality except for the idol that still was being used for worship. A modern temple has sprung up as if there was never any temple that is of 400 years' age. A few remnants of the temple parts, some broken idols, parts of temples amalak and some carved stones have been allotted a small corner out side the temple. This exhibits a slight love for almost an entire chapter in antiquity. Another new temple dedicated to Lord Shiva has also been built on near by elevated portion of the hill. There is a well paved pathway connecting the two. Previsouly there was no shop worth the name but presently a failry good market has come us. Perhaps the flow of the pilgrims and tourists has increased and to meet their demands the endevours of the traders have captured this lovely place as well. A well defined market street leading up to the main shrine with a few more addition of inns for those who halt for the night is an entirely new addition to this ages old complex.

A modern well built and furnished rest house is an extra attraction. As to how this building got created out of the fancy of public works department is not well understood! Was it really needed? With the change of times it appears that this hill summit will rather become a busy picnic spot or a crazy place for trekkers than a sight of solace for devotees as it was in the by-gone times.

CHAPTER - 22

IN SEARCH OF AN INSCRIPTION : No Loss No Gain

Earlier, whenever attempts were made to write the history of the erstwhile Mandi state, invariably the inscription on a rock at Salanu got a passing reference. The village is about three kilometer from a place, Manglaur, which is on the Kullu-Shimla highway via Jalori pass near the flourishing village, Balichowki.

Presently, this area has more social and economic affinity to Kullu district but in the early 10th century, a cadet of the ruling house of Mandi had settled at Manglaur and made it his capital for a few years.

The Raja was Bahu Sen who was the younger brother of Sahu Sen of the Suket state and had founded the nucleus of the principality, which later emerged as Mandi state.

Manglaur might have seen its days of royal patronage but now it is just like any small hill village and there is nothing, which is reminiscent of its palmy past. The main attraction is a newly constructed wooden temple with carvings of considerable merit dedicated to Shringi-Rishi.

Near the temple is an old deodar tree. The village is situated on the shoulder of the hillock with a river flowing at its foothills and it lends majesty to the place; and justifies the aesthetic sense of Bahu Sen to select this place as his capital. Otherwise also, it appears that the word Manglaur had a special fascination for our ancestors.

Near Roorkee, there is a Manglaur township in old Kurudesha. In the pre-historic Swat valley, there is a Manglaur, now in Pakistan and similarly, in southern Karnatak there is a place which goes by this name.

I had a keen desire to have a glimpse of this place and to observe some remains of antiquity. But for its scenic beauty, Manglaur could not add anything to my information of history and archaeology, Nearby is a village, Salanu and Salari, which in the old books, was said to have a rock inscription.

Not long back, I visited the place to see the inscription. As we ascended to the village from Balichowki; I had the pleasure of verifying what I had read long back. Personal verification after perusal of the books has its own satisfaction and in this hobby I failed here miserably. No one in the village was aware of such an inscription. A man who could understand the purpose of our visit and told that a stone, with certain words, was on the side of nearby rivulet and had been washed away by flood.

But even he had not seen it. The village has one conspicuous Shiva temple in Shikhara style which does not appear to be of old antique value and another place of worship on the entrance to the village is dedicated to an aboriginal disturbing spirit, the name of which our village guide was not disclosing, lest be got the wrath of the spirit.

It was being pleased by the offerings of iron trident, iron chains and nails etc., signifying that the goding is fierce and is feared by the people.

The inscription had its own importance as one at Khanihar near Dharamsala in Kangra district. This rock inscription was of second or third Century B.C. in Brahmi and Khrosti scripts, extolling the rule of the king of "Vatsa" dynasty.

Similarly, a coin of rulers of Kullu; had been discovered, with a legend in Brahmi and Khrosti script. So far, no one has made any attempt to explore this kingdom, stretching from Kullu to Kangra, possessing a currency of its own with prevalent double scripts in fashion i.e. Brahmi and Khrosti and a good number of stone inscriptions.

History might unfold many of its unknown chapters if some linkage can be discovered between these sources of history and archaeology.

I do not know whether the text of this inscription in original is available in the old files of the Epigraphica Indica. If traceable it will be a source of pleasure and profit to the scholars.

Accordingly to the translation of the inscription which had appeared in an issue of Epigraphic Indica, it reads as follows:

(i) That a Maharaja Sri-Chandes avara hastin, who was the son of a Maharaja Ishvara- hastin, and belonged to the family of Vatsa, conquered in battle a Rajjila- Bala and founded a town of which the name was Salipuri, possibly the present village of Salari situated near the site of the inscription. These names carry some significance if studied analytically.

In the inscription, village Salipuri can be easily projected at Shivapuri considering the Shiva temple at the village Salanu which is further derived from Salipuri or Salari.

(ii) The two names of the rulers, both son and father have a common suffix as Hastin and they were from a family of Vatsa. The prechristian eras inscription in Kangra also preserves this clan name proving there by that the entire geographic entity from Kullu border to Kangra were being ruled by Vatsa who were in active process to subjugating the chieftains like Rajjila Bala and others.

(iii) Presently the name Salanu has lost importance. The entire track is now called Bali-Chowki. Perhaps during the erection of the inscription it was known as Bali or Badi meaning there by the garden area belonging to one who was reigning over known as Rajjila. The name Bali or Bali Chowki found echo of old name Bala of Rajjila. Later chowki meaning a "post" was added recently to the name and even after the passage of centuries the place is keeping up some vestige of its name as epigraphed in the inscription.

It was an uphill task for us to locate the site of Salanu village and it was all the more difficult to find out the rock which carried the said inscription. Finally to our dismay, the disclosure of its dis-appearance was all the more disgusting whether it was flood which swept it away or it was an act of vandalism by some unscrupulous hands, or it might have been blasted. There is another possibility that some unsocial elements might have passed it on to the art thieves or antiquarian squad of thugs. Notwithstanding the fact that these are presumptions without any valid proof; this inscription would have been the oldest archaeological record in this area Salanu nearby Manglaur, the old capital site of present day Mandi state.

A joyful but funny incident was also in out lot during our sojourn to search the inscription. A man of average age was emphatic of its presence which accordingly to him he was witnessing daily near the footpath of his house. The information was a flash of ultimate hope for us. He took us to the place and pointed to the "Slogan" written on a rock in bold Devanagari Script reading "Hum Do- Hamare Do". He had carefully observed the redcross on our vehicle and thought we are on inspection to confirm the slogan writing campaign of medical department. Enough was enough and we returned home after failing in our mission or enterprise to unearth the oldest rock inscription of Mandi State. Our failure in preservation relics of the past can only be lamented as in this case.

CHAPTER - 23

THUS SPEAKS KOLASARA BOULDER : History and Legends

Does it sound modern and progressive to write about a single boulder may be very huge in dimensions simply made up of sand stone? May not. But if cobwebs of history and legendary past are woven around it! Yes, it is then definitely a meaningful dialogue, which hopefully keeps its importance alive. Such a big boulder is situated on the left bank of river Beas which is olden days was 2 Km. outside the town of Mandi. Now the intensive and extensive urbanization has made it a part of town as on the both side of the Beas, several hundreds buildings have been erected. Actually in itself it is still a solitary scenic place where the water of the Beas touches it on one side and a vast ground of white pellets from an uneven land on the other sides. The boulder is a massive structure having innumerable crevasses, curvatures and contours which the swift water of Beas have produced over it for thousands of years by striking hard its body mass. When the river is in its prime during the rains, the fleeting blow of the Beas which not only surrounds it but totally cover it and submerging it for a few hours of the days. Still its existence as a pristine, and primitive elephantine creature is waiting, sitting and relaxing in spite of all odds, emitting a very particualr luster which appear like that of rock salt range of mini hillock.

Presently on its right side a big modern colony has fast emerged and on the left side a gurudawara of splendid grandeur is being steadily enlarged which to begin with was a modest structure. The boulder is known as Kolsara. History does lend clues that the place on left side of the river got the nomenclature of Mandi- Kolsara once the capital shifted to this side of the bank. Perhaps the territory around the boulder was village Kolsara. The way the Raja invaded and destroyed the polity of this area was much hated and disliked for long-times and that is why the phraseology of Mandi Kolsara is the refuge of non loyal persons came to vogue.

Strange enough, in olden of the old times, not recorded in history but firmly attached in local psyche, it is place where Rishi Mandava had undertaken penance for self-purification. How and as to why, he took fancy for the site is not clearly known. Also it is said that it was word Mandava, that Mandi was derived from. From Mandavaya-Nagar to Mandi Nagar is a long journey and who knows how many centuries this span of time is spread? How far it is correct is also to be established! Various places are connected with a many a sages of lore in the hills and perhaps Rishi was really enchanted by the sublime silence of this place, he stayed here, undertook his tapasya is not recorded in any scripture but in the people's psyche, this lore has made deep indent which can not be dismissed casually.

In the whole area of the western Himalayas the history has witnessed mild wars and battlements amongst the ranas and thakurs. Commensurating the trend, both sides of the river had chieftains who were busy in encroaching upon each other's territory. The one at Bheuli on its right bank was gradually emerging as over-lord of the area. He had evil eye on the ranas of Gandharv, Sidhayani and Kanwal who were on constant conflict to capture the place where the present Mandi Town is situated. The ruler of Bheuli area thought of a plan. He took help from the tribes of cooks residing at Bhatoli which was the old name of Purani Mandi. The cooks are locally known a boties and their hamlet was famous as Batoli. On one early part of a day, near Kolasara dry wooden logs were burnt in plenty to raise a smoke screen. This facilitated the passage of soldiers to cross the river unnoticed and march ahead with their designs and desires to capture and add further pastures for them and their lord. The adventure was successful and the left bank of the river Beas was captured. This event may dates back to early sixteenth century when the present Mandi Town emerged as principal seat of power for the present ruling dynasty. Thus Kolsara proved a pathway for establishment of a raj which lasted till 1948 A.D.

The spouse of Raja Suraj Sen (1637 A.D. - 1664 A.D.) was Prakashwati and was familiar with the name Kolsara attached with Mandi. While cursing her disloyal and disobedient servants and courtiers on the death of raja, she is reported have said. Mandi Kolsara Harma-Khore-ri-paror. This curse has already got reference in this write up. It is a famous saying which the people of Mandi have not yet forgotten from generations to generations. People accepts its validity as well although the palace intrigues, loot and acts of usurpations are global phenomenon in all the emerging reigndoms of rajas.

The natures bounties of this site attracted Guru Govind Singh the tenth and last guru of the Sikhs who visited Mandi during the reign of Raja Sidh Sen

(1679 AD - 1727 AD). It appears both were like-minded and become intensely attached to each other. The raja had welomed him in his state as a guest of honour when he was consolidating the hill-chiefs in his favour against the Moghuls. Their prolonged meetings at Kolsara on the river bank were routine of the days. As it is said, one day the guru ordered for a earthen picher and allowed it to be floated in the water of the Beas. He asked raja's attendant to shoot it but in spite of all best efforts, the exercise went futile. On this guru pronounced: that your Mandi will escape from the evil forces as my picher has the bullets. Further anyone who will harm Mandi, the sky will blast them with gods fury. The raja was pleased with the boon and raised a gurudwara where the guru was residing. Later during the rulership of Raja Joginder Sen (1913-1948), it took a shape and was granted lands for its upkeep. Now enterprising and hardworking Sikhs have replaced that with a fortlike structure in which thousands of people can stay and are fed in its day long langar. Even presently some belongings of the guru are well preserved in this gurudwara i.e. one musical instrument, one firearm and a cot which guru was using during his stay over here. These items are out of proportion for a normal healthy man to handle proving thereby that Guru Govind Singh had unique physic and remarkable body strength to handle them.

Much water has flown down the Beas, but the Kolsara boulder is enough to make these forgotten chapters of history still alive and pulsating.

CHAPTER - 24

BRAHMOUR : The Ancient Brahmpura

Village Brahmour in the Chamba District of Himachal Pradesh is indentified as a remote, inaccesible and backward area. The village proper is situated in the comparatively open Budhal Valley surrounded by high hills. The mountains on the southern bank of the Budhal river are without trees, having high slopy pastures and grazing fields the northern bank offers a contrast, having hundreds of terracedfields gradually merging with ban and thick pine forests as the height increases. In the back drop, to the east, is the perpetually snow clad mountain known as Mani Mahesh or Kailash which enhances the aura of the place. The ladder-step fields of the village become brilliant red in September and early October, when an indigenous crop 'Phullan' is ready to be reaped and Brahmour is at its best during this part of the year. Many European scholars who have visited this remote seat of civilization have compared the scenic beauty of Brahmour to some of the finest in Switzerland.

During winter, the village remains several feet deep in snow and during rains remains cut-off from the rest of the world due to heavy breaches and land slides along the motorable road. Although recently connected with the district town Chamba, the bus service is irregular and unsatisfactory, either due to rains or snow.

Brahmour is about seventy Km. from Chamba, more than 7000 feet above the sea level and inhabited by about one thousand souls. It is homeland of the ethnic group, Gaddies and they call it Gadderan i.e. the land of Gaddies. Gaddies are familiar migratory shepherds of the Himalayas who come down alongwith their herds of goats and sheep which they call 'Dhan' (Wealth) in search of grazing pastures to the lower districts in the winter months. Gaddies are simple, gay and hardy people. Their women folk also accompany them in their distant journeys. Gaddi women possess pleasing manners and more often than not are beautiful to behold. The valley resonates with their melodies when ever they render voice to their folk songs.

Brahmour is the original seat of the government of the erstwhile Chamba state. From here, the Varmans ruled over these remote hills for four hundred years till the tenth century, when a more resourceful ruler shifted the capital to the lower Ravi Valley, the present Chamba. Brahmour enjoyed considerable peace and prosperity as is evident from what remains today. These remains consist chiefly of temples and their wonderful idols which date back to last fourteen hundred years. Their contemporaries are rare in whole of northern India. The oldest of them is the temple of Laxana Devi. It is a typically early wooden temple of western Himalayas and is of great archaeological interest due to its elaborately decorated facade, pillars and ceilings. It is a rare piece of Pahari Architecture. The object of worship in this temple is a fine three feet high bronze statue of Devi Mahishasur mardini (Slayer of the buffalo demon). This idol was installed by Raja Meru-Varman who ruled in 700 A.D. as is evident from the inscription on the idol. Another inscribed and three feet high bronze of Ganesha has been housed in a near-by modest hill temple. Similarly Brahmour has a life-size solid brass Nandi Bull (the vehicle of Lord Siva) which was also installed by the same ruler. The inscription are in Sanskrit although they are engraved in Sharda script in post Gupta style. There is another life size idol of Man-Lion incarnation of Lord Vishnu i.e. Narshinga housed in a Shikhara style temple. This idol does not carry any inscription but on iconographic study, it also seems to be the work of the same master craftsman who cast the other idols of Brahmour. In tradition and on paleorgraphic ground, his name was Gugga: a typical Pahari name. The Shikhara temples of Narshingha as well as the central temple of Main Mahesh can not be contemporaries of Meruvarman and Gugga as till that time, the Shikhara style of temples was not yet prevalent in the western Himalays. They date back to 10th century when shikhar style was being introduced in the hills. The temples and idols are in fine state of preservation and repair even after thirteen centuries. The rigours of snow and severe climatic conditions however are gradually eroding and damaging the well carved facade of Laxna Devi for want of proper protection. Till recently a part of Kardar Kothi of state regime was on one corner of the central table land of the village. It was of course in dilapidated condition but it is difficult to understand by what compulsion it was demolished. It was a fine piece of Pahari Palace and should have been preserved as a relic of local art and architecture.

The place is still difficult to approach. The tourists, scholars, archaeologists, hikers and 'thirayatris' should come fully equipped with their requirements. Even in fair weather alu and dal (potatoes and pulses) are not available in the local shops. Reason is the self contained economy of the place. Brahmour has a small P.W.D. rest house and a local dharamsala which may provider shelter to a visitor.

CHAPTER - 25

THE STUFF OF LEGENDS : Indelible Impressions

The T.V. Serial "Mahabharata" held the nation spell bound for almost two years. During this period the exploits of the Pandavas were avidly followed through out the length and breadth of the country. Now with the serial becoming a part of television history; the stories in the epic are bound to gradually fade in the viewers mind?

In Himachal Pradesh, however, there is hardly any place a which is not associated with the Mahabharata in general, and the Pandvas in particular. In Himachal the fragrance associated with Sita and Rama; Radha and Krishna is absent. It is the land of Shiva, Shakti and the Pandavas. So many temples, takes and springs are associated with the five sons of the Pandu who wandered in the hills during their exile or when they passed through the region on their way to heaven.

Khajjiar in Chamba district is well known for its scenic beauty. It is also assocated with the Pandavas. In the midst of thick deodar forests lies a small lake. Nearby is a wooden temple dedicated to a "Nag"- a cult still prevalent in the hills. It is believed that the temple was built by the pandavas. They are also believed to have meticulously carved their own images on the pillars of the temple.

Next, just adjoining the historical town of Chamba on the other side of the river Ravi stands a large hillock which resembles an inverted basket ("tokari"). It is known as Bhim-Ki-Tokari which fell from Bhim's hand when he was carrying up earth to build a castle. The basket took the permanent shape of the hill as we now see standing today.

In the nearby district of Kangra most of the shrines including that of Jawalamukhi, owe their existence to the Pandavas who built them during their exile. The historic Kangra fort is also said to be the creation of these epic heros. In the ancient days Kangra was known as Trigarta. In the Mahabharata there are several references to this kingdom ruled by two brothers who had fought on behalf of the Kauravas. One of them was Susharman Chand. He has been mentioned as a brave soldier in the epic.

In Mandi district one finds several places claiming association with the Pandavas. In Mandi town itself at the confluence of the river Beas and Suketi, there stands a huge boulder known as Chakdini Chattan. The people believe that the Pandavas had spent a night here. The steps leading up to the top of the boulder are said to have been carved by the epic heroes themselves. People's sentiments are so strong that a plan to blast this boulder had to be abandoned due to stiff resistance from the residents of Mandi.

Nearby in the heart of the fertile valley Balh there is a sacred shrine dedicated to goddess Kali at Hatgarh. Not only is the place associated with the Pandavas, but the scattered idols and parts of temple indicate that at one time Hatgarh was an important place. Again people believe that the Pandavas halted here during their sojourn in the hills.

Like in Khajjiar there is a picturesque lake in Mandi district known as Rewalsar. Complete with a small floating island. Situated nearby are seven small lakes. One of which is quite large and is known as Kuntabhayo lake, named after Kunti, the mother of the Pandavas. In the regional folklore it is mentioned as a spot where Kunti felt thirsty. Since water was not available the great archer Arjuna sent an arrow into the spot where the lake appeared.

The scenic beauty of Janjehli area of Mandi has remained unspoilt mainly because it is not mentioned in the tourist guides. Two boulders near Janjehli are so placed that people believe them to be marvelous structure created by the Pandavas. These boulders are known as Pandav-Shilla or Chukati-Jan, meaning shaking stones. It is a strange phenomenon seen no where else; which even the best-known scientists cannot explain. How and why the boulder weighing several tones shake when touched gently, and still not topple over? It is truly a mystery.

Further ahead towards Shikari Devi Dhar there is a "Narol" of Draupadi/ "Narol" is that pat of the palace where only women are permitted to enter.

Near Shikari is another place known as Budhakedar where the impression of a foot and tail of a bull can be seen in a cave. Again, a stange story has been woven around the cave. It is said that after the Mahabharata war; Yudhistra was afflicted with leprosy as a curse for killing members of his own clan. He was advised by sages to meet his fater Dharamraj in the Himalayas to get rid of the disease. Dharamraj had his own compulsions for not meeting his son.

Therefore, when Yudhistra approached him, he took the shape of a bull to hide his identity. But somehow the eldest Pandava saw through his disguise and caught him by the tail. The bull, however, managed to escape. It is said that the head of this bull can be seen in the Badri-Kedar area of Garhwal.

In far Kinnaur and Sirmour a number of mountain peaks and temples are said to be linked with the five Pandavas. In Shimla district the Kali temple at Sarahan is believed to possess coins used by the Pandavas. The famous temple of Hatkari is believed to be the creation of the Pandavas.

Some people believe that the entire Bilaspur district was the center of their activities. One village derives its name and is still called Panjagaon i.e. the five nearby villages belonging to the epical heroes. Even Kunjam pass in the inner Himalayas, connecting Lahaul with Spiti valley is known as the spot where Draupadi was the first to fall and die when the Pandavas and Dharma in the guise of a dog were journeying to heaven.

Who has not heard of Manali in Kullu district? The beautiful hill town is a favourite with visiting tourists. The famous Hidimba temple has been built on the site where Bhima and his demon wife Hidimba spent many a happy day in each other's company. Hidimba gave birth to a son Ghatotkacha who earned undying fame for his valour on the battlefield of Kurukshetra.

How much these accounts are authentic, no one know. But these tales do show the extent of the people's faith and devotion to the epic heroes. Since the Pandavas, during the exile were moving constantly to evade detection by the Kauravas they used to stay to a particular spot for the night and move on in the morning. In this way they travelled the entire area now known as Himachal Pradesh. Himachal on the whole remained culturally isolated from the mainstrea for a long time. As such the ancient myths, traditions and beliefs have survived intact over the ages and cannot be dismissed casually.

CHAPTER - 26

A POETRY CARVED ON STONE SLAB : A Joy Forever

The mueum at Chamba is a fine repository of art objects of merit accommodating all thematic varieties concerned with hill-life and living. As I entered, the left hall of its old wooden building (which has been demolished and an alternate concreat building has now been erected nearly) on well cut huge slab was a fascinating object of attraction with all the lines chiseled meticulously over it. The stone slab measuring 1'- 11 1/2" by 11 1/4" by 6' 1/2" brought from a place known as Sarahan of Paragana Saho not very far from Chamba town. It is inscribed on both sides with an incription in twenty lines consisting of twenty two stanzas of elegantly written Sanskrit poetry. It is remarkable both for its excellent preservation and fine execution. Most of the inscription is devoted to the praise of a lady, Somprabha (Moonlight) by name, a daughter of Kish Kindhika (the ancient name of the Himgiri Paragana). She was married to Satyaki, the son of Bhogata, evidently a local Rana who ruled over the part of Saho valley. Her husband in order to establish an unshaken friendship between her and the mountain- daughter i.e. Parvati, built a temple to mooncrowned Shiva. The temple referred to is perhaps that known by the name of Chandra-Shekhra (The moon crowned one) which still exists at Saho- a small village amongst the vast fields not far from the place where the inscription was discovered. Although having no date, the inscription has been assigned the date of 9th or 10th century on the basis of the study of the character of letters. Undoubtedly it dates back to the period when as yet the Chamba town was not the seat of power of the unbroken line of Varman kings and when independent ranas were still holding sway in the lower valleys of the Ravi and its tributary the Sal and others. It goes to the credit of this Sarahan Prashasthi which probably had the privilge of being the oldest inscription existing in Sarada script. As it was found near a watermill at a hamlet Sarahan, this beautifully executed eulogy (Prashasti) goes with the name of Sarahan although the temple of Chander Shekhra Mahadev is existing at Saho. Perhaps Satyaki had commissioned the temple at the present site of Chander Shekhra temple but it could have been a modest one and later Sahil Varman of Chamba had improved and renovated it to its present form. The object of worship is a huge stone lingam. How it was brought and placed on the padestal i.e. Yoni in those olden day is still a matter of wonder? The Shiva lingam is much bigger in girth and height as compared to that of temple of Manimahesh at Bharmour. There are fierce carved representations of 'Mahakaal' on the wall of the temples which are executed with great care and fineness. Chander Shekar temple at Saho is at par in its importance religiously with Chander Gupta, Trimukha and Gauri Shankar at Chamba Town, Mani-Mahesh at Bharmour and Nilkantha in the upper- Ravi valley on way to Kharamukh. Several derivations are in evidence about the refined cultural contours of this valley of Saho even prior to the establishment of the capital of Bharmour Kingdom at Chamba town. Firstly the ranas were well versed with Sanskrit and the script perferred was Sarada. The names were well articulated emanating good meaning. The Shiva cult was the main object of worship and there were good number of artists to construct the temples of classical style prevalent in the hills. The artists were well equipped to give shape and life to stone and the result of their work is the execution of carvings of Mahakaal, Ganga and Yamuna in Saho. Also they had a fine taste and the ability to execute such an elegant eulogy which still steam thunder, even after more than 1000 years of its existence. The word Sarahan used for villages in Himachal also carry some weightage in itself. It is one of three Sarahans I know besides many more, which did not get exposure. Sarahan near Rampur in famous for the temple of Bhimakali and was once capital of Bushair State. Second is one on the state highway linking Nahan with Shimla and third and by far the oldest is on the other bank of River Sal just opposite to the village Saho in Chamba. The full translation of the eulogy of Sarahan reads as follows:

OM SAVASTI (HAIL)

1. Victorious is Shiva, our lord, whose body is adorned with moonlight and whose affection is fixed on that half of his body consisting of the ever devoted Gauri i.e. Ardhanarishwer.

2. There was on the earth a man of laudable virtues, dignity and department-pure like the sickle of the glittering shudder of brightness (the moon)- whose form was an ornament of the world and who resembled a jewel of very clear pearls.

3. From him was born-even as Jayanta from (Indra) the prince of the immortals, and Karttikeya from (Shiva) who bears the half moon as his diadem- the illustrious SATYAKI who used to put away the sorrow of his dears ones-like unto Vishnu of abundant virtue and the victor over

his enemies host.

4. A daughter of the house of Kish-kin-dhikas lord, Soma Prabha by name whose form was an ornament of world, was his queen-even as (Durga) the daughter of Himalayas was the queen of three eyed God Shiva.

5. When the creator (Brahma) had fashioned her face a moon such as was never seen before of ever sparking splendour, devoid of blemish and fullorbed the hairs on his slinder limb stood up.

6. She, exceedingly lovely and rich in virtues attained by the cunning disposition of various ornaments still greater charm in the eyes of men of taste, like the muse of good poet.

7. Can she be the high time of the ocean of passion, or a cluster of blossoms on the tree of love or the presiding goddess of the realm of king Spring, or the sum of the beauty of three worlds?

8. Or a spell named "Mind Perplexing" capable of remdering the three worlds obedient? Thus lost in a multitude of doubts, one can not decide about her.

9. Beholding her with an eye, now sparking with joy, then pregnant with amazements; and then again confused with doubts, one was bewildered and full of imagination.

10. She bears a lock of hair, glittering like a bee, made by the Creator-desirous, as it were, to show favour to the flower armed (Cupid) that he may fetter (with it) the hearts of the three worlds.

11. By her who with the bent bow to her brow and with the arrows of her side long glances has attacked and completely conquered the hearts of mankind, Cupid has been rendered shelter less.

12. Her cheeks of a very pale hue full of the essence of beauty and loveliness, capable of causing delight to the night lotuses which are the eyes of her admirers, make on the people the impression of Hare-marked (Moon).

13. Her lip is not equaled by the ruby though endowed with (a like) redness; for the one partakes of hardness and has no moisture the other is soft-shaped and nector-distilling.

14. Her rows of teeth beem like diamonds; her slender arms are soft like lotus-stalks; her pair of breasts high, and watered with charm, appear like a caste of Cupid.

15. Her lotus like hands possessing the ruddy appearance of young buds, remain expanded in the brightness of her moonlike face, even when in contact (with each other), causing amazement among the people.

16. With flashing net of her ray like nails, gifted with whiteness, of spotless nature, exceeding captivating, she seems to scatter bundles of pearls in all directions.

17. The creator (Bramha) who was afraid that by carrying the burden of her breast, her slender waist might break, has fastened it with a girdle of multi tu-dinous folds.

18. The dolphin- bannered (Cupid), perceiving that she contains exquisite treasures of grace and dalliance and such like pearls has in order to fuard these, shaped her naval like a seal.

19. The eye roaming over her broad round hips is wholly be-wildered. She has things yellowish like the center of a lotus well-matched like two honest men.

20. If a tendril-like beam of the Nector-Shedder (Moon') fell on a widely expanded red lotus then would there be an image of the net of raylike on the rosy pair of her lotus like feet.

21. "May there be an unshaken friendship between her (Somaprabha) and the mountain daughter (Durga)" With this wish that prince (Satyahi) had this temple built to Shiva whose diadem is marked with the stainless sickle of the Moon.

22. Victorious be (Shiva) whose diadem is the cool rayed (Moon) and may this temple be of high renown, as long as the wealth bestowing (Earth endures) and may the illustrious Satyaki conquer the entire Earth.

This poetry in stone is a vivid discription of female beauty. Considering its date and the difficult topography of the then Saho, it appears the chieftain in that era had scholars of merits in his capital who could compose and produce such marvelous stanzas and also artists who could execute it perfectly on the stone block.

CHAPTER - 27

A PRINCESS OR GODDESS : An Enigma

Chamba- a beautiful small town of Himachal Pradesh is well known for its temples which belong mostly to the 10th century. Most of these shrines have been an attraction both for Indiana and European scholars. It is really difficult to understand as to how the temple of Champavati or Chameshwari has escaped the attention that this shrine deserves. Here is a holy place which contains in itself unique amalgam of considerable magnitude from historical, asthetic, legendary and cultural point of view. Chamba is said to have derived its name after the victory of Sahil Dev Varman, the Raja of Chamba dynasty who ruled from this place as the first king.

Originally the nucleus of erst-while state of Chamba was at Bharmour from where Sahil Dev came down to this town. According to the local tradition, it is said while the king was settling down in the lower Ravi valley as a conquerer, his daughter Champavati was with him. Charmed by the openness of this place, she persuaded her father to shift his capital to this place and in due course the new capital named 'Champa' after the princess as she was known by her first name. Later, over time the name changed from Champa to Champa and this became the chapter one of history of Chamba.

Simultaneously in the well preserved and broadly accepted authentic geographical description of Chamba rulers, it has found mention, that the Raja Sahil Dev Varman conquered this site after defeating the 'Kshatriyas' in the battle and thereafter established his capital in the land of Mahishasur-mardini. This reference has some relevance with an original temple of this goddess of slayer of buffalow demon. It is a fact that the icon which is an object of worship in this shrine named after Champavati is that of Mahishasur-Mardini.

There is another legend that refuses to be erased from the public memory is about the princess Champa who had a religious bent of mind and used to participate in the ceremonies with sadhus whose place of discussion used to be the preseent site of temple. Unable to appreciate the deep involvement of

Champavati with these religious predicaments, her father doubted that his daughter was going there for elopement. He chased her with a naked sword to kill her on the spot. But as the legend goes at the spot where the temple stands, she suddenly disappeared followed by an 'akashvani' that since he had doubted a 'divine' being that his daughter was; he would now have to construct a temple on this place to perpetuate her memory. Now if the temple is dedicated to his daughter, then as to why as icon Mahishasur-mardini had been installed? This has remained on enigma which so far none has tried to explain and explore; this pertinent fact of Chamba's history and antiquity. As a matter of fact the raja in question should have installed a human figure in the memory of his daughter rather than an idol of goddess. Therefore it can be conjectured with simple information that the idol was already there without a proper temple and the raja simply erected the shikhara style of temple, at the place of event. There is another version also in vogue that the original temple was made up of wood and was later on replaced by stone structure.

Situated in the heart of the town, near the much beloved flat land of chowgan, this temple is not freuently visited by local persons, pilgrims and art-historians. Neither it is rated in esteem as high a other temples of Laxmi Narain campus, Harirai and Chaumunda. It is surrounded on all sides by shops and houses and a narrow lane leads to this nagar temple of sand-stone with refined and beautiful carvings. Still in front of the sanctum is a sabhamandaps in wooden frame work. The idol of worship in the sanctum santoum is an icon of Durga-Mahisasur-mardini in back stone. The sculpture is now much disfigured and eroded by climatic vagaries and aging or ageing process. The face of the icon is almost totally obscured and has been replaced by a metal mask. Otherwise it is an executed sculpture of Durga standing on the body of demon buffalow in such a way that her feet is on the head and other foot on the hinder part of the body of animal. It appears that after killing the demon, she has just jumped on its body signifying her latest victory. The divine vehicle of devi is a standing lion behind her facing right side and on the left side is a disfigured figurine with 'chanwar' in hand attending for the comforts of the devi. Here the devi is with eight arms all equipped with the traditional attributes with a trident going deep in the body of the demon. Adorned with a jewelled costume and framed with a crust of medallations, her face with widely opened eyes and curved figure with full breasts and hips suggest quiet an elegant rhythm and the over all effect is harmony in motion. Stylistically the image may be placed in 9th or 10th century A.D. ie. the late Gupta period. On the whole, the idol as such is well built with life like plasticity and well laid down iconography of Devi Mahishasurmardini. Posterior of the main idol is well carved out to run with several deities in action and the central and the most prominent of Hindu pantheon being the lords of creation, preservation and destruction. In a central niche of the temple an icon of same goddess is shown thrusting the trident into the body of a buffalow from whose decapitated neck, the demon is emerging in human form. The trident is held in while the other two, sword and an indistinct object, the goddess is trampling the back of the demon whith her right foot. The lions the mount of the devi is pounding upon him on the right. The face of the main deity is much more mutilated and worn as is the case with all ageing sand-stone icon but even wih the arranged metal mask, the vitality and vigour of the carved out human figure in stone is very much evident even after the passage of a full millenium.

The pose and posture of this dhyan of the devi is not uncommon both in Chamba in particular and in Himachal in general. The unique metal image of Laxana devi at Bharmour, and other remarkable almost life size statue at Hatkoti in Shimla are of perhaps earlier conceptualizations and formations of 7th to 10th century which falls in the school of Late Gupta or Early Pratihara school of Art. A fine stone structure in the niche temple of Bajaura in Kullu is a remarkable piece of Art with elongated and thin anatomy of the unique relic of Pala Art of sculpture and similar one in metal is in Kao temple in Mandi District.

The theme of Mahishasurmardini as extolled in great length and **breadth in** Durga Saptashati or Devi mahatmya of Markandeya Puranja is very **dear to** Indian heartland as well. The Pallavas in Mahabalipuram, the Chalukya in Badauni, caves of Guptas in Udaygiri and Bhumara have dealt with same thematic description of Durga. The same impact had travelled to the distant Himalayas. On conjectural gorunds, it can be easily conceived that Sahil Dev of Chamba tried to preserve the memory of his daughter as Mahisashurmardini widely acceptable at large in India as well as in India colonies abroad. It is indeed a challenging task to ascertain whether the temple and idol were in existence prior to his era or commissioned ab initio by Sahil Dev Verman in 10th Century.

Although oldest of the older than any other spot of religious and historical significance this temple of Chamba is, regretfully not being projected in the proper perspective which it deserves. The temple, in short needs more care and greater attention from all historians, pilgrims and art lovers.

CHAPTER - 28

A TEMPLE OF PANCH DEV : An Exalted Encounter

The concept of 'Brahm' of post-vedic and unpanishadic era was gradually shaped into 'Tridev'. The creator is Brahma, the sustainer is Vishnu and the god who destroys is Shiva. Ironically Shiva the presiding lord of destruction has been universally accepted as great favourite of Indian psyche for whom innumerable temples and shrines are dedicated. Later when the religious schools of thought multiplied, more 'gods' were admitted into Hindu pantheons to accommodate two more principal deities. Surprisingly this addition is that of Shakti i.e. the divine consort of Shiva and Ganapati his son with elephant head. Thereby a fresh idea of Panch-dev got recognized in religious texts and scriptures. Wisely all the five were kept on same footing and got started to be worshipped in a same complex. Arrangement was designed to istal the most favourite god in the central and major temple whereas the rest four were accommodated in minor temples on the four corners of the principal shrine. In this way, all the five were being propitiated thereby the mutual antagonism and controversies were taken care of.

One such temple exists in Mandi Town of Himachal Pradesh which was built on the bank of the river Beas about one hundred and thirty years back during the reign of Raja Bijai Sen of Mandi who ruled over his state from 1851 to 1902 A.D. During the so called Delhi-Durbar held in Delhi in the year 1877 A.D. which confirmed the total sovereignty of the British over India, all the native state chiefs had participated. The outstanding outcome of this 'Durbar' was to give these 'chiefs' an exposure to the importance of public works. Bijai Sen, after his return, ordered the construction of road connecting Mandi with Pathankot by laying a road in his territory and commissioning a suspension bridge over the river Beas which flows between the two parts of the town. His act was not commensurate with the actions of earlier rajas who had more predilection of temple building process for centuries. The ladies in the royal house-hold could not reconcile with the altered state of activity and the grandmother of this raja and therefore along with the order of commissioning of bridge, the king made resources available to the state to construct the temple of Panch-Dev which is known as Sahibi-ra-dwala, presently popularly known as Ekadash Rudra Mandir which has Shiva as the principal god with eleven lingas arranged together with one more prominent linga surrounded by ten in a circle.

The total temple complex is built with sandstone and having a wide boundary wall with a twenty feet high main gate facing the rive side. The main gate has a toran depicting various Hindu gods in separate blocks. The bull inside the boundary-wall is a massive stone structure carved out of a big boulder. The sabha Mandap and garbhagriha are on a raised platform for which stone steps have been provided. Inside the sabha mandap on other bull made up of marble has been placed facing the Ekadash-Rudra in garbhagribha. The inside of the temple is plain in construction but from outside niche temples have been adorned with small icons of Matashya, Kurma, Varaha incarnations of Vishnu and statues of Durga and others. It appears on stylistic grounds that perhaps they are not the creations of local wrokers but have been imported from outside the Mandi state. One the four corner of the main shrine the front two small temples are dedicated to Vishnu and Surya whereas the back temples have an icon of Durga and Ganesh respectively. In the Ganesh temple, a side niche is meant to keep a small image of Kartikeya the other son of Shiva. All these statues of Vishnu, Surya, Durga, Ganesh Kartikeya along with the small bull inside the sabha-madap are made up of marble and are the production of Jaipur artists and are fairly chiseled to project the different 'gods' with their attributes. It could have been a rigorous exercise to procure, transport and install these icons when there were no modern facilities even at the command of the ruling chiefs. Still their fire of imagination and strong affinity for deism and religious endevours are praiseworthy.

It appears that the inspiration for the creation of a temple of Panch-devata was Narvadeshwar temple of Sujanpur-Tihra. Although the said temple is a flat roof building but is extensively decorated with Pahari murals. It is also dedicated to Lord Shiva but has four temples on its four corners. Raja Ishwari Sen the grandfather of Bijai Sen was kept captive by Raja Sansar Chand at Tira-Sujanpur and the ladies of the royal household were so much impressed by the conceptualisation of Narvadeshwar temple that they wanted to create such a temple in their own Capital also. Although both templs are similar in religious projections and perceptions but the majesty of the mural paintings of Narmadeshwar temple has been replaced by installing various icons of gods in stone. Moreover it was created in Shikhara style which lends elegance and grandeour of actual Hindu temple to this shrine.

For a couple of years the Sahibini-ra-dwala i.e. the temple of Sahibini as the lady creator was popularly addressed remained the singular monument of its specific style. After a while an other Ekadash-Rudra temple was constructed by one wealthy family of Mandi Town which is known as Dhwana-ra-dwala. Dhwanas might have earned a lot in their trade adventures and were rich enough to creat a beautiful edifice. This later temple is also provided with various niche-temples for ten incarnations of Vishnu but is without corner temples. Therefore it is exclusively a Shiva temple for Ekadash Rudra. In various Shiva temples of Mandi, these two remain unique to have been dedicated to Ekadash-Rudras and are still venue of various socio-religious gatherings.

CHAPTER - 29

GAURI SHANKARA ICON OF CHAMBA : Unrivaled and Peerless

Sahil-Dev-Varman of tenth century was the founder king of Chamba. Well known as warrior, builder of temples and having a keen bent of mind for religious practices. He was followed by his son Yogakarvarman who has the credit of bringing the marble slab from across the Vindhyas as is narrated in the genealogical records when he was heir-apparant. Posterity will remember him till his masterpiece of Gauri Shankar in bronze remains in one of the temple of Laxami Narain temple complex of Chamba Town. His period of rule can be regarded as a peaceful reign of Mediaeval Chamba, less powerful, but richer, more cultured and more refined than the rule of his father. It is therefore less surprising that his reign has left one of the great masterpieces of the highly refined, elegant art of the late Pratihara school of sculpture casting. It appears the art-activity in Chamba under him (AD 940-960) had become though less vigorous but remarkably refined. There are only two temples assigned to his times; the one erected by his queen Tribhuvanrekh at Bharmour for the icon of Narasingha and other for the sculpture under discussion. Both temples repeat the type introduced by his father; but are smaller, more elegant and richly decorated.

As such the Gauri-Shankar is one of the finest 'bronze' groups not only in the present Himachal Pradesh but in the entire Himalayan ranges and in whole of the Northern India. Who was the master artist who had cast this massive but elegant structure is not known. Was he one like Gugga probably a local trained by outsiders or exclusively by some outsider. Due to absence of inscriptions it is not evident but Bharmour statues clearly indicate the names of commissioning king and executing artist.

As a matter of fact, the earlier historian were right enough to designate this sculpture as a group rather than a solitary icon. It represents Shiva standing by the side of his divine consort Parvati i.e. Gauri and the bull Nandi stands behind both of them. Lord Shiva has four arms. The right lower hand has been affectionately placed on the neck of the Nandi and right upper arm and hand is raised to compose the Abhaya mudra with a rosary between the fingers. His upper left arm rests over the shoulder of Gauri and hand has been depicted in semi-fist formation but the left lower one has some vessel like structure. Gauri has only two arms the right with a rosary and in Abhaya-mudra and left bearing a water vessel in the palm like the Shiva statue. Shiva has three faces and resembles the famous Trimurti as is the internationally famous Trimurti Shiva of Elephanta. Both deities wear the high conic crown held together by a series of circlets characteristic of Medieval North-Indian Art, however combined with a diadem with three high pinnacles. The curious mannerism of the folds of Shiva's dhoti is a familiar as bronzes and sculptures of late Gupta and early Pratihara period possess. Similar is the Mekhla (belt) which is richly jewelled on the pattern of early Pratihara period. The Gauri has flowing hair as on the mask of Mujani Devi from Nirmand in Kullu which dates back to the tenth century. Gauri has a plain oval halo behind the head and back. In this case it may have been inspired by the name of the goddess, Gauri the bright fair one.

Not with standing all the merits this group of icons exhibit and keeping in view the aesthetic treatment of the figures, it reveals a highly refined and elegant tradition, familiar in many Pratihara sculptures of the tenth century, especially those of Harshanatha temple near Sikar, built by early Chahamanas, contemporaries of Yugakaravarman and Dodka Varman and like those latter practically independent vassals of the week late Pratihara emperors. But on the other hand there are indications that the artist was more than a clear imitator remarks Hermann Goetz. Unfortunately the figures are not in well proportions; the legs are somewhat short, head of Shiva too big, bull is too small may be not to overpower the whole composition of Shiva and Gauri. Fine as it is, it permits us to expect and even more beautiful art of metal sculpture in the former centres of Pratihara power and culture of which to-day only some temple ruins and not yet excavated mounds remain.

We have discussed the Brahamani-Nala-reliefs of Shiva-Shulpani which depict the original Bharmour deities. On the basis of that, this figure of Shiva seems to be a variant of the seventh century idol at Bharmour which was destroyed during the invasion by Tibetans also described as Kiras. So far the people and rulers of Chamba have not forgotten the glory of their erstwhile seat of power at Bharmour. Therefore at the new capital, a Shiva statue of same elegance and magnificence was ordered to be commissioned by Yogakar Varman even after four centuries had passed. Moreover the interesting aspect of co-existence of Shiva and Vishnu is evident in event of casting of this icon of Shiva. Laxami Narain was the presiding lord of Chamba Kingdom but it appeard Yogakar-varman was more a disciple of Shiva than Vishnu. At capital town he constructed a temple for Shiva and installed the icon of Shiva Gauri in it. His wife made a similar stone temple, it is not introduced by an invocation of Vishnu, but by a stanza in praise of Shiva, calling him, amongst various more general epithets, Vrishabhanka i.e. he who holds the temple of Gauri-Shankar temple of Chamba. In praising Shiva as Vrishabhanka, the maker of this icon Yugakarvarman, therefore, has had in mind only this image which by tradition and history is attributed to him. It also gives credence to the event that the Narsingha temple construction was a later date them Gauri Shankar's installation in its respective temple.

This Pratihara icon is unparalled in the art-history of Himalayas. Chamba the kingdom of Yogakarvarman in the perspective of the Himalayas, had been vast and important but in the all-Indian perspective it had no more than a small frontier state. But the very situation of this hill kingdom on the off the beaten tracks of world history and civilization has likewise been responsible for the fact that this brass group has survived from the hordes of invading iconoclasts. There might have been in thousands who got over the rich states of the North India. This group serves as a valuable masterpiece of its tribes which could not claim resume at the destructive hands of mighty armies.

CHAPTER - 30

A UNIQUE SCULPTURE : Solitary and Single

If I am not mistaken, not years but decades back, precisely somewhere in year 1975, I was quizzed by a gentleman fairly elder to me, brilliant in disposition, well read and widely travelled, about an icon in one of the niche temple of Mandi Town. I had a close look at this 3X2 feet statue coloured with sindhur but even with all the knowledge at my command, could not decipher it, and I made camera the search of its identity a challenge for myself. I snapped it in my and ensured my efforts to brood over it remained even alert on its track.

The statue is from a niche temple dedicated to Shiva, the great among the trio of Hindu pantheons of worship, who is the most popular object of worship all over having a great to its credit score, in that the number of temples dedicated to this God is ten times more than the combined numbers of temples of all other Hindu deities. The temple has two more seats of worship niches housing icons of Ganesh and Brahama which can easily be made out by those who are familiar with such idols. The temple is in shikhara style made up of sand stone. In the Compound, there is an icon of huge bull meticulously carved out from a single boulder. A modest 'ghat' stairs lead from the gate of the temple down to the left bank of the river Beas. The temple has been provided with a well defined strong boundary wall all around but there is no sabha-mandap. It is known as Mahant-Ra-Dawala because a family of Mahant had once constructed it. Perhaps it is a creation of one such noted family of Mahant who still survive by the same name possessing a comparatively huge house near the well-known temple of Ardhanarishwar. This temple is the first in a big row, spreading from the southern part of old Beas Bridge and going right to the Shiva Wawali. As one enters from the North end of the old bridge of the Beas this icon under discussion become conspicuous by its presence. Its presence may got ignored by all and sundary but my scholarly old person was caught by its spell and the he involved me in the process as well.

The icon is constituted of two persons. The person below is sitting in such a psoture as if it is about to rise. It has a hefty muscular built body with very bold and strong legs the right foot of which is firmly placed on the ground of the niche-temple; while on the toes of the left foot he is trying to lift his body wanting to stand. It is holding a shield (dhal) in its left hand while with its right hand seems to be supporting the body over its shoulder and perhaps that is why that can not be seen in the icon. The face has been modelled in such a way that it is not human but more akin to some demon or animal of the canine family. No other elements of decoration like the pendals or ornaments have been carved on this figure. Riding this figure is another in human form slightly smaller than the former. It is sitting on the shoulders of the lower one with its right foot on the right thigh of the demon and left is hanging freely up to the middle of chest and abdomen. The figure is rigid but sitting majestically facing skywards. Although neck is obescured due to this posture of the deity but it is supporting some garland like structure hanging up to the chest. It may be a snake with its hood in the centre but the weather and years have defaced that part too much to make out the features comfortably. The head is without any headgear, a mukut or turban but is well carved although disproportionately. Large ears are supporting ear rings like 'Kanaphatta' yogi. The deity has four arms on each side. The right arm is having a rosary, a club and two more obscure attributes whereas one left hand is in var mudra while others are supporting some attributes out of which one trident is conspicuously clear. The whole composition is folkish which may be the creation of local craftmen and is being smeared with sindhur for several decades since its creation. A close examination reveals that in its early years before being decayed the face of the deity had a smiling disposition. The figure is enclosed in a square bracket with out strong stone pillars which form the part of this miniature temple like structure known widely as niche temple.

In case the figure on top is taken to bear resemblence to Lord Shiva, then the lower one is definitely of some demon. Thereby it can be easily inferred that Shiva is sitting on the shoulder of the demon. In Durga-Saptashati, one of the incarnation of Devi has been described as Pretsanstha Tu Chamunda i.e. the Chamunda incarnation of devi sitting on the 'pret'. On that analogy he is He-Chamunda i.e. Shiva riding over the shoulder of pret. On the basis of this couplet, it become easy to interpret this icon which is unique and solitary one in such presentation and composition, otherwise also Shiva is known to have the company of Bhuts and Prets and this region of Mandi has Bhutnath as its presiding overlord in divine pantheon. Incidently Bhutnath was the first shrine commissioned to shiva when Mandi became the capital town of the state of the same name. Now pragmatically this sculpture is that of Shiva riding over a demon: a rare piece of conception and execution.

CHAPTER - 31

SIDH SHAMBU : An Untold Story

Mandi had witnessed a remarkable building activity during the rule of Sidh Sen whose period is a landmark in the history of this state. Somehow he had spotted such places which were far away from the constant humdrum and noisesome life of the towns when he was the ruling chief. Things have undergone tremendous change presently and the areas which were far away are now part of the main town. The temple of Sidh, Ganapati near the Government Hospital, which has been mentioned to be two miles away from the town is now surrounded on all sides by a number of houses. Similar is the fate of the lonely sites of Sidh-Bhadra and Sidh-Jalpa of his times.

At a stone throw from the temple of Sidh Jalpa is a Shiva Lingam of enormous size meticulously designed from a single boulder. Till recently this locality was a small flat land surrounded by shrubs and trees on the three sides with the swift flow of the crystal clear and ice-cold water of the River Beas on its northern boundary. Even now it retains its natural beauty but for the scanty water in the river which virtually presents a look of a small nala. The central Shiva-lingam is formed on a Jalahari chiseled in such a way that all worship water is drained out of the structure proper. Artistically the lingam is surrounded on all sides with a snake, the close associate of Shiva in a unique formation, wherein the broad head end and tapering tail projects towards Jalahari encircling the lingam. Two conspicious ridges have been fashioned between the snake and lingam proper representating either the 'janeu' or mala around the Shiva. The icon is on a single boulder but has been divided into two pedestals. The upper one houses the Shiva lingam which is the object of worship while the lower one is reserved for an image of bull the divine vehicle of the lord. The bull is in sitting rather lazily sleeping posture, as if in total relaxing mood. The whole environment was a classical example of jungle where the lord is in deep meditation therefore the artist has cleaverly designed his vehicle also in restful pose as if enjoying his holiday period. The whole concept of Meditation by the lord and relaxation on the part of servant is in tune with the pervading atmosphere. One simply gets amazed while standing and admiring this divine poetry in stone.

How the stone was executed into this structure. There is a legendry episode associated with.During the reign of Sidh Sen one Tibetan Lama by the name of Taranath was a royal guest. Taranath is a celebrated name not only in the Tibetan lores but far away in many a countries of Asia and Europe. He was born in 1573 A.D. and was a versatile scholar. He was prolific author of standard books on history and philosophy of Tibet. His work on the History of Indian Budhism is a sheer masterpiece of its own kind. As a translator of a grammar book like Saraswat was also a proverbial fresh rose in his buttonhole as till date it remains the undisputed reference book. It is said Sidh Sen was in his spell of meditation in Jalpa temple, when he visualized a person sitting on this boulder on the bank of the river Beas. The person in question was no one else than Tara Nath. It is narrated that a carcass of some animal full of maggots was nearby this legendary Lama and he was picking them up. With his benign touch the maggots were turning into piece of edible article of food. Fearfully Sidh Sen approached him and their first meeting turned into a long lasting friendship. Tara Nath remained the guest of Raja of Mandi for some time and with an act of appreciation or blessings handed over a magical book to the raja by dint of which he could perform super-natural acts for which Sidh Sen is widely remembered. To commemorate and immortalize his love on first sight with the Lama, the raja had ordered a carving of Sidh Shambu on the boulder where he had met Tara Nath. With the passage of time, the site is being neglected, but it encompasses in it a strange but recorded event of the history of the place signifying the scholarly love between two learned personalities.

Inspired by the creation of this image on the stone, a somewhat similar Shiva lingam was carved out on the ghat of the river Beas near the present temple of Ekadash Rudras in the town proper. In mid nineteenth century a Shiv temple of above name was commissioned and built by the grandmother of Raja Bijai Sen (1854 - 1902 AD) of Mandi. Later on the ghats and the stony ladders were constructed to connect the temple to the river bank. Here again the royalty was fired with a desire to erect a replica of Sidh-Shambu on the projecting ridge of the boulder touching the ever flowing waters of the Beas. The execution of the sculpture is simple with a Shivalingam placed in a jalahari pointing to the river side. There is no snake or any ornamental mala or janeu but the figure of bull facing the Shiva-lingam in sitting pose with flexed limbs is majestic. Although it has faced vagaries of weather for years together but the fineness and meticulous composition of this bull is praiseworthy. It is shown sitting alert to receive the order of the lord as and when it is commanded. As comparision to this the bull of Sidh Shabu appears to be sleepy and lazy and facing the river rather than lingam just opposite to this icon of Nandi the divine vehicle of the lord. The pages of the history repeat themselves and with its repetition, not only the events but the thought processes, the mindsets and conceptualisations of the eras are also reflected in the form of art objects, the religious configurations, icons and images created in the changed epoch.

CHAPTER - 32

A 'SHIVA' OR 'SIDHA' : A Peep into the Past

There was no motorable road connecting Mandi with its supurb Bhiuli which is now the new emerging modern colony of this town. About five decades back when 'Bhiuli' was a must visit for all in the younger age group, actually in the phase of life in school, its fair used to attract all of our age group. From the northern end of the suspension bridge over the Beas up to Triloknath temple the road was wide enough but not metalled. From the temple the pathway crossing the habitation of Purani Mandi was well laid with stone which still exists. On its father end upto Bhiuli was a narrow bridle path leading to the much wider Greenland of Bhiuli where the mela was regularly held on the first of Baishakh corresponding with the month of April in geogrian calendar. There were (are) many a landmarks of Purani Mandi which remained the seat of power of Sen dynasty roughly for two centuries, prior to their shifting to the capital on to the left bank where the town stands presently. To begin with there is a statue of Hanuman carved on the boulder which now has been provided an enclosure; followed by the nearby complex of Triloknath temple. From this point the narrow paved pathway moves away from the hub of activities of the Purani Mandi marked by a big tank of water which generally is taken as an indicator of place of importance. On one side of this tank is a small stone temple known as Thakur Dawala and on the other side the temple of Shitla Bhagwati. Just in front was a modest temple of Radha-Krishanan icons both in marble with slate roof structure. A modest Shiva temple is front of Shitla was also one to be counted with pride. Ahead was still a narrow lane opening up to the water source known as Chaibai and nearby there is a small temple which used to win over the fancy of all of us. As it was just on and near the paved street, no visit to the Bhiuli fair was complete without a short halt at this site. Down the memory lane, we had enjoyed our 'jholipakodi' at this site the taste of which along with its fragrance still allures my senses

This point of journey to Bhiuli was much awaited and feared as well. It was longed for its delicious delicacy to taste the 'jhol-ri-pakori' out side the home as well as feared and awed to have to look at a statue smeared black making it all the more awe-inspiring. To go near it or steal an attempt to touch it was to invite the rebuke from nearby house-holders from where the elders were always there to scold or scuffle you for this act of sacrilege. In those days of youthfull ignorance, god might have been just another being.

As I felt interested in the images and idols of our bygone era, it again flashed upon my mind and I went close to it not with fear but with a keenness to study its craftsmanship and the associated hidden meaning therein. The idol is almost life size, carved out of a single boulder. The icon is shown sitting with its both legs downward. A small figure of female is on its left thigh which is with folded hands. The icon has two arms. The right hand is supporting a rosary while the left is placed on the back of female figure. The face of the deity is broad and globular with conspicious ears which have been pierced and the holes so made are for the religious ring of 'Kanphatta' jogi.

Although the eyes are closed as of the image is in meditation but a sublime smile on the lips is easily decipherable. The head is shaven and a third eye in a shape of lozenge is carved on the forehead. Just above this is a half-moon or Ardh-chandra associated with Shiva sculpture and painting. The image has been provided with Rudraksha-mala and a necklace in which a small 'nad' is used as pendant. Where-as the half-moon is an attribution of Shiva, the pendant is associated with Sadhaka who has attained sidhi to emerge as Sidh. These Sidhas are also generally deitified and reach the realm of godhood. Here although the statue is worshipped as Shiva but there is likelihood of its being of Sidha clans or from Nath sect. Presently Gorakhnath and his guru Mateshendranath are no way inferior to Shiva himself, given their equally large number of disciples. Once they are deitified some of the attributes of the overlord also get associated with them. Otherwise also, Purani Mandi had families of Nath cult who were distinguished from others previously, but now seems to have mingled with the main-stream. Howsoever their influence over this area is revealed by this icon and its type which has survived a long passage of time. It is also to be observed that woman figure shown with the icon of Sidha in the same way as in the sculpture of Vishnu and Shiva with ther consorts. Nearby the three headed Shiva in the temple of Trilokinath has Parvati on his left thigh. Similarly sidha were shown with female figures with them as their 'Shaktis'. Moreover in the Brajayana the Tibetan school of Budhism, the gods as well as sidhas are shown in physical union with their consorts who represent 'prajna'.

CHAPTER - 33

THREE BRASS ICONS : Flight of Imagination

Whenever I recall my visit to a particular house situated in my own surroundings, I do not forget to take a glimpse of three icons which have a special space in my mind since childhood. All the three are so meticulously designed that they do cross the realm of art in such a way that gyrates them as object of worship in their own rights.

First is an icon of Garuda the divine mount of Lord Vishnu. It is eight inches in height with a stout standing figure of garuda the bird. Although given a human form and shape but its wings lend credence of its being a bird. Its face with prominent beak and angry looking eyes have been given special treatment with mukut on the head. The divine vehicle has two hands which are in folded composition having a serpent in between them. The figure has been cast with proper proportion of the body and from the feet upto above the head a rod has been fixed on the posterior of the icon. A provision to fix a disc of metal has been provided. This disc is meant to place a Vishnu icon or preferably Saligram Shila over it. In this way for the propitiatories of Vishnu a complete iconography has been provided in a miniature scale. Looking back into the history of the house, the icon has been kept for more than two centuries, previous to that it could have been elsewhere being an easily transportable item. On iconographic grounds, it is much more older fitting into classical frame rather than in folk origin.

In the same 'in-house-temple' there is a bigger icon of tiger which is six inches in height and eight inches in length from face to hind part. The tiger as compared to Garuda is of lesser antique value but still seems have behind it roughly two centuries' of history. The 'Simha' as the tiger is called is a divine vehicle of devi and this piece of object of worship also form part of a housefold devi temple. Again on the centre of the this divine mount a projection has been provided to hold a small plate like structure of brass. On this plate a 'Shriyantra' a geometrical manifestation of devi on a 'safatak' stone is still placed for daily worship. On this Yantra, a small mask of devi hardly less than one inch in dimension is placed which is made up of silver. The old pujari of the in-house-temple was of opinion that his object of worship is in this icon-complex rather in the main object of worship which is Devi Balasundhari's image in stone provided with silver mask to the devi and brass mask to the tiger Shriyantra was transportable to various religion ceremonies whereas the Main stone image is stationary and fixed in the almirah of a wall of the room.

On same pattern, but much more elaborate, is an icon of bull the divine mount of Shiva. Although bull is small about six inches length and four inches in height but the whole composition is roughly one foot in height. On the bull a flask like structure emerges from its back on which a fine flower of lotus is shown with well defined petals of the lotus. In the middle of this flower which is on the so called flask, a depression is provided to place the Shiva in red stone which is one spindle like formation. Strangely there are three definite spots on this Shiva lingam in red colour which are having blackish hue representing Parvati, Ganesh and KartiKeys i.e. the entire Shiva Pariwar. In the rear part of the bull from the pedestal level, a half an inch supporting flattened rod has been fixed on which is carved a snake which gradually fans out over the Shiva lingam. It is a cobra with a fanning hood. A ring has been fixed in the mouth of cobra to make place for holding a vessel of water from which water falls in drops over the Shiva-lingam. This is a common feature over most of the Shiva temples. It is said that the Neelkanth which is an other epithet to Shiva is constantly having the burning sensation in its entire self due to the poison which Shiva preferred during the puranic narration of Samudra-manthan. To produce some relief to the burning body of Shiva, the scriptures prescribed pouring of water constantly on Shiva icon; and therefore, this arrangement of a ring in the mouth of cobra to hold water vessel has been designed. This icon has been possession of a wealth due to sheer beauty and artistic magnificence. This object had became a part of large collection of various gods and goddesses for a daily worship of the devoted person.

Presently these objects may be of no importance to cursory observers but for a penetrating eyes, they provide narrations in metal of the great Hindu gods like Vishnu, Shakti and Shiva which have not been erased from the common Hindu psyche in spite of all the hum-drums of modern life.

CHAPTER - 34

SMALL BUT GREAT : A Shrouded Fact

The highest point of the mountain is known as Shikhar and the temples known as in Shikhar style or Nagara style are an epitome of the mountain. The heightest Shikar or the top-point of the mountain is invariably succeeded while founding, a temple complex in various parts of our country ruled over by various Kingdoms. Lingraj temple complex of Bhvneshwar is an excellent example where the central main edifice has many a temples all round it. Such temple complexes do exist in Himachal Pradesh of Western Himalayas as at Bharmour, Chhitrari, Laxmi-Narain temple complex in Chamba, and Hatkoti in Shimla. Similar pattern exists at Trilokinath temple of Mandi Town.

Trilokinath temple is one of the finest and oldest shrine in shikhara style in the Shivalik regions. Although it is attributed to come into existence round about 1520 A.D. during the times of Raja Ajber sen who ruled over a considerable terrains by adding several ilakas to his kingdom. Perhaps he was the first in the ruling Sen dynasty to deserve the entitlement of rajahood. All others prior to him due to their small tracts of kingdom can be classified not better that ranas. Ajbar Sen was the founder of present Mandi Town, who shifted his capital to the left bank of the river Beas, commissioned his palace and constructed the temple of Bhutnath. As the Triloknath temple complex possesses structures dating much prior to his era, it can be safely said that this massive structure was not erected by him but simply repaired in his time, may be by his rani Sultana Devi. An inscription in Sharda script still preserved in the temple, attributes that Sultana Devi a rani of Ajber Sen had ordered its erection.

Although this place was not under the domain of a powerful ruler but surprisingly the complex possesses many a evidences suggestive of its being a hot favourite place for artistic activities. Still three of them are places of worship where the object of worship is Shiva is linga form. In the massive main structure, the three headed Shiva is carved on sand stone in life size sitting on double vehicle representing bull and lion. As Parvati his consort is shown on the left of Shiva, the lion found its place being divine vehicle of Shakti. Out of surving three miniature temples one is of great artistic and cultural importance. It is having a lotus pedestal with River Ganga and Yamuna or the doorjam one on each side with their vahanas i.e. makar and kurma respectively. This temple is facing west where as the massive shrine is towards the East. The front enterance is of a smaller dimention and on the other three sides there are three niche temples having the icons of Durga, Vishnu and Surya. This arrangement is exactly on the pattern of earlier Jagat-Sukh temple of Kullu which has been dated to the eighth century. Altgough it derives its inspiration and conceptualization from Jagat-Sukh temple but the outform is decadent subscribing it to perhaps 11th century. The other two miniature temples are being used as the repository of the burning lamps kept in the memory of dead persons of Purani Mandi after the tenth day of the death as is a religious practice in the locality.

The small temple of Shiva under discussion remained obscure till the publication of book under the caption Antiquity of the Himachal in 1986 by Dr. Postel and others, which displayed its photograph in their text. Obviously it is to be demystified as to how on stylistic ground a temple structure of 11th century came into existence when Mandi as a state was in its infancy and had not yet consolidated into a principal power of the area. It could have remained enigmatic but for the explaination which make the matter a little plausible. When, Ban San of the 11th century was a ruler his capital was at Bhiuli only one kilometer from this place, some organized and clarion artistic and cultural activity was in progress in this place known as Bhatoli, famous for its cooks and might have some independent Thakur or Rana with same artisans from the plains as upto that time the polity of this entire areas was in the custody of several Ranas and Thakurs. The temple in question anactual prototype of Shiva temple of Jagat-Sukh but on miniature scale can match with the Vishveshwer temple of Bajaura and Gauri Shankar temple of Dashal. It is a fact that Bhatoli (Purani Mandi) was not powerful enough at that early date to commission such a piece of art which reflects the Imperial Pratihara style of the plains of the North India. Howsoever it can be contemplated that after the imperial control of the states situated in the northern plains weakened, local dynsties came to the fore all over Himachal Pradesh. With this the style also changed and became more provincialised and artistically decadent.

CHAPTER - 35

POETIC ICONS : Two Visions

The temple of Vishveshwar Mahadev is of outstanding merits in the Kullu Valley of Himachal Pradesh. Although the main object of worship of a stone lingam of Shiva but its three niche temples are preserving elegant and the finest of the images in this region. The north niche temple has a big almost life size slab of stone having a figure of eight armed statue of Mahishasur-mardini, a most popular image of Shakti in the Western Himalayas. The icon is a sheer poetic expression of the Devi in stone. She has been depicted in the act of killing the demon king by plunging her trident into its body. From the other hand she is holding the hair of his head as if trying to lift it upward. Her other attributes in six other hands are a vajra, an arrow, a sword, a bell, a bow and a khapar i.e. a cup of skull. The body of the goddess has been shown in terrible action. Two other demon figures are also shown near her feet. The duo may represent Shumbha and Nishumbha as per narration of Durga Sapatsati. Her real target in this composition is the buffalo demon with his buffalo head severed from the trunk, but a human figure is erupting out of the head part of the buffalo with a mace in his right hand. In this way the main episode of Sapatasati has been brought in entirety in a singular stone slab. Although presently the facial part is slightly damaged but the broad halo along with the decoration of head and neck lend a divine touch to this great piece of art. The slender but powerful bodies, the longish faces as well as over elongated limbs of the Pala art of the period of 8th- 9th century are very conspicuous in this art composition. The sculpture seems to have been executed by artists from Eastern India, as is depicted by the marvelous sense of anatomical configuration of volume to be seen in the arrangement of the arms and legs of the goddess and of the demon king whom she looks to have simply overpowered just a while ago.

With decline of the ruling dynasty of Kashmir who had patronised a art as well as great upheval in Indian main-land after the decline of the kingdom of Kanauj, the artists were looking for shelter in the courts of the kings of the western Himalayas. Also the artisans of the eastern states of Bengal also felt threatened by the repeated attacks of Gorakha armies of Nepal. Therefore through these refugees, Pala models began to got done in the hills in great numbers and finally succeeded in occupying a position no less important than that earlier held by the Kashmiri school of art. Such is the outcome of this image of Mahishasur-mardini. This indicates the renewed vitality and vigour of these refugee craftmen in their new ecology and environment. The quality of this work of Pala art is also in keeping with the canons of ideal beauty of Meruvarman's brass figure of Devi Mahishasur-mardiniat at Bharmour being worshipped as Lakshana Devi in a majestic early temple of 7th century which has an advantage of an inscription also. Here in Bajaura on stylistic grounds, by and large, this statue can be placed in the era of the middle of eighth century during the period of Yashovarman who might have had some vassal king controlling this tract of Himalayas.

In comparison to this icon of Devi, there exists another brass image of remarkable refinement in the upper Ravi valley of Bharmour which as already mentioned is worshipped as Lakshana Devi. It is a fine brass status about three and half feet high, on a metal pedestal of nine inches. The dedicatory inscription on the image reads that the illustrious lord Meruvarman has caused the holy image of the goddess Lakshana to be made by workman Gugga. Therefore, the image was made in the second half of the seventh century which was the most glorious period of the kingdom of Bharmour in the valley of River Budhal, a tributary of the Ravi. Here again the representation of the goddess is as Mahishasur-mardini, the slayer of the demon king Mahishasur as we have come a cross at Bajaura. Here the goddess is shown as putting her right foot on the head of the slain buffalo demon, after having run her trident into the neck lifting the whole body up almost vertically. The goddess wears a high jata mukuta (crown of matted hair) or rather an immense wig, the hair being piled upin a slightly oblique protuberance bould together by strings of pearls and jewelary articles falling down on the shoulders and neck in innumerable ringlets. A costly belt i.e. mekhala with attached pearls, strings and pendants, and a sort of pearl studded girdle pressing in the belly, holds a skirt of very fine muslin. A shawl falls down from the shoulders in innumerable fine folds, and a necklace of golden discs hanging from the strings of pearls, embossed bracelets from which dangle short strings of pearls and jewels, wristlets and anklets complete the costumes. The eyes of the goddess are inlaid with silver and as compared to Bajaura image of eight arms, the Lakshana Devi possesses only four. The upper right hand has the trident and the lower right hand has a khadga i.e. sword. In the left upper hand has a Ghanta (bell) and the left hand lower holds the tail of the demon buffalo king.

It is certain that the creation of this great piece of art goes to the credit of Meruvarman but unfortunately, the reign of this king has been dated by paleographic evidence only and so scholars differ on the subject. While some experts have placed him in the middle of seventh century A.D., others prefer the end of the century. There are still those who consider him to be roughly contemporary with the Kashmirir monarch Lalitaditya Muktapida (725-56 A.D.) with some sort of subordinate alliance with him. On stylstic grounds alone, the later views appears to be more plausible. In this period, Kashmir and Shiwalik regions were in close cultural contact as is shown by the architectural designs of temples at Bharmour and also by some of the most exquisite of the wellknown images of Shakti Devi at Chhatarari and bronzes of Bharmour including this Lakshanan Devi icon under reference.

The devi in the slayer of demon form can be traced first in the Udayagiri caves near Bhilsa (Malwa) and in the Gupta temple of Bhumara but became common under the Chalukya of Badami and the early Rashtrakuta. As a matter of fact this Bharmour image follows the iconographic concept of Chalukya period i.e. seventh century. Therefore while summing up, this exquisites icon is a legacy of late Gupta or early Pratihara art as compared to the stone image of Bajaura which was undisputedly carved uder Pala school of Art. Both these poetic representation in metal and stone will go a long way to preserve the landmarks of art activity in the regions of Western Himalayan Hills.

CHAPTER - 36

NAHAN : Grateful to the Royal Ladies

Till recently, Nahan a district town of Himachal Pradesh was known for the standards of cleanliness. Its lonely walks, three in numbers but all circular were really the creations of grand aesthetic imagination and as well as the finest natural resorts. The fact can only be visualized by those who have witnessed them in their glorious past. Added to them were four man made lakes, small in circumference but excellent in creation. One of them was known as Rani-Tall i.e. a lake of Rani. This meticulously maintained lake upto sixties had a wide road all around it with flower beds on its both sides. As the beds of flowers beds on its both sides. As the beds of flowers were always booming with seasonals, but perennials were also adding extra majestic contributions to beautify the place. In that era, when I first witnessed them, they were tenderly being attended by full time gardeners in sixties. Nearby the duck-houses and mini-bird sanctuary used to make the site more impressive and attrctive. The rhythmic walks in line by the ducks were being viewed by so many nature-lovers. Their suddenly occupying the water levels was a scene of beauty to behold. Fish culture was also being reluctantly but wisely assumed in early sixties. It is said, and even presently, it is fresh in memory of the old citizens, that the whole garden complex with its flowers, ornamental plants and trees and the artificial lake were fabricated for the females of royal house. This dream creation is attributed to one of ranies, but exactly who was she, is still surrounded in mystery. At scheduled dates and times, the ranies used to descend from their near-by ivory-tower fashioned as Rajput-fort down to enjoy the bounties of nature to this place through a tunnel. The exit part of the tunnel is still pointed near the Shiva's temple which is more in European architecture rather than in the age old temple style of India. This tunnel was the secret mean of transportation from fort to the flowering garden. According to the custom of that times, the ranies and rajkumaries of the royal house were not allowed to come out of the four walls of the palace fort. A strict purdah was the ultimate destiny for them. Therefore this place became synonymous for an open air flower house to them as well as a site to breath fresh air. The strictness of the purdah was to the extent that the place was made 'no entry' site for all the persons lest they cast evil eyes on the beauty of the woman with blue blood. For the rest of the time all the persons could enter and enjoy their time in this place of flowers and fragrance.

There is a open green place just below the P.W.D. rest-house. It is known as Chamba-ground. Again it appears to be associated with some Chamba princess who got married to the Sirmouri raja. The green flat lands are a rarity in the hills. The princess hailing from the land even beyond the Dhauladhar where Chamba is situated with its unique Chaugan in the heart of the town rather the heart of Chamba Town; got the place leveled on the pattern of Chaugan to keep the memories of her father's house alive with her new abode for a life time. This little gift of Chamba princess even up to this time come in full spirits whenever some functions are held on the premises of this ground. Presently a stadium is being constructed here to lend a modern touch to this memorable place. Looking back to the earlier years when the capital of the state was shifted to Nahan, the rulers were under the spell of a vairagi of Vaishanav sect. This legacy is still intact in the temple of Jagan-nath in the main market of Nahan where hundreds of Shaligram Shilas are still worshipped. But Vaishnava cult has remained unpopular in the hills, where the predominance of Shiva and Shakti are palpable everywhere. After Jagannath temple, the emergence of Kalisthanand of Kalisthan became the most favourite site of worship. The main Kali temple has a black stone lingam representing the goddess as the main object of worship along with a row of minor temple. It is still believed that this stone symbol of Kali was brought to Nahan by some princess of Kumaon who got married to Nahan's Raja. This small object was very dear to the yound charming princess which later lent charm to the entire population of the Sirmour State when this was enshrined in a modest temple known as Kalisthan. Now a modern building has come up which does not conform to the prescribed style and structure of temples as envisaged in our Vastu Shastra. In this way again an important and permanent site of community life which is Kalisthan is an indirect gift of the princess to this place.

Another land mark is Chatari. The ideallic Villa round which like Hospital and Military rounds used to be track of silence and solitude. In its scene ecology of thickly wooded oak and pine forests; there is a resting place known as Chatari. Just leaving behind the main track, walk for a while on goat road, and find a structure, erected for the ladies of the royal origin to relax outside the thick walls of the palaces. From this site one can get lost in the scenic panorama offered by the Poanta valley which begins right down. Both for a thinker and worker, it used to be place to contemplate and rest offering both peace and placidity to them. Presently the villa-ground do exist and so exist this place modified in from, but its naturality is being bitten and engulfed by the additions of concrete and steel structure which are emerging fast. The human lust is not sparing the bounties of mother Nature.

The last contribution from the fair gender of the Sirmour Royal House is a temple of knowledge and information dedicated to a princess of a Raja who was known as Mahima by her first name. She died in tender age. A beloved of her father, her demise was a great loss to her parents. To perpetuate her memory, Mahima Library a great monument of scholarship was commissioned by the ruler. It goes to the credit of Mahima Library to be the only library in Himachal Pradesh when it came in to being in 1948 A.D. to run in a systematic and scientific frame-work. The Library has thousands of rare books in Himdi, English, Sanskrit and Persian with several hundreds of bound volumes of old and reputed journals, periodals and daily-papers. Mahima Library remained a unique repository of knowledge which is still keeping its head high in the culturally decadent present ecosystem of out mind-set, where the persuits of knowledged are being demeaned.

CHAPTER - 37

SAMADHI OF A SAINT : Losing Sheen

There stands a stone structure damaged partly by human hands and partly by the vagaries of weather. It bears a tomb like appearance and was made of chiseled sand stones. Most of the stones have been removed and stolen from the site and not only bushes and shrubs but trees with deeper roots are now penetrating right from the top to the deep foundation of this structure.

Only three decades back it was in a respectable state of preservation. The persons hailing from the nearly areas of Mandi Town voluntarily kept it spick and span with regular effot. Really, it was in the meticulous care of the social activists of that generation. Known by the name of Chini-Muni-ki-Samadhi, it was built as a tribute to the saint of an era in history of Mandi, who hailed from Nath sect of Shaiv school of thought. His mortal remains were buried here after his death and not consigned to fire which is the common practice amongst the Hindus.

Chini-Muni came into prominence when as believed he granted boon to Raja Sahib Sen of Mandi that his progeny will be salvaged from termination. Actually he proved correct and he came so close to the royal patrongae that even the raj guru went into insignificance. It was made a compulsory and perpetual practice to donate annually one 'mun' of rock salt to his math from the ruling house. Also the math was established for him and his disciples behind the present. Sidh Bhadra temple along with large tract of land. Rock-salt was a unique possession at that time as it was only found in the terrain of the erst while Mandi State. Besides the hill states of Western Himalayas, from Kinnaur to Bharmour; it had a thriving market in Nurpur, Hoshiyarpur and even beyond Gurdaspur areas of Punjab. Although now it has fallen from grace for human consumption but at one time, it was the proverbial 'salt' of the diet.

The samadhi now is on its last leg, situated in an idyllic site just near the confluence of the river Beas with Khad Suketi. This dilapidated structure can be identified while moving from Mandi Town proper across the Suketi iron bridge on the path leading to padal ground and the Government College. Even in its state of decadence it unfolds certain pages of the local history the importance of which goes without saying.

The structure dates back to the period of Raja Sahib Sen or his successor Narain Sen of 16th century. The later was born as a handicapped child and by the blessing of Chunni Muni he gained normalcy. This tale has been told and retold from generation to generation in Mandi area. As an act of gratefulness to the miraculous power of this saint alongwith the perpetual grant of rock salt it was mandatory for all the inhabitants of the town and state of Mandi to donate three seers of grains to the disciples of nath saint every year.

At one point of time, in the history of this country; the Sidh and Nath held special sway on the psyche of our people in the entire country. Guru Gorakhnath had made his sect as a massive movement of religious and spiritual bliss for his countrymen and even the hinterland of Himalayas had not escaped from that influence and impact. Scattered all over the hill states there are several maharis or matha which are still held in high esteem. In Mandi state this sect was in constant touch with the rulers and his subjects. In the times of Raja Balbir Sen (1838 AD - 1851) one of his concubine constructed a temple of Shiva on the bank of river Beas and accordingly the presiding Chief of Chuni-Muni-math was entrusted the duties of pujari of the temple in spite of the fact that this work fall in the realm of Brahmins who were in large number in the town. The descendants of that pujari were till recent times performing religious service in this temple.

Sahib Sen was a ruler of Mandi who was always busy in acquiring territory for his state and his wife Prakas Devi craved for a son and for this she was performing various religious ceremonies all the time later. Thereafter a son was born to them. It was supposed to be the blessing of Deo Narain of Hurang. Therefore the child was given the name Narainsen. To their dismay the child was born handicapped and then came Chuni-Muni to bless upon him a healthy human form. After a reign of twenty years, Sahib Sen died in 1554 A.D. and there after Narain Sen became the raja of Mandi and expired in 1574 A.D. The samadhi on the demise of Chuni-Muni was erected by either of them. The history is silent about the time of its construction but this neglected structure which is fast dashing towards its destruction is a unique historical bond of the present with the past. Nothing is more derogatory than to witness the destruction of such a milestone of our history.

CHAPTER - 38

GHATS AMONG THE HILLS : Age Old Tradition

Parwanoo, a small, fast growing town is the gateway to Himachal Predesh. Beyond this industrial area, lie the green hills of the Himalayas. They present a pleasing sight, particularly during the rains-hill after hill covered with green plants, herbs and grass in the newly formed Solan district of the stte in Himachal Pradesh.

Solan was the capital town of the erstwhile Baghat state. Although at the time of its merger in Himachal Pradesh, Bhagat was a small principality ruled by a Raja, but in its old palmy days the large areas and parganas around it formed part of the erstwhile Patiala State. Baghat received heavy blows from the Sikhs, Gorkhas and then British aggressions, yet it managed to maintain its identity, though very much reduced, as a land of "ghats" from which the name Baghat was derived.

A number of villages in the area have their names ending in "ghat"; Chambaghat, Kandaghat, Kairighat, Vaknaghat, Bhararighat, Darlaghat, Shallaghat and Danughat are the few you find on the main highway. Besides, there are many others like Oachghat, Shaktighat, Piplooghat and Loharghat in the interior.

When road and Rail links were not known the sturdy hillmen had a hard time going from one place to another. They had to go uphill on one side and then descend on the other to reach the valley or village. The highest point on the way was a halting station for rest and refreshment and the place was described as ghat. The word "pass" is the English equivalent of what ghat is to the hill people of this region. In some other parts of Himachal "galoo" is used to described such points.

Besides Baghat, Solan district has the remnants of the old aristocracy in the scattered forts on hilltops and the fortress palace of the Raja of Baghat at Arki, the crumbling huse of the ruling family of Kuthar and the scattered and partly ruined fort palaces of the Royal houses of Nalagarh. They speak of the era when these place were the seat of power and those living in them held authority over the lives of the residents of the area.

In fact, so much of antiquity or of archaeological value can be found in these hills for which the inner Himalayas are famous though few wall paintings of the Pahari school in the fortress palace of Arki have survived the havoc that the Gorkhs brought to this area.

Nature has been bountiful in this part of the country but so has been the ugly presence of poverty. The people have been exploited by men from the plains in more ways then one. Since the formation of Himachal Pradesh and particularly the creation of Solan district the face of the area has been changing. Both in terms of agricultural produce and industrial progress, the district of Solan has carved out a place for itself.

Scientific and technological improvements have converted agriculture into a profitable proposition and the farms in this district produce some of the best tomatoes, peas, cauliflowers, cabbage, beans and other vegetables. This has changed the socio-economics structure of its society and the downtrodden class of yesterday now own beautiful farms and houses with modern facilities.

From Parwanoo to Shimla the highway is studded with modern, tastefully decorated hotels both in the private and public sectors besides a number of moedest catering places for low and middle-income tourists. Solan, which ws a sleepy small town about two decades age, is now full of zest.

In the interior, places like Kasauli, Subathu and Dagshai still retain their old regal character. Kasauli, although it possesses a majestic aura, needs better maintenance and care. It can develop into a popular health resort. Similarly, Sabathu and Dagshai are ideally situated as tourist resorts.

The British had their own reasons for turning to this area. The extreme climate of the plains forced them towards the hills. In the changed context this land of "ghats" is moving on the road to prosperity through agriculture, industry, tourism and advanced education.

CHAPTER - 39

TEMPLE ARCHITECTURE : A Magnificiant legacy

All over India, the variations in the temple styles form a conspicous feature. We know a lot about Puri's Jagannath, Konark's Surya and Bhuvaneshwar Lingraj temple complex emitting the grandeour and exquisiteness of our cultural heritage. Down South the temples of Tamil Nadu especially that of Madurai's Minakshi and Rameshwaram's Ramnath temple offer a typical variety of Southern Architecture of temple formation. The North has been plundered by the Muslim invaders and their main attack was on the temples and the statues. In this way North India stands poor as its glorious shrines were raised to the ground repeatedly and the wealth looted times and again. Hopefully the Western Himalayas offer certain osis of hope while traversing this area carefully. Partly, its terrains being difficult and its economics also not being prosperous this area escaped the onslaught of iconoclasts. In the lap of Kullu Valley, at Jagat Sukh which was the capital town in the early history of Kullu rulers; still stands a small temple dedicated to Shiva which is a prototyple for a bigger shrine of the northern plains of India. As Jagat-Sukh had an enormous potentials for art activities in its palmy days we could conjecture to have had a Shikhar styple temple of Sandhaya Devi near this temple of Shiva Gaurishankar of Jagat Sukh. Still the modest pent roofed structure of Sandhya Devi possesses several stone icons which formed part of the massive stone temple. Several 'amalaks' are also seen scattered in the temple complex indicating to the existence of the temple which either got destroyed due to poor care and utter negligence or could not withstand the vagaries of weather.

In the category of Shikhara style, the masterpiece at Bajaura temple extolls the art and architecture envisaged by the migrated artists of the North India. Bajaura temple only has a garbhagriha but another shrine of excellence having a sabhamandap added to garbhagriha is that of Baijnath temple in the shadow of Dhauladhar at the town of the same name. In Shikhara style the Laxami Narain temple complex at Chamba, Mani-mahesh and Narsingh temple at Bharmour, several Shiva temples of Mandi are the reminiscent of the elite art-compositions.

The most wonderful and unique in itself is the rock-cut temple of Masrur in Kangra made in post-Gupta tradition of the eighth century and equally old are the pent roofed temples of Hatkoti in Shimla, Lakshana Devi at Bharmour. Shakti Devi at Chhatrari and Bijli Mahadev near Kullu. Western Himalayas witnessed a style between the typical Shikhar style and pent roofed temple and that can be described as Domed temples of deformed Shikhar styles. They are typically an admixture of Hindu, Sikh and Muslim architectures. Jwala-mukhi in Kangra, Chintpurani in Una, Shiva temple of Nahan near Pucca Johar, Kameshwar and Tarna temple are deformed shrine formations. Several flat roofed temples are more often than not seen as Budhist monastries of Lahoul and Spiti, Shiva temple of Mangarh in Sirmour, Ramgopal temple at Damtal and the most decorated temple of Narbadeshwar in Tirra-Sujanpur in the Hamirpur area of Western Himalayas.

Simultaneous activities of temple construction can be visualised which is pure and simple the native variety of temples. As wood and stone were in plenty, therefore in place of chisselled stones of Shikhar styles, the local materials were made use of abundantly to erect the temples in Pagoda style and sometimes the pagoda and pent roof were combined in such a way that in the Satluj Valley, there developed an unique amalgam of its own variety. This admixture of both pagoda with pented roof emerged at its best in the old capital of Rampur-Bushehar State at Sarahan near to the snowy mountain ranges of Kinnaur. It is in several storeys and its roofs are slanting and slightly concave. Such roofing styles were reserved for the mansions of 'gods' and 'rajas'. This pented roof variety was made possible even while constructing the Damdama palace which Suraj Sen who ruled over Mandi State.

The simple pagoda style temples are the product of local conception and execution. Such temples with pyramidical tiered roofs take the shape of pagoda. In such structure, the diminishing roofs rise one above the other and the top one generally emerges round rather than squarish taking a funnel like shape. It goes to the area of Kullu to possess such temples in their best form at Manali, Nagar and Khankhan dedicated to Hidimba, Tripur Sundari and Aadi-Brahma respectively.

Adjoining the Kullu-Mandi borders, in the midist of high snow ranges is a temple of Parashar rishi made up of wood and stone all locally procured and erected in pagoda style. This temple is so fascinating in formation and surrounding that Ms Penelope Chetwood, the author of the book Kull- The

End of the Habitable World compared it to Taj Mahal and Konark's Surya temple. How far is she correct? She was correct to assess the brilliance of the local artists to translate the body-language of Nagara style's sophistication of several centuries under patronage of rich royal dynasties to this small work of folk art in the hinterland of the Himalayas by comparatively poor rulers Ban Sen a ruler of Mandi's Sen dynasty is said to be the builder of this monument in mid-thirteenth century. The selection of the site is a great accomplishment. A three liered structure near the bank of lake with floating islands and the majestic reflection of the temple is the crystal clear water of the lake all add to infer the aesthetic approach of the builders. The temples has marvelous carvings on the deodar wood in abundance. The doorframes are perhaps the superb. The angular meander with garland-bearers harks back to such early monuments as Ajanta, and interwind serpents are the motifs of Pratihara art. The figural representations like garland bearers, adorers and Bhradramukha as also the deeply undercut and luxuriating scrolls bespeak a vigorous tradition. Similar carving are seen on door of Devi nearly temple of Nau-panau. Several mythological scenes have been carved besides the decorative arts. The churning of ocean, on the panel over a carved window is a good example of the knowledge and craftsmanship of the artist. Similarly Durga Mahishasur-mardini over the window is a bold wooden relief having deep-chispelled curvaceous forms being gradually replaced by flat and angular shapes. This composition seems to be of a later date, the original being replaced by this. The theme of 'churning of oceans' was very popular with Himalayan wood workers. The same scene on the wooden frames at Markuladevi temple at Udaipur of the erestwhile Chamba State is more detailed and well executed. Now this area falls in the new district of Lahaul Spiti. There is a very severe and sober face of deity on the door frame of Parashar temple. This face or mask later became the pacemaker of metal-mask so popular in the hills.

Inspired by the wood carvings of Parashar, another masterpiece of woodwork is the temple of Magaru-Mahadev at Chhatari in Mandi District. A bold figure of Indra, the king of the gods on its Eravat Elephant has been carved by well experienced hands along with many mythological characters and events. A wooden portrait of Raja Dashrath controlling a chariot of ten horses is very conspicuous. War scene of Mahabharat and seperate portraits of Pandava heroes can be easily located. The tales and events of Krishna along with the ten incarnations of Vishnu have been included. A beautiful and majestic panel depicts a royal personnel toiling the fields being shown in typical hill terraces. It has been deciphered as Prithu; the first sovereign of the earth from when the word 'Prithavi' has been derived.

It appears that the art work in wood had its most glorious phase in Himalayas. Both the artists of native skill along with wandering migratory workers of outside world have worked side by side to produce and protect these wooden temples. Who knows how many of such treasures may have been lost in forest fires and due to lightening but some of the surviving building exemplify the heights of glory touched by them. Perpetual process of replaing and repairing is a scene even witnessed in the present times but the eminence reached in old structures remains unparalled.

Herman Goetz: a German scholar has described most ancient woodwork of preeminence in his book under the title the Early Wooden Temple of Chamba including the temples of Lakshana Devi at Bharmour, Shakti Devi at Chhatarari and Mirikula Devi at Udaipur. All the three temples are still surviving after overcoming seasonal hazards of centuries and can still serve as monuments of great achievements. Those who can not travel all the make way to witness these valuable pieces of art and art heritage can go through the exhaustive work of Dr. Goetz who has paintakingly narrated them for all who are concerned with our cultural heritage. Goetz's opinion about the carvings of Lakshana Devi temple is a big tribute to the craftmen. According to him, "For an exact explanation of Indian religious images the identification of their costumes, hair styles, crowns and various emblems is necessary, but only an approximate explanation of the decoration is now possible." Comparing Shakti Devi's shrine with that of Lakshana Devi he observes that but their decoration is somewhat richer and more elegant, the designs more fluid and variegated; but also more mannered, and the individual motifs more interesting, though less numerous. While concluding on the Mrikula Devi Temple at Lahaul his summing up is noteworthy. The interiors however, presents one of the most extra-ordinary views. The richness and the interest of the carvings exceed the monuments of both Bharmour and Chhitrari, though the artistic quality can not compare with them. I owe gratitude to Dr. Hermann Goetz to enthuse me to personally visit these out of the way places of unforgettable experiences and exalted richness of creation.

CHAPTER - 40

SNOWCLAD MOUNTAIN TOPS : Threesome Kailash

Himalayas' real beauty lies in its snow-capped mountains. Kailash on the foothill of which is Mansarovar is an esteemed place of purity and sublimness. Here is, as believed, the abode of Lord Shiva and His divine consort Parvati. This Kailash of ours is widely known in all corners of the country and abroad. Now in reality the journey to Mansarovar is known as Kailash-Mansarovar Yatra. Surprisingly, in the Western Himalayas as covered in this book; there are three more kailash known for being the abode of Lord Shiva. All the three are snowcapped mountain tops attracting large number of trekkers, pilgrims and mountain lovers. Presently they fall in the political domain of Himachal Pradesh which is a hilly state of India. It is worthwhile to note that Shiva does live here, but in people's estimation, his dress and decorative fit in with the prevailing costumes of those areas. Shiva in Churdhar has a big white loya, topa and langota made up of wool as his garment of choice whereas the Shiva on Kinnaur-Kailash has a predilection for the clothings designed in Kinnauri fashion. The third is at the Manimahesh peak near the historic village of Bharmour, where Shiva put on the attrie of the Gaddies with long chola and black dora around his waist. These Shivas are down to earth the product of local beliefs and perceptions and have nothing to do with the lives and lores of Shiva's narration in 'Pauranic' scriptures.

Chur-Ki-Dhar falls on the border of erst-while Sirmour State and another native state of Chopal which presently is a part of district of Shimla. Here resides the devata Shirigul presumed to be a derivative of Shaivism on the Choor peak which is visible from Shimla. Hence the Shiva or the Sirigul is represented by lingam, as is done all over the country. In local psyche Shiva is no other than Shirigul. There are various legends connected with Shirigul who is supposed to possess supernatural powers or say magical powers over ailments and their curses. Various unusal feats were performed for pleasing this lord of Shrigul cult. It is attributed to him to construct water channels on the both sides of Choor mountain. Although Choor mountains is projected to be his main seat of residence but villages are adorned with temples dedicated to this form of Shiva. Bijat is supposed to be his prime-minister who in his own right has exclusive temples built for him besides several as subordinate to Shrigul. Besides Bijat a goddess Bhangani is his sister. She has an important shrine at Haripurdhar from where a clear glimpses of Choor-ki-Dhar are easily deciphered. Choor, is spelt as chaur in the survey of India maps though popularly pronounced as Choor. The local native name is Chur-Chandni-Ki-Dhar i.e. the hill of the silver bangle. According to the Survey of India reports at Chaur mountain, hornblende sehists and amphibolites occur as aykes cutting the Jutogh beds and less commonly as sills parallel to the bedding of Jutug sedimentary formations. They do not appear to invade the Chaur or Chor granites and are never seen cutting the under lying chail and Jaunsar series. Their extent is very limited rarely exceeding 91 meters. They neither have any particular direction not horizon. The peak of Chaur mountain 3,647 M (11,966 feet) from a prominent feature south-east of Shimla and is composed of gereissose granite, the chor granite which is probably of late palaeozoic age.

Regarding this Choor-chandani-ki Dhar an enthusiastic writer has said "travellers agree that no mountain scenery not that of Alps, nor any in the Cancasus, Andes or other famed highlands of the world is remotely comparable in splendour and sublimity with what the Himalayas offer in almost any of their valleys, but here the place in Sirmour is really the wonderland of the HImalayas and in this state the highest hill is Chur-Ki-Dhar. It is described as the divine Kailash the winter abode of Shiva, the region to which the Aryan Hindu look with longing and reverence, for there are the dwellings of his gods. There they were enthroned in serene and unattainable majesty; their they regarded the hidden store-house of their choicest gifts to men, for there lay the mysterious caves of Kubera, the god of wealth, the keeper of gold, silver and other precious ore. There, at the height of some twelve thousand feet, on the top of the hill is a little piece of even ground. In its midst, straight springs up water in large quantity and on one side it is a Shiva temple where the pilgrims make offerings of gold and silver, and sheep and goats are sacrificed to please the deity of mountain top which is Shirigul the local Shiva, the destroyer of the three of the worlds." This is how goes the impressions of a European. Recent observation of a scholar of the repute of M.S. Randhawa are also worth recording. He says- a conical snow covered peak is visible from Chandigarh in the months of December to march towards north-east. Hemmed in by the upper Shivaliks of Kasauli and Sirmour it appears very distinctive. Few people in Chandigarh know its name, and also the fact that it is the nearest snow-peak to the capital city of Delhi. On enquiry I learnt that it bears the picturesque name of Chur-Chandni-Ki-Dhar- the mountain range of silver bangle- and is in the territory of the district Sirmour of Himachal Pradesh."

Perched in the lap of the high Himalayas, the mountainous, rugged and craggy terrain of Kinnaur is a land of beauty and fascination and also boasts proudly of possessing a Kailash of its own. Kinnaur in itself provides an abiding field for study, research and artistic endeavour for the sociologists, anthropologist, theiologians, scholars, writers and artists the attractive tribal inhabitants of Kinnaur, where the Hindu and Budhist cultures blend and meet in their picturesque villages and hamlets, with frescoed monasteries and wood carved temples. One such place of common faith is one of the highest peak of the region at 6473 M known as Mountain Kinner Kailash or Raldang. Here the former nomenclature is entirely of Hindu origin and the later has the Tibetan connotation; likewise its inhabitants generally have two names. Kinner Kailash rises from the base of the Sutlej river (1900 M) to its spectacular height in a sheer wall of rock, ice and snow, over looking the opposite bank of the district headquarter that was Kalpa in 1975, from where I had the view of Kailash of the incomparable beauty and majesty. The characteristics dome shaped summit in Kinner Kailash with its northern shoulder is also clearly visible from Kufri (Near Shimla) standing aloof amidst its lesser surroundings satellites tops separating the valley of Baspa from that Tidong and has for its crown pointed summits and in its lap immense expanse of snow. The description of Gerard is note worthy. "Some idea of it may be formed by imagining an assemblage of pointed peaks, presenting a vast surface of snow, viewed under an angle of 27 degrees, and at a distance of not more than five miles in a direct line." He further noted than there is a mountain of same name Reldang, which has an elevation of 30° to 32°. It rise to the height of 12000 feet above the town, or 21,000 higher than the sea," and to show the idea the natives have of the Eastern Kylas, I need only mention Reldang Kylas."

Again here in Kinnaur also this Kailash is an abode of Shiva and Parvati his divine consort. Kailash and Khaskar opposite Kalpa have a sacred character, one is believed to be peopled by the souls of the dead and other the residence of Shiva. According to the prevalent belief, in certain seasons music is heard in these places and the older generations have a faith that a pool is surrounded by mountains near the Kailash, where stands a temple dedicated to Shiva, and other deities have their dwellings in the neighbourhood of the mountain tops. They are of opinion that many years back a holy monk came to this place to worship Shiva. Having done so he asked for some favour, and thereby incurred the god's displeasure with the result that he was turned into a rock, which is visible from Kalpa. This rock is tinted white at sunrise, red at mid day and green at sunset. This may be due to some optical phenomenon caused by light waves being reflected by the rock. In the faith and belief of the Kinnauras one who makes a complete circuit round Raldang Kailash obtains the realization of a wish. The jorney is rather difficult and tough and can only be attempted in July or August; on these path covered by snow where normal human foot may never hope to tread. I met a good number of young peoples who had circumambulated the Kailash and gone up to this rocky top where even the snow does not settle; this being slopy and perpendicular. Even the mere sight from the old building of hospital at Kalpa was in real sense a very satisfying experience. The changing colours cast a unique and amazing charm each and every time when one attempts to look at this majestic site.

The splendid mountain systems and ranges, coupled with the river basin determines the natural geographical division of the Himalayas. In the Chamba district, the Northern-most part of Himachal Pradesh, at the point where the Pangi range first touches the district territory, it forms of the Mani Mahesh branch, to the south which divides the Bara Bangahal as far as Ravi. In the basin of the Budhal a smal tributary of the Ravi, there is a lofty mountain which remains snow-clad throughout the year and is called Kailash again an abode of Shiva. This is Bharmour-Kailash, and is held in great reverence by the peoples of Chamba and Kangra alike; and is approachable from both sides. I became familiar and was charmed by the sheer conical formation of this hilltop while on my way to Bharmour in year 1970. By that time the place was connected with the district headquarter Chamba partly by bus-road, kacha jeep worthy pathway and thereafter by briddle jorney on foot from Bharmour, a town of antiquity to the Mani Mahesh lake.

We had started from Chamba town and passing through Mehla, Rakh and Durghati reached Kharamukh. Although the road was not comfortable and all through our jeep was tossing and tumbling. This discomfort was compensated by having the fierce spectacle of the Ravi, on the bank of which the road led us all the way up to Kharamukh. Here Ravi is known by its Vedic name of Iravati. While on our way we had a glimpse of the primitive methods of crossing river by iron trollies and wooden bridges made of one or two planks of deodar. Confluence of the River Tundah and River Budhal are also on the way leading to Bharmour. There are spots which do lend natural beauty to the place and are awe-inspiring. At Kharamukh, we had to unload the jeep and cross the suspension bridge, as it could not take load of jeep with passengers and baggage to bear the burden. On of the farther end again, we made use of the jeep which now had an uphill journey on a narrow track of newly constructed jeep route. Half way between the Kharamukh and Bharmour, the first glimpse of the Mani Mahesh Kailash could be had but soon the clouds formed a screen between us. Steadily the terraced fields of the village Bharmour and its temples make your tempo more vigourous with a sense of achievement that the populated village is not very far. The distant view of Bharmour is eyecatching as is the glory of its temples and statues of great antiquity. From Bharmour the Mani-Mahesh lake is approached thorugh Hadsar, Danchoh and ultimately the lake which is sacred for the devotees. It is about 13,000 feet above sea level in the midst of snowy peaks, the highest of these being the Mani Mahesh or Bharmour Kailash. The lake remains submerged in the ice and cold water. From Bharmour it is 22 miles and thereby from Chamba it is about sixty miles. In 1970 upto Hadsar it was bridle path and in 1983 it was jeapable but beyond Hadsar which is famous for an old Shiva temple up to Dhanchoo it is a steep ascent. At Dhanchho, the pilgrims assemble for night halt before their approach to the lake. Dhanchho is known for a beautifull waterfall an unique site to behold. Between this place and the sacred lake, there are many a small places of worship. The water of lake is the feeding center for Hadsar stream which rises lower down and joins the Buddal which is a tributary to the Ravi and they have their confluence at Kaharamukh. It is said that the Mani Mahesh Kailash has not been yet conqured by human being and no successful attempts have been reported so far.

Although showered with highbrow philosophical thoughts, the love for nature, hills, the dales, the mountains, the snow peaks, the rivers, the tress and lakes have made lasting impressions on the Indian psyche. These Kailash tops are nothing but unending store house of snow for centuries together but their fascination and spell on the minds on Indians is thoroughly blended with high and pure dedication or religions, they being presumed the place of stay of the highest of the high gods. None of these places can boast of any place of worship made by humans hands. It is the pure and simple creations of nature surrounded by innumerable tales and legends which still persists with a lot of positive influence.

Kinner Kailash and Chur-Ki-Dhar have a limited sway but the Mani-Mahesh peak attracts pilgrims in large numbers. Those who can not be fortunate enough to be at this rough and tough place, a suggested substitute for them is the mighty temple dedicated to Mani Mahesh at Bharmour. The temple is made of stone in Shikhara style and there are two such temples still existing at Bharmour the largest and biggest is that of Mani Mahesh Shiva and the later of Narshigha. The Mani-Mahesh temple is on a huge pedestal with an enormously big Shiv lingam placed on a Yoni. It was erected by Raja Meru Varman of 7th century. Scholars doubt its being of that antiquity but it is secured in Sharda script on the brass bull facing the Shiva lingam that the bull and temple of Mani Mahesh are the creation of Raja Meru Varman. A visit to this temple is a must before the pilgrims pave their way to the exact site of the lake which is on the base of the conical mountain known to us as Mani Mahesh Kailash to differentiate it from other Kailashs of Himachal Pradesh and the main Kailash Mansarovar of international repute.

CHAPTER - 41

A SAD MEMORABILIA : Rumination

In the erst while Mandi state, now in Himachal Pradesh the area lying south of the Beas, up to the basin of the Satluj in the Dhauladhar mountain range, was known as Saraj. The whole range was thickly wooded with Himalayan jungles of Deodar, Chil, Fur and Oak. In between in the valleys were small habitations with terraced fields small yield of crops which used to be insufficient even for the personal need of the household. In the southern tip of this vast tract of land were two garhs or ilakas which were famous as Magru and Mangarh adjacent to each other. Magru was reached in good old days by crossing the Magru Pan at a height of seven thousands feet above sea level. This was the easiest and nearest approach and trade route from the capital of the state i.e. Mandi Town via Baggi, Gohar, Thunag and Janiahali leading to Rampur Bushair. From Janjahali to the Magru Pass it was almost straight ascent taking normally 3 hours and deep descent to reach Chhatari the heart of Magru a place known for its early wooden temple of Magru-Mahadev with profuse wooden carvings of considerable merit. In between, from Magru pass to Chhatari, small villages like Lassi and Rumani are worthy of mention. Now Chhatari, which usually takes three to four days to reach, has been connected with bus service from Mandi via Karsog.

As both these garhs were strategically located, being on the borders of states of Suket, Kullu and Bushehar, it needed a lot of protection from the invaders. The recurrent warfare was constant phenomena of the then polity so Raja of Mandi used to post a state official there for keeping a vigil on the intruders to protect his boandaries. One such official was Ramji Khatri of Mandi Town. Till his life span during the time of Raja Ishwar Sen he guarded the state frontiers and on his death his son Shridhar took his place. Probably 'Bist' was his designation and that is how we were respectfully addressed by the people of Magru and Mangarh although in the old and written records the word 'Kaith' was also added as a prcfix to the name of my ancestors. Shridhar had long innings in this land and laid down his life while fighting with the invaders of Bushehar. He was cremated there only as transportation of his body was not possible to his home town, being a four days' march. As according to Hindu custom a bank of a river or rivulet is considered a pure spot for cremation, so his body was consigned to flames on the bank of a small rivulet near Swan/Katheri and the rivulet adopted his name as mark of respect to the brave warrior, which later came to be referred as Shridhar-ra-nala i.e. the rivulet of Shridhar. Shridhar had two sons Lohar and Jorawar. The former was a valuable child in a dynasty which was not having a progency. Therefore on birth, he was sold to a person of Lohar trade formally and there after was given that name. Jorawar got the village of Swan and the land and house were passed on to his son Haranu Ram who lived up to the early fifties. Lohar got the village of Katheri and was my grand father. He died in young age when his son Kaith Ganesh Dass was in his teens. It appears that my father inherited very little from his father. It was a general practice in his time to lend money and grains to the village folks of Magru and Mangarh and collect it at an appropriate time with interest which according to the old records kept at our house at Chaura was one percent per moth and for grains one fourth of the total weight per year. I had heard in my child-hood that when my father came back from his first collection of his visit, it amounted to a negligible sum and passed on the money to his widowed mother Saraswti. It is said she threw it back at him in a fit of anger and that gave my father a lesson to earn more to live respectfully. Thereafter most of the time of the year, he used to maintain his trade in this hinterland of Himalayas and generally used to retreat to Mandi Town in the winter when that area used to become snowbound. After the death of my great grand father Shridhar, it appears we were divested from official position and thereafter our profession was a trade involving money and grain-lending. It may appear something extra ordinary and non-professional but keeping in view the then economic and geographical situation, the profession seemed to be a boon to the local inhabitants and simultanenly gainful trade to the money lenders. In such situations like draught and flood, the relief's could not be rushed as is possible today. So the granaries or the stocking houses of our's known as 'Kathyar' were the only and natural relief to the people. The money was so scare that person who used to act as load bearers from this area to the town used to get one rupee silver coin plus a loadful of rock salt from Drang mines, as much as the man could lift to meet the need of entire year plus ration for to and fro journey similarly whenever money was needed there were no local person, bank, mutual cooperative society or agent to arrange money to the needful persons. By his hard and strenuous work, my father earned a lot and was considered to be one of the wealthy men of the town. He had his 'Kathyars' at Katheri. The 'Mela' or 'Jach' of Chhatri is well known for since centuries. Prior to the beginning of this mela in rainy season, generally falling in August, a big dance night was held at village Chaura about a Km of two from Chhatri. His wife i.e. my step-mother was very keen to see this all night-dance festival where hundreds of men and women used to dance together till the next dawn. Once she could not get a good place to get a good view of the dance and had to struggle hard to get a seat and was taunted by other onlookers to possess her own house at that place. After this incident she persuaded her husband to own a house at Chaura. My father agreed to her contention and purchased a piece of land from same gosain:— perhaps a person from Nath cult and paid him in silver coin spreading all over the area which seems to be an exaggeration. He started the construction of a double storey house which was not in the folk style but like modern house but built of stone and timber with earthen floor without any cement. My step mother who was having a small son died and could not see her cherished dream of owning a house at Chaura. Her son Mangat Ram later travelled every year to this house for a short stay till his death in 1991 but for his last two-three year's of his life. After the demise of his early wife, my father married my mother who had five children but I am the only surviving one, other died in infancy. It was she under whose supervision the house was completed and got the final touches and furnishings. She used to tell me with pride that such house is nowhere in the entire garhs of Magru, Manguru, Bagara and other territories where we had our trade. It was her desire to have "this type of house" at Mandi Town as well. In my childhood she used to mention it time and again till my father was alive who died in 1946 when I was about ten years old. After his death she never mentioned about the house although my father had arranged sufficient materials for construction. His constraint was a piece of land of his choice. He was very choosy in this respect. Neither he wanted to go in for a upcoming colony to own the hosue nor to accept a unsuitable site which he used to examine from many angles. In his old age and eventually in late years of life, he got his femur fractured and I still have a dim memory of his limping and walking with the help of a stick. He died and that smashed the whole tempo of my mother. Her only ambition remained that I should be brought up with good education so that along with me and my family she could live in the shadow of old glory. Now when I am on the thresh-hold of my retirement from government services, my desire to see the cremation place of my warrior great grand father Shridhar came alive. I had been to Chaura in my childhood once along with my father and mother, when I was not even a school going kid. Later after his death twice or thrice I visited the place during summer vacations alongwith my brother. When I was in first year of MBBS, I visited the place again and repeated the visit in 1980, whereas my brother visited the place regularly. Now the turn of events has forced me to come here as a pilgrim. A visit to Shridahr-ka-Nala was irresistable, non-fading and ever exciting and this desire of mine, all through my active carrer remained un fulfilled.

Nevertheless, the solitary and singualr approach to the site, later on, was the usual tale of repentance and regrets. No habitation, no cultivation, only a bank of thirfty water channel with the eternal solitude in wilderness and the proverbial, silence of graveyard. The boulders are surviving witnesses of the scene of the old conflicts and tearful cremation. Nothing more than a watershed between the native state of Mandi and rival state of Kullu over shadowing the far flung areas of Shimla Hill states of the bygone days.

BIBLIOGRAPHY

1	Aggarwal, Vasudev Saran	:	India as Known to Panini, Vanarasi, 1950.
		:	Evolution of Hindu Temple, Varanasi, 1965.
2	Archer, W.G.	:	Indian Paintings in Punjab Hills, Landon, 1972
3	Bannerjee, Jintender Nath	:	Development of Hindu Iconography, Calcutta, 1936
4	Bose, S.C.	:	Geography of Himalays, New Delhi, 1972
5	Chetwood, Penelope	:	Kullu, the end of Habitate World, New Delhi, 1972
6	Chhabra, B.Ch.	:	Antiquities of Chamba State Part II, New Delhi, 1957
7	Commarawamy, A.K.	:	Rajpoot Paintings, Oxford, 1916
8	Cunningham, A	:	Archaeological Survey of India Report 1872-73, New Delhi, 1871
			Ancient Geography of India Landon, 1877
9	Dange, S.A.	:	India from Primitive Communism to Slavery, New Delhi, 1949
10	Eschmann, Anncharlott, Kulke, Herman, Tripathi Gaya Charan,	:	The cult of Jagannath and the Regional traditions of Orrissa, Delhi, 1978
11	Fraser, J.B.	:	Journal of a Tour through part of snowy ranges of HImalaya mountain, Landon, 1820
12	Francke, A.H.	:	Antiquities of India Tibet Part I&II Lanon, 1926
13	French, J.C.	:	HImalayan Art, Landon, 1931
14	Goetz, Hermann	:	The Early Wooden Temples of Chamba, Leiden, 1955
15	Gazetteers of the		
		*	Chamba State, Lahore, 1904-Revised, 1963
		*	Kangra District, Lahore, 1983-84-Revised 1917
		*	Mandi & Suket, Lahore, 1094
		*	Mandi State, Labore, 1920
		*	Shimla Hills State, Lahore, 1934
		*	Sirmour State, Lahore, 1934, Revised 1969
		*	Suket State, Lahore, 1927

		*	Kinnaur, Shimla, 1971
16	Griffin, L.H.	:	The Rajas of Punjab Vol. I & II, Reprints, Patiala, 1970
17	Huchinson, J	:	Guide to Dalhousie, Chamba and Inner Mountain between Shimla and and Kashmir, London, 1923
18	Handa, O.C.	:	Art and Architecture of Uttaranchal, New Delhi, 2003
		:	History of Uttaranchal, New Delhi, 2002
		:	Naga Cults and Traditions, New Delhi, 2004
19	Harcort, H.F.P.	:	The Himalayan District of Kooloo and Lahoul and Spiti, Lahore, 1871
20	Kapoor, B.L.	:	Gods of the High Hills, New Delhi, 2001
		:	History and Heritage of Western Himalayas, Delhi, 2001
		:	Himachal: Itihas aur parampara, Delhi, 1976, Reprint-1994
21	Khandalwala, Karl	:	Indian sculptures and paintings, Bombay, 1938
		:	Pahari Miniature Paintings, Bombay, 1958
22	Khosla, G.D.	:	Himalayan Circuit, Landon, 1965
23	Man Mohan	:	History of Mandi State, Lahore, 1930
24	Martin Paul, Dubost	:	Ganesha: The Enchanter of the Three words, Mumbai, 1997
25	Madan Jeet Singh	:	Himalayan Art, Macmillian, 1971
26	Mishra, D.P.	:	Studies in the Proto History of India, Orient Longmen, 1971
27	Moorcraft, W; Trectbeck	:	Travels in Himalayans Provinces of Hindustant and Punjan, Reprint Patiala, 1937
28	M. Postel, A. Neven, K. Mankodi	:	Antiquities of Himachal, Bombay, 1985
29	Mehta N.C.	:	Studies in Indian Paintings, Bombay, 1926
30	Panikkar, K.M.	:	A Survey of Indi a History, Bombay, 1963
31	Rapson, E.J.	:	Indian Coins, New Delhi, 1966
32	Rai Krishan Dass	:	Bharat Ki Murtikala, Varanasi, 2032 (Vik.)
33	Randhawa, M.S.	:	Kangra Valley Paintings, New Delhi, 1954
		:	Chamba Paintings, New Delhi, 1967
34	Roeirich, Nicholas,	:	Himalayas, Abode of Light, Bombay, 1947
35	Rose H.A.	:	Glossary of Tribes and Castes of the Punjab & NWFP, Lahore, 1919
36	Shastri Hiranand	:	Historical Documents of Kully, ASR 1907-8-9,

BIBLIOGRAPHY

		:	Calcutta, 1911
37	Singh, R.C. Pal	:	Census of India, 1961
		:	H.P. Village Survey of Bharmlour.
		:	H.P. Village Survey of Chhitrari
		:	Shimla, 19
38	Singh, Govardhan	:	Art and Architecture of Himachal Pradesh, Delhi, 1980
39	Vogel, J. Ph.	:	Catalogue of Bhuri Singh Museum of Chamba, Calcutta, 1909
		:	Antiquities of Chamba State, Calcutta, 1911
		:	Temple of Mahadev of Bajura, Kullu, ASR-Calcutta,
40	Vogel, J.Ph & Huchinson, J	:	History of Punjab Hill States Part I & II, Lahore, 1933
41	Vidya lankar, Jai Chandra	:	Bhartiya Itihas Ki Mimansa, Allahabad, 1950
42	Vidya lankar, Satyaketu	:	Bhart Ka Prachin Itihash, Mussouri, 1967
43	Zimmer, Heinrich	:	Myths and Symbols in Indian Art and Civilization, New York, 1946